Forgotten Bombers

of the Royal Air Force

Forgotten Bombers
of the Royal Air Force

KEN WIXEY

ARMS AND
ARMOUR

Below: The second prototype Manchester, L7247, of 1940. It has Frazer-Nash nose, tail and ventral turrets (the last was later replaced by an FN7 dorsal turret), a small 'shark'-style fin and revised wingtips. It was also experimentally fitted with a servo-elevator balance tab below the starboard elevator. (Rolls-Royce plc, Derby)

Arms and Armour Press
An Imprint of the Cassell Group
Wellington House, 125 Strand, London WC2R 0BB

British Library Cataloguing-in-Publication Data:
a catalogue record for this book is available from the
British Library

ISBN 1-85409-306-1

Designed and edited by DAG Publications Ltd. Designed by
David Gibbons; layout by Anthony A. Evans; edited by Philip
Jarrett; printed and bound in Great Britain.
All line sketches drawn by the author (not to scale).

Acknowledgements
The author is extremely grateful to the following indi-
viduals and organisations for their generous help in
providing valuable information and photographs for
this book: Andrew Delgaty (BAe, Brough); Bob
Wilcock (RAF retired); Brian Pickering (Military Air-
craft Photographs); Brian Stainer (Aviation Photo
News); David Charlton (BAe Airbus, Filton); Don
Bruce (RAF retired); Dr Mark Nicholls (Cambridge Uni-
versity Library); Fairey Holdings Ltd; Ministry of
Defence (Air Historical Branch); Mrs M. Hunt; Peter
Hicks (Rolls-Royce Heritage Trust, Derby); Peter Pavey
(Rolls-Royce AITD, Filton); RAF Museum; Short Bros
Ltd; T. I. Jackson Ltd (late of Yate); Vickers plc. To Ron
Mackay I am especially indebted for loaning me pho-
tographs from his collection which, apart from his
own sources, include credits for Bruce Robertson,
Canadian Armed Forces; Dick Ward; F. T. Roberts; J. D.
R. Rawlings; Jerry Scutts; L. Wilde; Peter Baldock and
the Stirling Association.

Beauforts and crews of No. 22 Squadron, Coastal Command, at Thorney Island in 1940. This was the first RAF unit to fly
Beauforts and the first to lay mines in enemy waters. (Ron Mackay)

Contents

Introduction

Ask the average man or woman in the street to name a British bombing aircraft of the Second World War, and the reply would probably be Lancaster or Mosquito. But ask them the name of the aircraft from which the Lancaster directly evolved, and it is doubtful if they could provide the correct answer.

Again, how many of the general public would know the type of aircraft in which two British airmen were flying when, for their gallantry, both earned a posthumous Victoria Cross – the first awarded to RAF aircrew in the Second World War?

The de Havilland Mosquito became famous for its speed and daring attacks against enemy targets in daylight. But that was not until 1942. Previously, Bomber Command relied heavily on the Bristol Blenheim for daylight raids on Germany, occupied Europe, Middle Eastern targets and Japanese objectives in the Far East. Despite great odds, Blenheim crews were dedicated to their tasks, and three Victoria Crosses were won by them, two posthumously. Previous publications have extolled the part played by Blenheims in RAF history, but it is included here because, although it was a hard-hitting maid of all work, the Blenheim is seldom remembered by the public, who are only familiar with the more glamorous types covered by the media.

The Bristol Beaufort was another type which enjoyed little limelight. A torpedo bomber, it also carried bombs and mines, and a Beaufort pilot, too, was awarded a posthumous Victoria Cross.

Blackburn's Botha, also designed for torpedo or conventional bombing, served with only one RAF unit and was not used operationally after 1940. Nevertheless, its use on armed patrol duties has earned the Botha a place in this book.

The film 'Target for Tonight' brought fame to the Vickers Wellington, the public being made well aware of the 'Wimpey' and its operations. But what of its two Bomber Command partners, the Hampden and Whitley? How many people today connect the term 'Flying Suitcase' or 'Flying Panhandle' with the former, or know that two Victoria Crosses were awarded to Hampden crews? Would they know that the Whitley was Bomber Command's mainstay heavy night bomber until 1942, the first to drop leaflets on Berlin and the first to attack Italian targets by flying over the Alps? It is doubtful whether the Hampden and Whitley are remembered other than by aviation historians.

Naturally, the Avro Lancaster remains a symbol of RAF bombing capability in the Second World War, and deservedly so. Likewise its partner, the Handley

Below: Had Britain gone to war in 1938, the RAF's heavy night bomber force would have relied mainly on biplanes such as this Handley Page Heyford, K3500/R of No. 99 Squadron. (MAP)

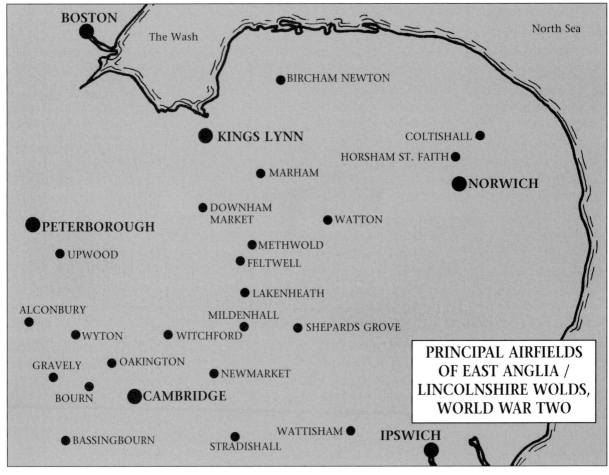

PRINCIPAL AIRFIELDS OF EAST ANGLIA / LINCOLNSHIRE WOLDS, WORLD WAR TWO

Page Halifax, is fairly well known, but the third four-engine heavyweight, the Short Stirling, has never really won the public acclaim it deserves. Yet it saw plenty of action, and was the first British four-engine heavy bomber to attack an enemy target. The type flew bombing operations until well into 1944, and two Stirling pilots were posthumously awarded the Victoria Cross for their bravery.

Mention the geodetic construction designed by Barnes Wallis, and some people think of the Wellington bomber (a fact brought home by a scene in 'The Dam Busters'). But how many recall the Wellington's immediate predecessor from Vickers,

Left: The Boulton Paul Overstrand was the RAF's only type of medium bomber until Blenheims arrived in June 1938. This Overstrand is the prototype, J9186, a converted Sidestrand. (Rolls-Royce Bristol)

Below: The first of the many – just in time! HM King George VI visits RAF Harwell in May 1938. In the background, left to right, are a Handley Page Harrow, Armstrong Whitworth Whitley III, Vickers Wellesley and Bristol Blenheim I, and in the foreground is Fairey Battle K7628 of No. 105 Squadron. (Mrs M. Hunt)

the Wellesley. The first RAF aircraft to use geodetic construction, it gained a long-distance record for Britain and saw action against the Italians in the Second World War.

Another unsung type which performed yeoman service, mainly in the Middle East, was the Bristol Bombay bomber-transport. Yet, like its similar contemporary, the Handley Page Harrow, the Bombay was little known to the public during the war years.

Most of these bombers, as part of the RAF's late 1930s expansion programme, were destined to see action against the Axis powers, but they were quickly overshadowed by more famous British and American replacements, some of which would become household names. Yet without its early monoplane bombers (and fighters, for that matter), which appeared only just in time, the RAF may well have had to face the enemy in 1939 with obsolete biplanes.

It is hoped that this book will appeal to members of the public who wish to know something of early Second World War British bombers. Forerunners of the more famous Lancaster, Halifax and Mosquito, they formed a nucleus from which RAF Bomber Command was able to expand into its eventual awesome might.

Armstrong Whitworth
Whitley

The first British bomber to fly over Germany following the outbreak of war, the first to cross the Alps to attack targets in Italy, and one of the first to drop bombs on an enemy land target and later Berlin itself, was the twin-engine Armstrong Whitworth A.W.38 Whitley. It also took an active part with RAF Coastal Command in the early campaign against U-boats, helped develop techniques used by British airborne forces and, manned by civilian British Overseas Airways Corporation (BOAC) crews, assisted in delivering much-needed supplies to Malta. Yet unlike its contemporary, the Vickers Wellington, and the succeeding Handley Page Halifax and Avro Lancaster, the Whitley received few accolades from the British public.

The ancestry of the Whitley can be traced to the twin-engine A.W.23 bomber-transport built in the Coventry suburb of Whitley to Air Ministry Specification C.26/31. Flown initially on 4 June 1935, the A.W.23 (K3585) was powered by two 700hp (522kW) Armstrong Siddeley Tiger VI air-cooled radial engines. Accommodation was provided for 24 armed troops, with alternative arrangements for the bombing role.

Realising the bomber potential of the A.W.23, Armstrong Whitworth Aircraft (AWA) chief designer John Lloyd revised the layout as a pure bomber for service with the Czechoslovakian Air Force. Designated A.W.30, the projected machine had a much slimmer fuselage, the gross weight being reduced to 18,650lb (8,460kg). No drawings of this design survive, but, like the A.W.23, it would have featured patented AWA light-alloy wing construction, a retractable landing gear, and manually operated gun turrets in the nose and tail positions. The A.W.30's layout was to be an important influence when development of the A.W.38 Whitley heavy bomber began.

Meanwhile, RAF requirements and political expediency in 1932 had resulted in Air Ministry Specification B.9/32, intended to cover medium-bomber replacements for RAF service in accordance with the Geneva Disarmament Conference ruling. Eventually this produced the Vickers Wellington and Handley Page Hampden, but by 1934 a heavy night bomber was required to replace the RAF's ageing Vickers Virginias and Handley Page Heyfords. The Geneva restrictions still being in force, there was suggestion of a B.9/32 layout with interchangeable wings and empennage, while another scheme envisaged the temporary use of Vickers Vildebeests as night bombers. Indeed, one Vildebeest was given the Nivo (dark green) overall finish standard on contemporary night bombers and flown on trials with No. 7 Squadron, flying Virginias. Common sense prevailed, however, and in June 1934 Britain officially denounced the Geneva weight limitations, which

Below: The progenitor of the Whitley, Armstrong Whitworth's A.W. 23, K3585, with its landing gear lowered. The numeral 8 on the fuselage side is for its appearance at the RAF Display at Hendon on 29 June 1935. (MAP)

cleared the way for a more practical specification to be drawn up by the Air Staff for a new heavy bomber.

This specification, B.3/34, called for a heavy night bomber with a wingspan not exceeding 100ft (31m), this then being the maximum that could pass through RAF hangar door openings. A bomb load of up to 2,500lb (1,135kg) was to be carried for 1,250 miles (2,011km) at 15,000ft (4,575m), the maximum speed at that altitude being 225mph (362km/h). Provision was to be made for one 1,500lb (681kg), or two 1,000lb (545kg) bombs, or a larger number of small bombs, while guns were to be located in nose, tail and midship positions as defensive armament. The five-man crew was to include two pilots (one doubling as navigator), two gunners and a wireless-operator/gunner.

Specification B.3/34 was submitted on 23 July 1934 to AWA, Fairey Aviation, Vickers (Aviation) and Handley Page but, at a meeting on 1 August between the four companies and Air Ministry officials, some requirements were altered. Maximum speed was reduced to 205mph (330km/h), a lower climb rate was agreed and the stipulation that 1,500lb (681kg) and 1,000lb (454kg) bombs be carried was deleted. However, development costs could not be agreed, and the Air Ministry forsook its normal procedure of ordering several competing prototypes. The contract would be awarded to a single company and, from the four in the offing, AWA and Vickers were left in the running. Vickers proposed a modified B.9/32 employing Barnes Wallis's geodetics, but Air Ministry officials were unsure of the then new and untried structure (the Wellesley did not fly until 19 June 1935, and the Wellington on 15 June 1936). Consequently the B.3/34 contract went to AWA, and on 14 September

Above: The prototype Whitley, K4586, in silver finish and powered by two Armstrong Siddeley Tiger IX engines. (Author's collection)

1934 two prototype A.W.38s were ordered, it being suggested by the Air Ministry that John Lloyd adapt his earlier A.W.30 design for the Czech Air Force to suit RAF requirements. The A.W.38 was to be named Whitley, after Whitley Abbey near Coventry, the city in which the aircraft was designed and built, although much of the work was later transferred to AWA's new site at Baginton.

By this time political unrest in Europe had caused Britain to consider rearmament and RAF expansion programmes. Normally a new aircraft design was tested as a prototype before a production order was placed, but the scenario had changed dramatically by May 1935 and one RAF expansion programme being implemented, Scheme C, demanded an increase in RAF bomber squadrons to 68 by March 1937. To fulfil the requirements of this programme, the Air Ministry received government approval to sign contracts for new aircraft types 'off the drawing board'. As a result, AWA received an initial order on 23 August 1935 for 80 Whitley Mk. I heavy bombers. Under contract No. 421118/35 these would be built in two batches of 34 (K7183–K7216) and 46 (K7217–K7262), although the latter would eventually emerge as Whitley Mk. IIs.

The first prototype Whitley, K4586, made its initial flight on 17 March 1936 from Baginton in the hands of AWA chief test pilot Alan Campbell-Orde. Early flight tests were satisfactory and devoid of serious problems, but although the Whitley clearly had a much better performance than the biplanes it was to replace, it left a lot

11

to be desired for a new bomber which would be entering service in the late 1930s. On 27 June K4586 made its public debut in the New Types Park at the RAF Display at Hendon before flying to the Aeroplane and Armament Experimental Establishment (A&AEE) at Martlesham Heath, Suffolk, for trials. It achieved 192mph (309km/h) at 7,000ft (2,134m); 180mph (290km/h) at 3,000ft (915m), and 183.5mph (295km/h) at 16,500ft (5,029m). At an all-up weight of 21,094lb (9,577kg), some 1,000lb (454kg) less than the original design maximum, K4586 took 15 minutes to reach 10,000ft (3,050m), its service ceiling being 19,200ft (5,852m). Using 66 per cent power and cruising at 160mph (257km/h), the Whitley prototype was able to carry a full bomb load for a distance of 1,500 miles (2,414km). With auxiliary fuel tanks fitted in the bomb bay the range increased to 1,900 miles (3,060km), but this resulted in a reduced bomb load, a longer take-off run, a supposed cruising speed of 135mph (217km/h), and implied a fourteen-hour mission.

The Whitley had an extremely thick cantilever wing in the mid-wing position which, like the rest of the machine, had a distinctly angular outline. Flaps were not in vogue at the time of the Whitley's initial design stage and, to allow the lowest possible approach speed and landing run, the wing was given an 8.5° angle of incidence. This gave the aircraft its characteristic nose-down attitude in flight, although, even before the prototype flew, hydraulically-operated split flaps had been incorporated in the design, stretching along the wing trailing edges from the Frise-type ailerons to the fuselage. Power for K4586 was provided by two 795hp (593kW) Armstrong Siddeley Tiger IX fourteen-cylinder, two-row air-cooled radial engines, enclosed by long-chord NACA cowlings with rear exhaust collector rings and driving de Havilland three bladed controllable-pitch propellers.

Because of the wing's high angle of incidence and the subsequent adoption of split flaps, the Whitley proved easy to land, which later made it popular with RAF aircrew who operated it mainly on nocturnal sorties. Touchdown speed was only 63mph (101km/h), and landing distance 1,275ft (389m) over a 50ft (15m) screen, although use of the wheel brakes reduced the actual landing to 630ft (192m). For take-off at the normal loaded weight of 21,660lb (9,834kg), a run of less than 900ft (274m) was sufficient at a speed of 70mph (113km/h).

When K4587, the second Whitley prototype, appeared, it had been constructed in accordance with

---

ARMSTRONG WHITWORTH WHITLEY MK. III DATA

Manufacturer
Sir W. G. Armstrong Whitworth Aircraft Ltd., Baginton, Coventry

Type
Five-seat long-range heavy night bomber

Powerplant
Two 845hp (630kW) Armstrong Siddeley Tiger VIII fourteen-cylinder, two-row, air-cooled radial engines with two-speed superchargers

Performance
Maximum speed, 193mph (311km/h) at 14,250ft (4,343m). Cruising speed, 164mph (264km/h) at 15,000ft (4,575m). Initial climb, 900ft (274m)/min. Climb to 15,000ft (4,575m) at a gross weight of 26,500lb (12,031kg) in 44min. Service ceiling, 17,000ft (5,182m). Range with standard fuel and 3,650lb (1,657kg) of bombs, 1,190 miles (1,914km)

Weights
Empty, 16,234lb (7,370kg). Loaded (maximum take-off), 26,500lb (12,031kg)

Dimensions
Span, 84ft (25.60m). Length, 69ft 4in (21.12m). Height, 15ft (4.6m). Wing area, 1,137sq ft (105.63sq m). Landing gear track, 18ft 10in (5.7m)

Armament
Two 0.303in (7.7mm) Vickers GO machine-guns, one each in power-operated Frazer-Nash nose turret and AW.38 tail turret, plus two 0.303in (7.7mm) Browning Mk. II Star machine-guns in FN17 ventral turret. Two 2,000lb (908kg) bombs in fuselage and six 250lb (114kg) and six 112lb (51kg) or six 120lb (55kg) bombs in wings

ARMSTRONG WHITWORTH WHITLEY MK. VII DATA

Manufacturer
Sir W. G. Armstrong Whitworth Aircraft Ltd., Baginton, Coventry

Type
Six-seat long-range maritime reconnaissance bomber with ASV Mk. II radar

Powerplant
Two 1,145hp (854kW) (take-off) Rolls-Royce Merlin X twelve-cylinder, liquid-cooled vee engines with two-speed superchargers

Performance
Maximum speed, 215mph (346km/h) at 16,400ft (4,999m). Cruising speed, 195mph (314km/h) at 15,000ft (4,572m). Climb, 12,000ft (3,658m) in 22min. Service ceiling, 20,000ft (6,096m). Range (with auxiliary tanks), 2,300 miles (3,701km)

Weights
Empty, 19,600lb (8,890kg). Loaded (maximum take-off), 33,950lb (15,400kg)

Dimensions
Span, 84ft (25.60m). Length, 72ft 6in (22.1m). Height, 15ft (4.57m). Wing area, 1,137sq ft (105.63sq m). Landing gear track, 18ft 10in (5.7m)

Armament
One 0.303in (7.7mm) Vickers GO machine-gun in power operated Frazer-Nash nose turret and four 0.303in (7.7mm) Browning machine-guns in power-operated Frazer-Nash tail turret. Maximum ordnance load, up to 5,995lb (2,719kg) of bombs and/or depth charges

ARMSTRONG WHITWORTH WHITLEY PRODUCTION

First prototype K4586 to Specification B.3/34
Second prototype K4587 to production Specification B.21/35

WHITELY MK. III (TIGER ENGINES)

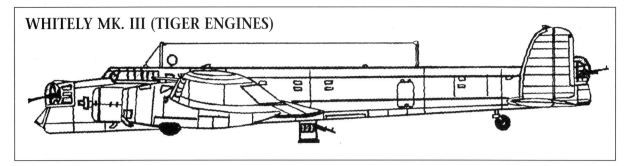

Specification B.21/35 covering the production version, and was powered by two 935hp (697kW) Armstrong Siddeley Tiger XI engines. Its first flight was from Baginton on 24 February 1937, piloted by Charles Turner-Hughes, who had replaced Campbell-Orde as chief test pilot during 1936. With the Tiger XI engines K4587's top speed rose to the required 205mph (330km/h) of B.3/34, and within a few days of this flight the delivery of production Whitleys began.

With RAF expansion in full swing, Scheme F was introduced in 1936 to allow further extension of the programme, and on 13 May AWA received orders for another 240 Whitleys under contract No. 522438/36. The number of production Whitleys now ordered totalled 320, it being anticipated that all would be delivered by the end of March 1939. By then, it was thought, a new generation of bombers to Specification P.13/36 (the Avro Manchester and Handley Page Halifax) would be available, and no more Whitleys would be required. However, early in 1937 it was clear that AWA was behind schedule with Whitley production, and it was estimated that by 31 March 1939 only 200 would have been built. Consequently, on 30 April 1937 AWA was officially informed that 120 of the last 240 Whitleys ordered were cancelled forthwith. In due

---

Initial production batch of 80 Whitleys = 34 Mk. Is (K7183–K7216) and 46 Mk. IIs (K7217–K7262)

Second production batch of 120 = 80 Mk. IIIs (K8963–K9015), 33 Mk. IVs (K9016–K9048) and seven Mk. IVAs (K9049–K9055). Another 120 Whitleys initially included in this batch (K9056–K9175) were cancelled

Third production batch = 312 Mk. Vs (N1345–N1528 and P4930–P5112). For security purposes some numbers were omitted in each sequence from N1345 onwards. P4949 was used as the Whitley Mk. VII prototype

Fourth production batch = 150 Mk. Vs (T4130–T4339)

Fifth production batch = 600 Mk. Vs (Z6461–Z6980, Z9119–Z9529 and AD665–AD714)

Sixth production batch = 300 Mk. Vs (BD189–BD674)

Seventh production batch = 100 Mk. Vs (ED283–ED410)

Eighth production batch = 150 Mk. Vs (LA763–LA951)

The following aircraft were completed as Whitley VIIs for Coastal Command: Z6960–Z6969; Z9120–Z9124; Z9135–Z9139; Z9190–Z9199;

Z9364–Z9383; Z9516–Z9529; BD423–BD434; BD561–BD574; BD620–BD625; BD675–BD693; EB282; EB327–EB336; EB392–EB401; LA794–LA798; LA813–LA817. Some Mk. Vs were converted to Mk. VIIs, two examples being Z6633 and Z9138

The following Mk. Vs were converted as freighters for BOAC: Z6660/G-AGDW; Z9208/G-AGDU; Z9216/G-AGDV; BD360-BD362/G-AGCF/G/H; BD382-BD384/G-AGCI/J/K; BD385-BD387/G-AGDX/Y/Z; BD388-BD390/G-AGEA/B/C.

Total number of Whitleys built = 1,814 including two prototypes and 1,466 Mk. Vs

RAF WHITLEY UNITS

Bomber and Coastal Commands
No. 7 Squadron (Whitley Mks. II and III)
No. 10 Squadron (Whitley Mks. I, IV and V)
No. 51 Squadron (Whitley Mks. II, III, IV and V)
No. 58 Squadron (Whitley Mks. I, II, III, V and VII)

No. 77 Squadron (Whitley Mks. III and V)
No. 78 Squadron (Whitley Mks. I, IVA and V)
No. 97 Squadron (Whitley Mks. II and III)
No. 102 Squadron (Whitley Mks. III and V)
No. 166 Squadron (Whitley Mks. I and III)
No. 295 Squadron (Whitley Mk. V)
No. 296 Squadron (Whitley Mk. V)
No. 297 Squadron (Whitley Mk. V)
No. 298 Squadron (Whitley Mk. V)
No. 502 Squadron (Whitley Mks. V and VII)
No. 612 Squadron (Whitley Mks. V and VII)

Special Duties
No. 138 Squadron (Whitley Mk. V)
No. 161 Squadron (Whitley Mk. V)

Training and Glider Towing
No. 10 Operational Training Unit, Abingdon, with a detachment at St Eval (Whitley Mk. V)
No. 1 Parachute Training School, Ringway (Whitley Mk. II)
No. 21 Heavy Glider Conversion Unit, Brize Norton (Whitley Mk. V)

course, however, circumstances resulted in substantial numbers of later Mk. V Whitleys being produced at AWA.

Structurally, the wings and empennage of the Whitley were similar to those of the earlier A.W.23, the Whitley's span and chord being slightly less. A patented innovative form of construction using light alloy was employed, the front and rear web spars being corrugated vertically, with top and bottom sheets corrugated spanwise to form a basic torsion box. Steel struts replaced conventional ribs as internal bracing, and the whole torsion box and built-on wing leading edges were covered by alloy sheet. Surfaces aft of the rear spar had fabric covering, as did the metal framed Frise-type ailerons. Split flaps with a maximum deflection of 60° stretched from ailerons to the fuselage. The low-aspect-ratio wings themselves were of unusually thick section, and incorporated additional bomb bays.

Located low on the rear fuselage, a broad tailplane carried twin fins and rudders. These vertical tail surfaces had curved leading edges and were strut-braced to the fuselage just ahead of the tail turret.

The Whitley's fuselage was a light-alloy semi-monocoque structure covered by Alclad sheet flush-riveted to longitudinal stringers supported by curved, open-section framing. Most of the fuselage had relatively curved sides formed by alloy frames and, in cross-section, resembled a barrel rather than an oblong with rounded corners as is often thought. The only really 'slab-sided' portion was in the area of the tail turret. Built in three parts, the fuselage comprised a nose section bolted to two large frames fixed to the centre-section spars, a middle portion stretching from the centre-section to the tailplane spar, and a rear section containing the tail gun turret and tailplane centre section.

Retraction of the main landing gear forward and up into the engine nacelles was actuated by Lockheed jacks, the main leg shock absorbers compressing to reduce stowage space. Thus the Dunlop wheels projected slightly beneath the nacelles and minimised damage in the event of a wheels-up landing. A fixed, castoring, self-centring tailwheel was located beneath the rear fuselage. Outboard of the nacelles in each wing leading edge was a contoured fuel tank with a capacity of 182 Imp gal (827lit), a third tank in the fuselage above the wing centre-section holding 154 Imp gal (700lit).

Defensive armament initially comprised two 0.303in (7.7mm) Lewis machine-guns mounted one each in nose and tail turrets. These were fitted to an AWA mounting inside Perspex covered cupolas rotated by means of the gunner's feet, gun elevation and depression relying on his relative posture. As these turrets were limited to the installation of a single gun, it would not be long before they were replaced by more effective types.

When the first production Mk. I Whitleys rolled off the line no wing dihedral was incorporated, but a dihedral angle of 4° was quickly adopted and applied to all production machines, also being incorporated retrospectively as a modification to all early Mk. Is. Owing to an initial shortage of turrets, some Whitley Is flew with metal fairings over the nose and tail gun positions, but turrets were later fit-

Below: The first production Whitley, K7183. Note the early-type A.W. front turret and small serial numbers on the rear fuselage and fin but large white serials under the wings. (MAP)

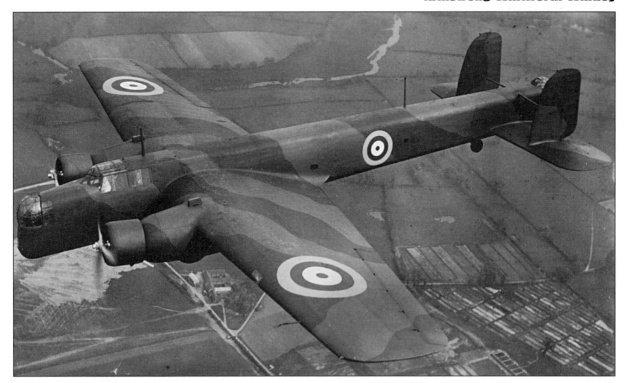

Above: Early production Whitley I K7191 on a test flight near Baginton in 1937. It later served with No. 10 Squadron. (Author's collection)

ted by Airwork Ltd. Only the first dozen Whitley Is had AWA A.W.13 (nose) and A.W.12 (tail) turrets fitted, each housing a Lewis gun (22 magazines per gun) mounted on a pedestal. These turrets were eventually superseded by Frazer-Nash hydraulically operated nose and tail turrets, the Lewis guns being replaced by 0.303in (7.7mm) Vickers gas-operated (GO) machine-guns.

A lengthy bomb bay extended from below the cockpit to the wing trailing edge, while the wing bomb bays were located inboard and outboard of the engine nacelles aft of the rear spars. This enabled the Whitley I to carry six 250lb (113kg) or twelve 112lb (51kg) bombs in the wings in addition to its 2,000lb (908kg) or four 500lb (227kg) bombs in the main bomb bay (later two 2,000lb (908kg) bombs became part of a Whitley's maximum load). As an alternative, two 66 Imp gal (300lit) auxiliary fuel tanks could replace two bombs in the main bomb bay, and reconnaissance flares were carried in a separate bay to the rear. The bomb-bay doors were wooden frames with metal covering, and were kept shut by means of elastic bungee, opening under the weight of bombs as they were released. The normal bomb load for a Whitley I was initially 1,500lb (681kg), a maximum 4,220lb (1,916kg) load being practicable later and comprising four 500lb (227kg) bombs in the fuselage bay, six

250lb (114kg) bombs in the inner wing bays and six 120lb (55kg) bombs in the outer wing bays. If 132 Imp gal (600lit) of fuel replaced two bombs in the main bay, the bomb load was reduced to 3,220lb (1,462kg).

At its normal operating weight of 21,876lb (9,932kg) the Whitley Mk. I could attain a top speed of 184mph (296km/h) at 15,000ft (4,575m), and a cruising speed of 152mph (245km/h) at that altitude. With a 1,500lb (681kg) bomb load the range was 1,370 miles (2,204km), but, if flying overloaded at a gross weight of 25,120lb (11,404kg), a 3,220lb (1,462kg) bomb load could be carried 1,840 miles (2,961km), or a 4,220lb (1,916kg) load a distance of 1,500 miles at cruising speeds of 152mph (245km/h) and 135mph (217km/h) respectively. However, at this excessive weight it took over 40 minutes to reach 15,000ft (4,575m), and the service ceiling was limited to 16,000ft (4,877m).

After 34 Whitley Is (K7183–K7216) had been completed, the remaining 46 machines from the first production batch emerged as Mk. IIs (K7217–K7262), a modified Mk. I (K7209) serving as the prototype. Whitley IIs were powered by Armstrong Siddeley Tiger VIII radials with two-speed superchargers (the first in RAF service) rated at 845hp (630kW) for take-off. Provision was made to install a retractable Frazer-Nash FN17 ventral turret, but this was fitted mainly in Whitley IIIs, other versions having a large blanking plate across the aperture. The standard bomb load for the Mk. II was 3,500lb (1,590kg), comprising four 500lb (227kg) bombs in the fuselage and six 250lb

PHOTO "THE AEROPLANE"

Above: In this view of Whitley K7191 the lack of dihedral on this early production model is apparent. Note the early type of RAF upper wing roundel. (Author's collection)

(114kg) in the wing bays. Overload weight was now 26,500lb (12,031kg), the performance being similar to the Mk. I, with slightly better speed and ceiling figures but a shorter range. Delivery of Mk. IIs finished in August 1938, fulfilling the first contract for 80 aircraft.

Eighty Whitley IIIs (K8936–K9015) followed under contract No. 522438/36 to Specification B.20/36, the prototype being converted Mk. I K7211. The Mk. III differed in having its main bomb bay adapted to carry two 2,000lb (908kg) bombs, as well as six 250lb (114kg) bombs in the wing bays. The established defensive armament on this variant was two 0.303in (7.7mm) Vickers GO machine-guns, one each in a Frazer-Nash power-operated nose turret and AWA A.W.38 tail turret, with six magazines each. Twin 0.303in (7.7mm) Browning Mk. II Star machine-guns were mounted in a Frazer-Nash FN17 retractable ventral 'dustbin' turret with 1,000 rounds per gun (rpg). Despite its wider field of fire (it was rotatable through a full 360°) the 'dustbin' turret proved a hindrance, weighing around half a ton (508kg) and creating unacceptable drag in its lowered position. With identical Tiger VIII engines and little difference in empty or overload weights, performance of the Whitley III was on a par with that of the Mk. II.

Efforts to provide more power resulted in plans for updating a Whitley to have Bristol Pegasus XX engines, but these never materialised. A scheme to fit Rolls-Royce Merlin twelve-cylinder liquid-cooled vees did, however, and Whitley I K7208 was passed to Rolls-Royce at Hucknall at the end of 1937. After conversion, K7208 made its first flight from Hucknall with a pair of Merlin IIs on 11 February 1938. With nose and tail gun positions faired, K7208 flew to the A&AEE for trials during April/May 1938. At a gross weight of 20,000lb (9,080kg) its top speed was 239mph (385km/h) at 16,000ft (4,877m). This resulted in two more Whitley Is, K7209 and K7211, having Merlins fitted for trials. The main criticisms were poor cabin heating and a high level of noise, but these discomforts were outweighed by the important benefits offered by Merlin-powered Whitleys.

Of the original 200 Whitleys ordered, the last 40 were Merlin-powered, 33 (K9016–K9048) being designated Mk. IVs and having two 1,030hp (768kW) Merlin IVs driving three-bladed Rotol constant-speed propellers. Their top speed at a gross weight of 25,900lb (11,760kg) was 244mph (393km/h) at 16,400ft (5,000m), cruising speed was 220mph (354km/h) at 15,000ft (4,572m), climb to 15,000ft (4,572m) took 16 minutes, normal cruising range was 1,250 miles (2,011km), and maximum range 1,800 miles (2,896km). A bomb load of 7,000lb (3,178kg), comprising two 2,000lb (908kg) and twelve 250lb

Above: This excellent view of Whitley I K7208 shows the curved leading edge to the fins, the added dihedral, the faired rear turret position and the port entrance door in the fuselage. (Rolls-Royce plc, Derby)

(114kg) bombs, gave an overload weight of 30,000lb (13,620kg) and a range of only 350 miles (563km). Cruising at 192mph (309km/h) at 15,000ft (4,575m) with a 3,300lb (1,498kg) bomb load, the range was 1,255 miles (2,020km).

The last seven Whitleys from this batch, K9049–K9055, were Mk. IVAs powered by uprated Merlin X engines producing 1,010hp (753kW) at 17,750ft (5,410m). The first flight of a production Whitley IV was made on 5 April 1939, an important step in defensive armament in this version being

Below: Here, Whitley I K7208 has arrived at Hucknall, where its two Armstrong Siddeley Tiger IX radials are to be replaced by Rolls-Royce with a pair of Merlins. Note the faired front turret position and the landing lights in the wing leading edge. (Rolls-Royce plc, Derby)

replacement of the old manually-operated tail turret by a new Frazer-Nash power-operated type. This turret, first tested on Whitley I K7183 in May 1939, housed four 0.303in (7.7mm) Browning machine-guns with 1,000rpg and 4,000 rounds reserve, the most potent rear defence of any bomber then in service. A handful of Mk. IVs which retained the old AWA tail turret were known by the AWA type number 206. Fuel tankage was improved with the installation of two extra 93 Imp gal (423lit) wing tanks inboard of the engines, bringing total normal fuel capacity up to 705 Imp gal (3,205lit). Also on Whitley Mk. IVs the old hinged bomb-aiming nose panel was replaced by a Plexiglas 'chin' extension, which increased the overall length by 24in (61cm). This vee-shaped window was also retrospectively fitted to some earlier Tiger-engined Whitleys.

The Whitley's five-man crew consisted of pilot, copilot/navigator, nose gunner/bomb-aimer, wireless operator and tail gunner. In Mk. IIIs fitted with the ventral FN17 turret, wireless operators doubled as 'dustbin' gunners. The copilot/navigator was provided

Left: A close-up of the Rolls-Royce Merlin II installation in Whitley I K7208 at Rolls-Royce, Hucknall. This view clearly shows the mounting frames, exhaust manifolds and vee-formed cylinder blocks of the starboard engine. (Rolls-Royce plc, Derby)

Below: A full frontal of the Rolls-Royce Merlin installation in the port wing of Whitley I K7208 at Rolls-Royce, Hucknall. (Rolls-Royce plc, Derby)

with a seat which pushed back and swivelled, giving access to a chart table aft of the captain. Access to the front turret was via the cockpit and under the right side of the instrument panel. Before the introduction of the fixed 'chin' window, bomb aiming was through a window in a vertical panel which hinged outward to allow a clear downward view. Entry for the crew was through a door in the rear port side of the fuselage, ingress to the aircraft's forward area being along a cat-walk fitted over the bomb bay and through the wing centre section where it crossed the fuselage. The tail gunner reached his turret via a gangway, negotiating the tailwheel mounting and tailplane centre-section en route.

By 1938 the Air Ministry realised that hopes for production of new Manchester and Halifax bombers were receding fast, and only Whitleys could fill the heavy-night-bomber gap. Consequently in April 1938 contract No. 75147/38 was issued to AWA for a further 148 Whitley IVs (N1345–N1528), which in fact were built as Mk. Vs. Retaining the Merlin X engines of the Mk. IVA, the Mk. V incorporated several modifications. The rear fuselage aft of the tailplane was extended by 15in (38cm) to give the tail gunner an improved field of fire from the Frazer-Nash power-operated four-gun turret, fin size was reduced by replacing the original curved leading edges with straight ones, the direction-finding (D/F) loop was enclosed in a streamlined fairing, and rubber de-icing boots were incorporated in wing leading edges. The maximum bomb load was 7,000lb (3,178kg), with two 2,000lb (908kg) bombs in the main bomb bay on front starboard and rear port racks as an alternative to four 500lb (227kg) bombs. Six 250lb (114kg) bombs could

Above: In this close-up of the port Merlin II installation in Whitley I K7208, note the panelling, the location of the landing gear, the faired turret position and the aircraft's nose-down attitude. (Rolls-Royce plc, Derby)

be carried in the inner wing bays, but the outer wing bays were seldom used, so Whitley Vs rarely carried their maximum bomb load. Nevertheless, this version was later cleared to a gross operating weight of 33,550lb (15,232kg).

In April 1938 an emergency production programme was introduced generally (Scheme L), requiring 12,000 aircraft to be produced within two years. This induced the Air Ministry to end Whitley production and order 64 Wellingtons from AWA, but production problems in September resulted in the Wellington order being replaced under contract No. 75147/38 by 64 Whitley Vs. A further 100 Mk. Vs were ordered after an extension of Scheme L, leaving AWA with orders for 164 Whitley Vs (P4930–P5112). On the outbreak of war the Air Ministry intended to add AWA to the P.13/36 (Avro Manchester) production scheme, but by the end of 1939 another 150 Whitley Vs (T4130–T4339) had been ordered under contract No. 38599/39. The Ministry envisaged that all 662 Whitleys so far ordered would be delivered by January 1941, and that AWA could then join what it was hoped would be a major P.13/36 heavy bomber production programme. By March 1940 a provisional order for 300 Manchesters had been placed with AWA, but the war situation

decreed that production of existing types was of primary importance, and two months later an additional 300 Whitleys were ordered. Indeed, Lord Beaverbrook, the recently appointed Minister of Aircraft Production, directed that five existing types of aircraft be given top priority. These were the AWA Whitley, Bristol Blenheim, Hawker Hurricane, Supermarine Spitfire and Vickers Wellington.

Chosen mainly because it was the only heavy bomber immediately available for RAF service, the Whitley V was built in larger numbers than any other version. The May 1940 order for 300 machines was doubled to 600 (Z6461–Z6980) under contract No. 106962/40, which covered remaining Whitley V orders. The first 300 of these (BD189–BD674) were built partly because of doubts arising over Avro Manchester production owing to problems with the Rolls-Royce Vulture engines. This brought total Whitley production orders to 1,562 machines, it being expected that all would be completed by March 1942. When the Manchester/Vulture problem was overcome with the four-Merlin Manchester (renamed Lancaster), it was decided that Whitley production at Baginton would be superseded by Lancasters. But further delays occurred and two more batches of Whitleys were ordered, 100 (ED283–ED410) in 1941 and a final 150 (LA763–LA951) in 1942, the first AWA-built Lancaster being rolled out in August that year. Including the two original prototypes and excluding the 120 cancelled from the first 1936 order, 1,814 Whitleys were built.

Above: A good side view of Whitley IV K9025, showing the glazed 'chin' characteristic of Whitleys thereafter, the curved leading edges to the fins and the 1938-style camouflage and markings. (Rolls-Royce plc, Derby)

Of those machines produced at Baginton during 1941/42, 146 emerged as Mk. VIIs for RAF Coastal Command. The Whitley had been first introduced to Coastal Command in September 1939, when No. 58 (Bomber) Squadron temporarily transferred to Boscombe Down, its Whitley Mk. Vs operating anti-submarine patrols over the English Channel. In 1940 this unit returned to Bomber Command, but two years later again flew patrols over the Western Approaches. Numbers 51 and 77 Squadrons also operated their Whitleys on maritime patrols. The type's suitability for oceanic patrol work, owing to its range and endurance, resulted in development of the Mk. VII, a long-range version intended specifically for maritime reconnaissance and anti-submarine duties with Coastal Command.

Powered by Merlin X engines, the Mk. VII was a revamped Mk. V with extra tankage in the bomb bay and rear fuselage which increased fuel capacity to a maximum of 1,100 Imp gal (5,000lit), giving a maximum patrol range of 2,300 miles (3,700km). Other changes included the addition of long-range air-to-surface-vessel (ASV) Mk. II radar, with its dorsal aerials (four atop the fuselage and others laterally and beneath each wing), and the necessity for a sixth crew member to serve as radar operator. The gross weight was 33,950lb (15,413kg) and this, together with the drag-inducing ASV aerials, reduced the top speed to 215mph (346km/h) at 16,400ft (4,999m) and the cruising speed to 195mph (314km/h) at 15,000ft (4,572m). This made the climb rate similar to that of the Mk. III, 22 minutes being required to reach 12,000ft (3,658m) at normal weight. The prototype Mk. VII, P4949, a converted Mk. V, was followed by 146 production machines in the Z/BD/EB and LA serial ranges. Some Mk. Vs were converted to Mk. VII standard.

During 1937 Whitley prototype K4586 went to the Royal Aircraft Establishment (RAE) at Farnborough for experiments to determine the requirements for hard-surface runways on RAF bomber airfields. The Whitley was operational from grass at a weight of 22,000lb (9,988kg), but the new heavy bombers then in the design stage (Short Stirling, Avro Manchester and Handley Page Halifax) were expected to weigh upwards of 40,000lb (18,160kg) and possibly exceed a gross weight of 53,000lb (24,062kg). To investigate this problem the RAE fixed a heavy steel beam between K4586's main landing gear units, extra large Dunlop wheels and tyres having been fitted and the track increased from the usual 18ft 10in (5.7m) to 24ft (7.3m). These experiments were of a non-flying nature, and at an initial weight of 24,000lb (10,896kg) the Whitley taxied under its own power. Extra steel members could be added to the beam to bring the

total weight to 40,000lb (18,160kg), and in December 1937 K4586 was taxied at that figure. Similar tests followed at Odiham and Stradishall and, despite measured 6in (15cm) wheel tracks being created by the Whitley, it was decided that bombers weighing 40,000lb (18,160kg) gross could operate from RAF grass runways with few problems! Nevertheless, by September 1939 hard runways had been laid at nine RAF Bomber Command bases, and when the war ended in 1945 there were 450 British airfields with tarmac or concrete runways.

The possibility of a shortage of light metals necessary for aircraft production caused AWA to consider producing wooden wings for the Whitley. Plans for such an eventuality promptly appeared in the design office, an all-wooden wing of identical dimensions and layout to the metal wing being drawn up. The only metal used was steel tubing for the torsion-box internal bracing. The wooden Whitley wing was tested under static conditions, and it was asserted that a larger bomb load and increased fuel capacity would result from its adoption. However, the need to produce wooden airframes for Whitleys never arose, and the idea was abandoned.

To compete with the high-powered Rolls-Royce Merlin and Bristol engines, Armstrong Siddeley designed a 21-cylinder air-cooled radial with the cylinders arranged in three rows and in line with each other, each line having an overhead camshaft. Named Deerhound, this very compact engine was first tested

in 1936 and produced 1,115hp (831kW), it being expected that further improvements would produce 1,500hp (1,119kW). To accommodate this engine AWA designed the A.W.39, an update of the Whitley with an exceptionally thick wing in which a pair of Deerhound engines would be buried. It was to be heavier than the Whitley, with a Boulton Paul dorsal gun turret and a 5,000lb (2,268kg) bomb load. A cruising speed of 230mph (370km/h) at 15,000ft (4,572m) was envisaged, and a range of 1,500 miles (2,414km). In the event this design was dropped and a standard Whitley bomber, the 27th production Whitley II, K7243, served as the testbed. With twin Deerhound engines installed it took off from Baginton in the first week of January 1939, flown by C. Turner-Hughes. The output of the Deerhound was increased in development stages to 1,350hp (1,007kW), but it was plagued by persistent overheating problems caused partly by a reverse-flow cooling system whereby air entered the cowling at the rear of the engine via a large frontal scoop. Cylinder finning was also poor, and a modified cylinder was under development when, in early March 1940, K7243 crashed with fatal results owing to its RAF pilot inadvertently winding the tail trim fully back. With this accident the Deerhound's future was bleak, and further development was abandoned.

The Whitley began its RAF career on 9 March 1937, when K7184, the second production Mk. I, was delivered to No. 10 Squadron, Dishforth, Yorkshire, where Whitley Mk. Is replaced the unit's Handley Page Heyford biplanes. By mid-June No. 10 Squadron had a full complement of twelve Whitleys. The next twelve machines went to Heyford-equipped No. 78 Squadron, also at Dishforth. Two of the 34 Whitley Mk. Is built were kept back for trials, however, leaving eight for delivery to No. 58 Squadron at Linton-on-Ouse, to replace its old Vickers Virginia Xs. This unit was finally brought to full Whitley strength early in 1938 with the delivery of four Mk. IIs. During 1938 No. 51 Squadron (Linton-on-Ouse) and No. 7 Squadron (Finningley) each received twelve Whitley IIs apiece, and during August delivery of Whitley IIIs commenced, No. 10 Squadron replacing its Heyfords at Driffield and No. 77 at the same base exchanging its Vickers Wellesleys for Whitley IIIs in November. Whitley IIIs then re-equipped No. 51 Squadron, which transferred its Mk. IIs to No. 97 Squadron at Leconfield while this unit awaited a full complement of Mk. IIIs. Whitley IVs fully equipped No. 10 Squadron only, this unit taking on charge 21 of the initial 22 produced. Its Whitley Is were sent to equip No. 166 Squadron at Leconfield, then on Heyfords. Some Mk. IV Whitleys went to Nos. 51 and 78 Squadrons, the latter unit operating all seven of the Whitley IVAs produced. With delivery of Mk. V Whitleys starting in August 1939, these two units were brought to full strength on Merlin-engined Whitleys. By October ten of No. 78 Squadron's Mk Vs had transferred to No. 77 Squadron, which, together with Nos. 10, 51, 58 and 102 Squadrons, became fully equipped with Whitley Vs during the opening months of the war. Subsequently Whitley Vs, the most prolific variant, were to operate with fifteen units of Bomber Command.

Autumn 1939 saw the Whitley squadrons being allotted to No. 4 Group with headquarters at Linton-on-Ouse, but only five of the nine Whitley squadrons involved could then be considered as suitable for operational night bombing. These were Nos. 10, 51, 58, 77 and 102 Squadrons. Of the other four, No. 7 Squadron had re-equipped with Handley Page Hampdens, No. 78 was converting from Whitley Is to IVs and would not be ready for operations until 1940, and Nos. 97 and 166 Squadrons (Group pool units) were to merge as No. 10 Operational Training Unit (OTU), specialising in Whitley training.

At the outbreak of war 32 Mk. I, 43 Mk. II, 76 Mk. III, 33 Mk. IV, seven Mk. IVA and five Mk. V Whitleys were in RAF service, mostly with Bomber Command's No. 4 Group, with Sir Arthur Coningham in command. This was then the world's only fully trained night bomber force, an all-Whitley concern which had ten Mk. IIIs up on the first night of the war (3/4 September 1939). Aircraft of Nos. 51 and 58 Squadrons took off from Leconfield, heading for the Ruhr and north-west Germany on a reconnaissance mission and carrying loads of propaganda leaflets,

codenamed 'Nickel' to drop over Germany. Six million pamphlets weighing thirteen tons (13,208kg) were released over Hamburg, Bremen and other Ruhr cities that night, the Whitleys being first Bomber Command aircraft to penetrate into Germany. Leading the raid was Squadron Leader J. J. A. Sutton of No. 58 Squadron in Mk. III K8973/'K', with Whitleys K8938, K8941 and K8982 of No. 51 Squadron and K8964, K8969, K8990, K9006, K9009/'M' and K9013/'W' of No. 58 Squadron.

The leaflets were in bundles tied with string, which was cut before their release via either the flare chute or ventral gun turret (where fitted). The pamphlets were part of the British government's propaganda campaign, and complied with its policy at the time forbidding the bombing of German territory. Leaflet raids were carried out on the first seven nights of the war, a further seven followed during September and, on the night of 1/2 October 1939, three Whitley IVs of No. 10 Squadron dropped leaflets on Berlin, this being the first Bomber Command sortie over the German capital. As one Whitley arrived over Berlin at 22,500ft (6,858m) the oxygen supply failed, causing two of the crew to collapse. The rear turret's mechanism had frozen, preventing the gunner from opening his door

Below: A head-on view of the last Whitley IVA, K9055. Only seven Mk. IVAs were completed, and all served with No. 78 Squadron. (Author's collection)

Above: The eighth production Whitley V, N1352, later ditched while returning from raid on Trondheim on 18/19 April 1940. (Author's collection)

Below: Two Whitley Vs, KN-J and E of No. 77 Squadron, RAF Bomber Command, in 1940 finish and coding. (Author's collection)

Above: Whitley V T4131/–/W in RAF Bomber Command matt black night finish, circa 1942. Note the row of bombs painted beneath the nose turret, indicating the number of raids carried out. (MAP)

and leaving the copilot to assist the two unconscious crewmen. One he dragged forward to connect up with the oxygen supply, before managing to drop two-thirds of the leaflets and then collapsing himself. But soon the pilot had brought the Whitley down to 9,000ft (2,743m) and everyone had recovered. The timing and navigation on this mission was remarkable for its day, the three Whitleys leaving base at three-minute intervals and arriving back exactly three minutes apart.

The difficulties experienced by those early Whitley crews as they rumbled over Germany each night, dropping their paper loads, is a monument to human courage and fortitude. For example, on the night of 27/28 October 1939 weather conditions over the targets of Dusseldorf and Frankfurt were appalling. They were so bad that the official report afterwards referred to the sheer amazement caused 'when it was realised that aircraft in such a condition of "icing-up" could still be controlled'. In those Whitleys using the ventral turret to discharge leaflets it proved impossible to lower the turret owing to the intense cold, the temperature being between –22° and –32° Celsius. One Whitley's starboard engine caught fire and was switched off as the aircraft flew through thick cloud with ice some 6in (15.2cm) thick on the wings. The Whitley dived to 7,000ft (2,133m) before

pulling out thanks to the strenuous efforts of both pilots, who then found the rudder and elevators immovable. A radio message was sent advising of the situation, but as the instruments were thick with ice the wireless operator could not tell if he was transmitting or not. After levelling out, the Whitley was still losing height at 2,000ft (6,096m) per minute, the port engine having also stopped. This was not surprising, considering 4in (10cm) of ice was visible protruding from inside the cowling! The leading edges of the propellers and the windscreen were also thickly coated with ice, and the pilot ordered the crew to bale out. However, there was no reply from the front or tail gunners (both had been knocked unconscious during the initial dive), and the order to abandon the aircraft was cancelled. By then the Whitley was in a shallow high-speed dive, and the pilot opened the top hatch to try and see where they were, the copilot, who was at the controls, peering from an open side window. They finally emerged some 200ft (61m) over a forest, skimmed the treetops and crash-landed in a field, the Whitley finishing up with its port wing against a tree on the far side. None of the crew was injured, and they stayed overnight inside the aircraft. Next morning the crew realised they were in France, and were quickly made welcome by the locals.

The crew of another Whitley managed to drop their load of leaflets although oxygen starvation forced the navigator and wireless operator to lie on the floor every few minutes to rest. Heating in the cockpit was non-existent, and everyone was frozen, the pilot and navigator butting their heads on a hard surface to experience an alternative feeling to that of frostbite and lack of oxygen. Descending to 8,000ft (2,438m) while homeward bound did not solve the icing problem, windows becoming completely coated, lumps of ice from the propeller blades striking the sides of the nose and continuous movement of the controls being necessary to prevent their freezing up. Even so, this gallant crew brought their Whitley safely back to base.

On the night of 19 March 1940 Hornum seaplane base on the island of Sylt received the first British bombs to fall on German territory when Whitleys from Nos. 10, 51 77 and 102 Squadrons attacked the base, together with a number of Hampdens from No. 5 Group. Two months later, on the night of 10 May, Whitleys from Nos. 77 and 102 Squadrons raided the German military transport routes between Germany and Holland, thus dropping the first British bombs on the German mainland.

With Italy's entry into the war on the side of Germany, Whitleys were soon in action against the new enemy, and on 11 June 1940 Nos. 10, 51, 58, 77 and 102 Squadrons flew their Whitleys across the Alps to attack Turin and Genoa in the first RAF bombing raid on Italy. Two months later, on the night of 25 August

Below: This Whitley V, T4149, has rocket-assisted take-off gear beneath its wings. It was used at RAE Farnborough for glider-towing experiments with a special towing yoke at the tail. (MAP)

1940, Whitleys from Nos. 51 and 78 Squadrons flew alongside a force of Hampdens and Wellingtons to carry out the RAF's first bombing raid on Berlin. By this time, of course, the British government had completely removed all restrictions on the bombing of Germany and, with the RAF bombing offensive now increasing in intensity, the Whitley undertook its full share of operations. These continued until the spring of 1942, when on the night of 29 April the last Whitley operation by Bomber Command was flown by No. 58 Squadron in an attack on the docks at Ostend.

In the meantime, Whitley VIIs had entered Coastal Command service late in 1941, and on 30 November a No. 502 Squadron Mk. VII (Z9190/'YG-B') operating out of Chivenor, Devon, used its ASV radar and weapons to track and destroy the German submarine U-206 in the Bay of Biscay. Other Mk. VIIs served with No. 612 Squadron at Reykjavik, Iceland, this unit having previously flown Whitley Mk. Vs as a stop-gap measure. During November and December 1942 No. 58 Squadron also flew Whitley Mk. VIIs until they were replaced by Handley Page Halifax IIs, while No. 53 Squadron flew Whitley Mk. VIIs during the first half of 1943. Whitley Mk. VIIs ended their Coastal Command service in the early summer of 1943, when No. 612 Squadron began operating Wellington VIIIs.

Whitleys also proved useful as paratroop carrying aircraft, both for training and operations. During 1940 No. 1 Parachute Training School at Ringway began using Whitley IIs for training, the aircraft having had

Armstrong Whitworth Whitley

their rear turret replaced by rather primitive 'jumping-off' platforms. This method was then superseded by modifying the redundant 'dustbin' turret well to serve as an exit for paratroops. The first British paratroop action of the Second World War involved Whitleys from Nos. 51 and 78 Squadrons. Known as Operation Colossus, this was an attack by men of the Special Air Service (SAS) on the aqueduct at Tragino, the object being to cut off the water supply to Southern Italy. Twelve months later, on the night of 27 February 1942, Whitleys from No. 51 Squadron took part in Operation Biting, the famous airborne troops raid on the German radar station at Bruneval, northern France. A dozen Whitley Vs dropped their paratroopers bang on time at the chosen spot, and as a result valuable radar components were captured and the station destroyed before the soldiers returned home courtesy of the Royal Navy.

Whitleys were also modified as glider tugs, a number serving with No. 21 Heavy Glider Conversion Unit

Right: Whitley VII BD622 of No. 612 Squadron, RAF Coastal Command, in an early colour scheme and fitted with ASV radar. (MAP)

Below: In the 1943 Coastal Command colour scheme, Whitley VII LA794 shows off its ASV radar antenna to good effect. (MAP)

Opposite page, bottom: Whitley IIIs continued in employment as paratroop trainers for some time during the war, like this one dropping its parachutists from the ventral aperture. (MAP)

Above: This Whitley V (ex-BD386) was one of fifteen converted as freighters for BOAC's wartime use in 1942. Registered G-AGDY, it was returned to the RAF as BD386 in 1943. (MAP)

at Brize Norton, where they towed the large Airspeed Horsa transport gliders. This role was undertaken wholly by Whitley Vs, and initially the rear turret was removed to allow towing gear to be installed. This system proved unsatisfactory and the turret was retained, a specially designed metal towing attachment being fitted beneath.

Fifteen Whitley Vs were converted by AWA as 'civil' freighters for use by BOAC. Their fore and aft turrets were removed and replaced by fairings, while additional tankage in the bomb bays increased the range to 2,500 miles (4,023km). A Britain to West Africa run was initially flown, but later the Whitley freighters operated out of Gibraltar on night supply flights to besieged Malta until replaced by Lockheed Hudsons in August 1942. Finally, these BOAC Whitleys were considered for the dangerous Leuchars-to-Stockholm flights, but proved unsuitable. All fourteen surviving Whitleys (one was written-off at Gibraltar) were then returned to the RAF.

Perhaps one of the Whitley's lesser-known tasks was that of dropping supplies and agents to underground resistance groups in occupied Europe. Whitley Vs operated with Nos. 138 and 161 Special Duty Squadrons on clandestine night missions, one such sortie being undertaken by Whitley Z9230 of No. 138 Squadron on the night of 30/31 July 1942. Piloted by Squadron Leader Davis DFC, it was over Holland on duties linked with the Dutch underground movement when, at 0058, it was attacked and shot down by a Luftwaffe Messerschmitt Bf 110

nightfighter from III/NJGl, flown by Leutnant August Geiger, one of Germany's top nightfighter pilots.

With the exception of Mk. Vs, all Whitleys were declared obsolete by 1944, the Mk. Vs being similarly classed in 1945, although the last Mk. V built, LA951, survived until 1947 after being retained by AWA to tow their A.W.52G tailless glider. It is sad that no example of the Whitley has survived, because despite its lack of glamour and limelight, this grand old aircraft played an important part in laying the foundation upon which the RAF's night bombing offensive was built.

Finally, a Whitley recollection from Bob Wilcock (ex-RAF) relates how his late brother, Flying Officer Doug Wilcock, was posted to No. 10 OTU at Abingdon to start bomber training on Whitleys. Part of the course was spent at St Eval, Cornwall, where the OTU had a detachment of Whitleys flying anti-submarine patrols over the Bay of Biscay. Each patrol, lasting up to ten hours, counted as one-third of a bombing sortie when a crew's tour of 30 operations was calculated. Doug Wilcock said that these patrols were mostly boring, and showed how cold a Whitley was aloft. The only relief came when the sandwiches and thermos flasks appeared.

Avro
Manchester

The first aeroplane to be named Manchester was a twin-engined biplane bomber of 1918 built by A. V. Roe and Co Ltd (Avro) at its Hamble works near Southampton. Two prototype Avro 533 Manchesters were produced, but owing to problems with the ABC Dragonfly engines intended for the type, the first machine, F3492, had two 300hp (223kW) Siddeley Puma high-compression water-cooled engines. As the Avro 533A Manchester Mk. II it first flew in December 1918, but it was late 1919 before the troublesome ABC Dragonfly engines were ready for installation in the second aircraft, Manchester Mk. I F3943. By the time the manufacturer's and Service trials had been completed, Air Ministry interest in the Avro 533 Manchester had lapsed.

Two decades later, similar circumstances occurred regarding a powerplant for the second Avro type to be named Manchester, the Type 679, although the end result was very different. The Avro 533 Manchester of 1918–19 had been developed from Avro's 523 Pike and 529, both proven airframes powered by established engines – 160hp (119kW) Sunbeams and 190hp

(141kW) Rolls-Royce Falcons respectively. In contrast, the 679 Manchester prototype, L7246, which first flew from Ringway (later Manchester Airport) on 25 July 1939, was the product of the marriage of a brand new airframe to equally new, underdeveloped engines in the form of two 1,760hp (1,312kW) Rolls-Royce Vultures.

The new bomber resulted from 1936 reports that the German air force (Luftwaffe) was rapidly expanding into a potent war machine capable of posing a serious threat in any future conflict. British politicians reacted by placing orders with industry for army, navy and air force weapons and fighting equipment. These measures included an invitation from the Air Ministry for British aircraft manufacturers to submit designs for a twin-engine tactical medium bomber (*sic*) covered by Specification P.13/36, the prefix 'P' signifying a tac-

Below: The original bomber named Manchester was this twin-engine Avro Type 533 (F3493) of 1918. One of three built, it was powered by two ABC Dragonfly engines and designated Mk. I. (MAP)

tical aircraft. The new aircraft was to be an all-metal monoplane, more powerful than the Armstrong Whitworth Whitley, Vickers Wellington and Handley Page Hampden bombers about to enter RAF service, and it was initially proposed that the ordnance load should consist of either 8,000lb (3,628kg) of bombs or two aerial torpedoes. The Air Ministry was assured by several aero-engine manufacturers that powerplants equal to the task would certainly be available by the time the new bomber reached production status.

Specification P.13/36 itself makes interesting reading when one considers the type of aircraft required. Dated 8 September 1936, it calls for a medium bomber capable of worldwide use and able to exploit long range and heavy bomb loads by means of catapult launching (often referred to as 'frictionless take-off'). To minimise time spent over enemy territory the highest possible cruising speed was essential, and of primary importance was the provision of adequate facilities for interchanging fuel and bomb loads, according to whether load carrying or range was the priority. All-round defence was essential, with power-operated gun turrets in nose and tail positions. The bomber was to be suitable for day and night operations worldwide, to have the best possible bomb aiming and navigational equipment, and to have good facilities for maintenance to be carried out in the open. If possible, the basic design was required to combine the Medium Bomber, General Reconnaissance and General Purpose Class (sic) of aircraft, and consideration was to be given to the carrying of two torpedoes.

Below: Avro Manchester prototype L7246, which first flew on 25 July 1939 with Rolls-Royce Vulture engines. Note the original design of twin fins and rudders. (MAP)

With regard to performance, the speed was to be not less than 275mph (442.5km/h) at 15,000ft (4,572m) on two-thirds maximum power at maximum cruise rpm. With a normal load, including 1,000lb (453kg) of bombs, and a 1,500ft (457m) take-off, the range at 15,000ft (4,572m) was to be not less than 2,000 miles (3,218km). When loading was increased to include 4,000lb (1,814kg) of bombs and a 2,100ft (640m) take-off, range was to be not less than 2,000 miles (3,218km) at sea level. With a maximum load, including 4,000lb (1,814kg) of bombs, and where accelerated take-off (catapulting) was used, it was stipulated that the range should be not less than 3,000 miles (4,828km) after 30 minutes, maximum power at sea level.

It was expected that, under maximum load, a range of some 2,000 miles (3,218km) would be attained carrying 8,000lb (3,628kg) of bombs. In any event, the maximum range of the new aircraft was to be not less than 3,000 miles (4,828km), and the service ceiling under normal load was to be at least 28,000ft (8,534m). The design was to include British engines which had passed their Service type test. Accommodation was to be provided for two pilots (one acting as navigator, front gunner and bomb aimer), one radio operator, and on long flights an extra pilot to act as relief pilot or navigator.

Armament was to comprise two guns in a nose-mounted power-operated turret controlled by the second pilot, and four machine-guns in a power-operated tail turret, with 1,000 rounds per gun and a reserve of 6,000 rounds. Maximum bomb load could consist of 16 x 250lb (113kg), 16 x 500lb (226kg) or 4 x 2,000lb (907kg) bombs. It was hoped that the new bomber would be able to carry two 18in-

MANCHESTER MK. I

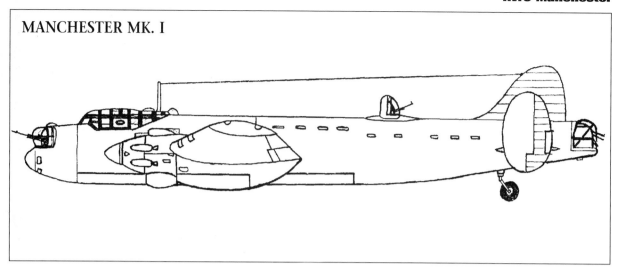

AVRO TYPE 679 MANCHESTER MK. IA DATA

Manufacturers
A. V. Roe & Co Ltd., Newton Heath, Manchester; and Woodford Aerodrome, Cheshire. Metropolitan-Vickers Ltd., Trafford Park, Manchester

Type
Seven-seat medium/heavy bomber

Powerplant
Two 1,760hp (1,312kW) Rolls-Royce Vulture 24-cylinder X-type liquid-cooled engines

Performance
Maximum speed, 265mph (426km/h) at 17,000ft (5,180m). Cruising speed, 185mph (298km/h) at 15,000ft (4,570m). Service ceiling, 19,200ft (5,850m). Range, 1,630 miles (2,623km) with fuel load of 1,160 Imp gal (5,273lit) and 8,100lb (3,674kg) bomb load; 1,200 miles (1,931km) with 882 Imp gal (4,009lit) of fuel and 10,350lb (4,694kg) bomb load

Weights
Empty, 29,432lb (13,350kg). Loaded (maximum take-off), 56,000lb (25,401kg)

Dimensions
Span, 90ft 1in (27.46m). Length, 69ft 4in (21.13m). Height, 19ft 6in (5.94m). Wing area, 1,131sq ft (105.63sq m)

Armament
Eight 0.303in (7.7mm) Browning machine-guns mounted two each in nose and dorsal turrets and four in the tail turret. Maximum bomb load, 10,350lb (4,69Skg)

AVRO MANCHESTER PRODUCTION

Two prototypes (L7246 and L7247), built by Avro under Contract No. 624973/37/C4(c) of 30 April 1937. Works Order No. 5667

200 production Manchester Is (L7276 to L7584 inclusive), ordered under Contract No. 648770/37/C4(c) of 1 July 1937. Works Order No. 5723. An amendment to this contract dated 20 September 1939 ordered a further 200 machines, but on 29 May 1941 the Air Ministry reduced the total of Manchesters to be built from 400 to 157. Of these, one machine, L7517, was destroyed by fire before delivery. From L7527 Manchester airframes on the production line were converted into Lancasters.

In 1939 Metropolitan-Vickers received Contract No. B108750/40, Works Order No. 8060, for the production of 100 Manchester Is in the serial range R5768–R5917. Of these, R5768–R5780 were destroyed in the factory by an enemy air raid on 23 December 1940, these serials being re-allocated to other Manchesters further up the production line. In the event only 43 machines (R5768–R5841) were completed as

Manchesters, the remainder becoming Lancaster Is on the production line. Conversions to Manchester IAs by Avro included L7276, '77 and '79–L7294; L7296–L7299; L7301, '05 and '08; L7385 and '86; L7389–L7391; L7394–L7398 and L7417–'18. Conversions to Mk. IAs by Rollaston Aviation and Tollerton Ltd were L7399–L7402 and L7415–'16.

RAF MANCHESTER UNITS

No. 9 Squadron, 5 Group. Coded WS
No. 44 Squadron, coded KM
No. 49 Squadron, 1, 3 and 5 Groups. Coded EA
No. 50 Squadron, 5 Group. Coded VN
No. 61 Squadron, 5 Group. Coded QR
No. 83 Squadron, 5 and 8 Groups. Coded OL
No. 97 Squadron, 5 and 8 Groups. Coded OF
No. 106 Squadron, 5 Group. Coded ZN
No. 207 Squadron, 5 Group. Coded EM
No. 408 Squadron (Canadian), coded EQ
No. 420 Squadron (Canadian), coded PT
No. 25 OTU
Nos. 1654, 1656, 1660, 1661 HCUs
No. 1485 BGS
Nos. 1, 3 and 8 AGSs
Also various establishments i.e. AFDU, AOS, A&AEE, TDU and the Lancaster Finishing School (LFS).

Above: The small original central fin is clearly visible in this view of the second Manchester prototype, L7247, taken in 1940. (MAP)

diameter (457.2mm), 18ft 2.5in-long (5.6m) torpedoes as an alternative.

It can be seen that Specification P.13/36 contained numerous requirements which would provide Avro's design team, led by Roy Chadwick, with the problem of designing an aircraft the like of which they had not produced before regarding configuration, stressed skinning, weight and power. They had to produce an aircraft exceeding 20 tons (20.32 tonnes), capable of carrying a heavy bomb load at very high speed considering its size. There was also the task of including new and sophisticated hydraulic and electrical systems, plus the latest technical equipment available. There is little doubt that, for its time the Avro 679 Manchester represented a major step forward in bomber design, but a factor of considerable disadvantage to the design team was the immediate threat of war breaking out. This greatly restricted development time, and resulted in arrangements for quantity production being made before either of the two prototypes flew. Consequently preparations were well advanced by the middle of 1938 for extensive Manchester production at Avro's Newton Heath works, Manchester, as well as at Woodford, Cheshire, and at Metropolitan-Vickers Ltd at Trafford Park, Manchester. Thus the stage was set for Avro's new twin-engined bomber, and when it emerged the airframe itself proved to be an outstanding design.

However, the same could not be said for the embryo Rolls-Royce Vulture engine chosen to power the new bomber. At quite an early stage, certainly before the RAF accepted its first Manchester into service, proposals had suggested installation of four Bristol Pegasus or Hercules radials, or four Rolls-Royce Merlin in-line engines to power the new machine. But top-level decisions were made to go for two very powerful engines rather than four of the 800 to 1,000hp (597 to 746kW) category then available. Ironically, after the Vulture engine proved such a liability in service, reversion to the four-engine layout was undertaken with excellent results, as will be seen.

The basic problem lay in the haste with which the Vulture had to be introduced. With war imminent, Rolls-Royce could not devote enough time to the new powerplant because of commitment and absolute priority being given to Merlin engine design and production. Despite testing of the Vulture at Hucknall with a 2,010hp (1,499kW) rating at 9lb (4kg) boost using 100-octane fuel, Rolls-Royce could not guarantee reliability of the new engine in the limited time available for its development. One major teething problem concerned fatigue failure of connecting-rod bolts, and early trials with Vulture-powered Manchesters were to prove disappointing to say the least. Indeed, one test report made it clear that the Vulture engines were just not producing enough power for the Manchester.

The Vulture itself was created by mounting two sets of Rolls-Royce Peregrine V-12 cylinder blocks to use a common crankshaft. With 60°/120° spacing between the blocks, a 24-cylinder engine of 'X' cross-section was produced with a 5in (12.7cm) bore and 5.5in (13.97cm) stroke. Design of the Vulture started in September 1935 and the first tests were carried out during May 1937. By August 1939 an updated Vulture II was producing 1,800hp (1,342kW), and production started in the following January. However, connecting-rod failures continued to plague the engine, and it was necessary to reduce the maximum rpm, first from 3,200 to 3,000 and eventually to 2,850. On paper the original estimated power rating was 1,710hp (1,275kW), and a

Above: The second production Manchester, L7277, with a larger central fin replacing the original small type. (MAP)

calculated rating gave 1,845hp (1,376kW) at 5,000ft (1,524m), but the final level power produced was 1,760hp (1,312kW) when driving a Rotol three-bladed, constant-speed metal propeller. Even so, in-service accessibility to the Vulture was poor and it was prone to catching fire in flight. These factors, coupled with other teething problems, resulted in inferior engine performance and deplorable reliability. It was not surprising, therefore, that Rolls-Royce switched its attention to more viable engines and ceased production of the Vulture in April 1942, after 508 had been built, mostly for Manchesters.

Meanwhile, Avro's design team had submitted several plans for the Type 679 Manchester, the first in September 1936 depicting a twin Vulture-powered layout with a 69ft (21m) long fuselage, 72ft (22m) span wings tapered in planform and thickness, twin fins and rudders inset on the 20ft 9in (6.4m) span tailplane, nose and tail turrets, a raised cockpit canopy and twin main wheels on oleo legs forming the retractable undercarriage. In 1937 a drawing was produced in which two Bristol Hercules air-cooled radial engines replaced the Vultures, the entire layout now being very much altered. Superseding the tapered wing was a broad-chord centre section with straight leading and trailing edges, outer tapered wing panels with rounded tips, a more angular tailplane of greater span with oval fins and rudders fitted as endplates, and single main wheels with high-pressure tyres. The fuselage was now deeper, and a glazed bomb aiming position protruded beneath the front gun turret. This design approached more closely the eventual Manchester outline. The wingspan was given as 80ft 2in (24.4m) and the length as 68ft 8.5in (21m).

Other competitors for P.13/36 included Handley Page with its H.P.56, intended for twin-Vulture installation but extensively redesigned, as doubts rose about the Vulture, to take four Rolls-Royce Merlins and become the H.P.57 Halifax. A shoulder-wing design from the Bristol Aeroplane Co, which would have flown at 15,000ft (4,572m) carrying an 8,000lb (3,628kg) bomb load at 315mph (507km/h) and was to be powered by Bristol Hercules radials, was turned down by the Air Ministry. Also rejected was a design by Hawker Aircraft Ltd, in which twin Vulture engines were mounted in a mid-wing layout of 87ft (26.5m) span. Its length would have been 72ft 8in (22.18m), and it had twin fins and rudders. Thus Avro's 679 Manchester was sole survivor in the P.13/36 competition, the Air Ministry inviting the company to build two prototypes, L7246 and L7247.

On the Manchester prototype's initial flight, Avro test pilot Captain H. A. Brown realised that the new Vulture engines were not producing sufficient power and, because of its high wing loading, the aircraft was difficult to handle. During a series of extensive trials at the A&AEE, Boscombe Down, L7246 revealed a tendency to lateral instability, while the Vulture engines proved their inability to produce sufficient power for the new bomber. To counteract the instability a small, shark-like fin was added atop the rear fuselage, complementing the twin endplate fins and rudders, but this was soon replaced by a larger and more aesthetically pleasing fin. Trials continued at Boscombe Down, but on 12 December 1939 L7246 crashed in a nearby field and suffered superficial damage. After repairs it was sent to Farnborough for trials in accordance with Air Ministry requirements for the possible catapult launching of Manchesters.

A 'frictionless take-off' system specially designed for the Manchester was chosen from three plans drawn

Above: Manchester L7288/EM-H of No. 207 Squadron early in 1941. (Ron Mackay)

up by the RAE at Farnborough for catapult take-off and arrested landing trials of Avro's new bomber. All three designs were hydro-pneumatically operated and robust enough to launch a fully loaded Manchester regardless of wind direction. Plan 1 showed the rear fuselage raised on a wheeled support, the main landing wheels resting on a railborne wide-track dolly. In plan 2 the main support was moved forward beneath the front fuselage, the dolly being pulled from ahead of the catapult. Plan 3 had two wheeled supports located one each beneath the nose and centre fuselage, spreading the force applied on take-off. Scheme 2 was chosen, and L7246 spent much of its career at Farnborough in efforts to perfect the catapult system for launching a heavily-laden Manchester. Ironically, an Air Ministry directive of July 1938 cancelled the requirement for catapult-launch stressing on production Manchesters.

Because of the Vulture engine troubles, Avro began studying plans for a Manchester Mk. II powered by two 2,100hp (1,566kW) Napier Sabre engines, one airframe being earmarked for delivery to Napier's Luton factory in Bedfordshire. However, the Sabre engine itself was proving troublesome, and this project was abandoned. Another airframe went to Filton for installation of two 2,520hp (1,879kW) Bristol Centaurus

radial engines, but it is believed that this machine was never air-tested.

Avro's design team did not only consider powerplant alternatives. Among several plans drawn up was one in which defensive armament for the new bomber consisted of eight 20mm Hispano, or Oerlikon, cannon mounted in a massive double turret by Boulton Paul which provided dorsal and ventral positions with four guns in each. The nose and tail turrets were to be faired in. Other turret arrangements by Bristol Aeroplane Co (Armaments Division) and Nash & Thompson (Frazer Nash) were also studied, but the swollen fuselage section resulting from these proposed installations was unacceptable. It was decided, however, to fit a retractable two-gun ventral turret aft of the bomb bay, and a 'dustbin' type was installed on the second prototype Manchester, L7247. This turret was quite physically demanding to operate, and contained a poor form of periscopic sight. One might think that the vulnerability of the Manchester's belly, with its blind spot below the aircraft, might have led officialdom to persevere in developing a more sophisticated type of ventral turret for this bomber, but it was not so.

Meanwhile, the second prototype Manchester, L7247, made its maiden flight at Ringway on 26 May 1940. The empennage included an original type of third 'shark-fin', although this was quickly replaced by the larger fin used on the first prototype. All defensive

pressed oval section and comprised five portions designed to ease production and transportation. A light-alloy stressed-skin covering was used. The flight crew were housed together in a forward cabin enclosed by a bulletproof glazed canopy, warmed by ducted air passing through a small coolant radiator housed within the wing. Both pilots were provided with armoured back plates, and a pivoted armour-plated bulkhead was located just ahead of the front spar. Initially a crew of five was allowed for, but later a seven-man crew flew in Manchesters, consisting of pilot, second pilot, navigator, wireless operator and three air gunners (nose, tail and dorsal). The doors enclosing the vast bomb bay were hydraulically operated, the impressive hydraulic system being innovatory at the time, as it was also used to retract the landing gear and operate split trailing-edge flaps and the radiator and air intake shutters.

The mid-set wings comprised two main spars built from channel-section light alloy, with extruded upper and lower beams joined by an Alclad sheet web. The light alloy wing ribs, pressed out in three sections, were stiffened by flanges and had vertical stiffeners. The wing leading edge had extra spanwise stringers beneath the metal skinning to provide additional rigidity. Split trailing-edge flaps were fitted to the wings in four sections. The empennage consisted of a metal-framed tailplane and twin endplate stressed-skin fins, with metal-framed, fabric-covered elevators and twin rudders. Metal trim tabs were fitted to the rudders and elevators, and all tail unit leading edges had de-icing. The rearwards-retracting main landing gear was by Dowty, and had twin oleo legs cross-braced to each main wheel. The tailwheel was non-retractable.

Full production of Manchester Is to Air Ministry Specification 19/37 commenced straight from the drawing board, the first production aircraft, L7276, emerging from Woodford in July 1939. This machine was sent to the A&AEE on August 5 1940, but owing to a hold-up in component supplies and a few minor defects, the second production aircraft, L7277, did not appear until late October the same year. This also flew to the A&AEE at Boscombe Down for Service trials, while the third production aircraft, L7278, was sent to No. 27 Maintenance Unit (MU) at Shawbury. There it would eventually be prepared for service with No. 207 Squadron, the first RAF unit planned to become operational on Manchesters. Five other Manchesters (L7279, L7282, L7283, L7284 and L7286) were temporarily diverted from RAF Bomber Command delivery to undertake an extensive series of Service trials.

Meanwhile, a 1939 order for 100 Manchester Is, placed with Metropolitan Vickers (Metrovick) at Trafford Park, Manchester, resulted in their first machine, R5768, passing its acceptance trials during December 1940. However, on the night of 23 December 1940 German bombers attacked the city of Manchester; the

armament was incorporated in L7247, including Frazer-Nash FN5 (nose) and FN20 (tail) power-operated turrets as well as the aforementioned ventral turret (FN21A). Each turret housed two 0.303in (7.7mm) Browning machine-guns, but because of the drag induced by the ventral turret it gave way to an F7 dorsal turret (Blackburn Botha type), lowered somewhat on the Manchester as a drag-reducing aid. For some reason the original metal covering for ailerons and elevators had now been replaced by fabric, and on L7247 experimental servo elevator balance tabs were fitted. Also new wingtips added an extra 9ft 11in (2.7m) to the span, the overall span now being 90ft 1in (27.4m). This final modification greatly improved the Manchester's qualities, despite persistent trouble from its Vulture engines. It was considered a delight to fly in its updated form, and was doubtless the best contemporary British heavy bomber design. Its excellent overall layout facilitated maintenance and allowed a comparatively simple method of production. A factor in the Manchester's favour was the storage of all fuel in wing tanks, giving it the ability to carry a heavy load of ordnance in a bomb bay nearly two-thirds the length of the lower fuselage.

The all-metal Manchester was designed to have a high degree of structural strength combined with great load-carrying capability. Emphasis was also placed on comfort and protection for the crew. A semi-monocoque structure, the fuselage was of com-

Metrovick works were hit and the company's first twelve Manchesters (R5768-R5780) destroyed. In the event these aircraft were later replaced by a dozen new Manchesters with identical serial numbers.

When No. 207 Squadron re-formed at Waddington on 1 November 1940, its initial purpose was to introduce the Avro Manchester to operational service. After the arrival of squadron personnel on 8 November, the first Manchester, L7279, flew in on 10 November from No. 6 MU at Brize Norton. Like all early production Mk. Is this Manchester had the large central fin, a 22ft (6.7m) span tailplane and 1,760hp (1,312kW) Rolls-Royce Vultures. The phasing-in period with No. 207 Squadron revealed that when the FN7 dorsal turret was rotated in flight, airflow disturbances caused severe vibration in the central fin. This was reported to the Air Ministry by Waddington's Commanding Officer, Air Commodore Sir John Boothman, but some time elapsed before any modifications were undertaken. Other faults were now occurring regularly – hydraulic failure, defective propeller feathering controls and tail flutter. With all this added to recurring Vulture engine failures caused mainly by a growing number of engine bearing faults, it was little wonder that the Manchester began to earn an evil reputation.

At the end of 1940 No. 207 Squadron could provide a token force of eight Manchesters, this figure rising to eighteen machines by 24 February 1941. On that day the squadron was ordered to put six Manchesters into the air for the type's first operational sortie, a night attack on a German Hipper-class cruiser moored in Brest harbour. All six bombers returned, but unfortunately one, L7248, had developed a hydraulic fault and crashed while attempting to land at Waddington. On the night of 27 February five Manchesters from No. 207 Squadron took off on a bombing raid, but one

was forced to turn back owing to a leaking hydraulic system. Navigators who flew on early Manchester sorties complained that the Perspex nose panels were inadequate for accurate checking of bomb runs and damage inflicted. This resulted in a new clear-view panel being inserted into the glazed chin of the Manchester, and also in the later Avro Lancaster.

On 13 March 1941 No. 207 Squadron suffered its first loss to enemy action when L7319 (X for X-ray) was shot down by an enemy fighter only five miles from base on the outward run. Another of the squadron's Manchesters, L7302 (R for Roger), was reported missing three weeks later on 8 April after failing to return from a bombing mission. A second Manchester unit, No. 97 Squadron, had been re-formed from a nucleus of No. 207 Squadron, its first Manchester having arrived on 12 February 1941. This squadron too was up on the night of 8 April, when four of its aircraft attacked Keil. By then, however, Manchesters were suffering so badly from engine problems that it was considered prudent to ground their units temporarily so that suitable modifications could be carried out. Indeed, No. 97 Squadron had already been nicknamed 'the 97th Foot' because its Manchesters spent far more time on the ground than in the air owing to engine failures. The official temporary 'stand down' came into effect on 13 April 1941, and the opportunity was taken to modify Manchester bomb bays to carry the 4,000lb (1,814kg) bomb familiarly known as a 'Cookie'. Manchester L7379 of No. 207 Squadron made the type's initial successful flight carrying a 'Cookie' and, after a return to operations,

Below: The Frazer-Nash dorsal turret and larger central fin are clearly visible on Manchester L7380/EM-W of No. 207 Squadron. (MAP)

Above: A 1941 shot of Manchester I L7427/OL-Q of No. 83 Squadron, with Rolls-Royce Vulture engines and the large central fin. (Aviation Photo News)

an early-May raid saw Manchesters L7377 and L7378 of the squadron each carrying a 'Cookie' to drop on Cologne.

In spite of thorough investigations into Vulture problems, engine trouble continued to plague Manchester operations, and a further week was lost in June 1941 when it once again became necessary to ground all Manchesters for more engine modifications and full overhauls. After they had returned to the air for a week, yet another grounding was required to rectify engine malfunctions. By July Vulture engine performance and reliability was so shocking that some Manchester units had to make up their numbers with older Handley Page Hampdens, by which time No. 207 Squadron, the first Manchester unit, was down to only two Flights, A (operational) and B (training and/or crew conversion). A return to operations by Manchesters in more reasonable numbers on 7 August was followed once again by the familiar tail flutter and serious vibration. This time a more complex modification programme was carried out which resulted in the Manchester IA. This updated variant had the large central fin removed, tailplane span increased to 33ft (10m), endplate fins and rudders increased in size, Vulture engines boosted from 1,760hp (1,312kW) to 1,845hp (1,376kW) for take-off, and the gross weight increased from the first prototype's 45,000lb (20,412kg) to 56,000lb (25,401kg). Standard armament on the Mk. IA comprised twin 0.303in (7.7mm) Browning machine-guns in nose and dorsal turrets, and four similar guns in the tail turret. A crew of seven was carried, the range being 1,200 miles (1,931km) with a maximum bomb load of 10,350lb (4,694kg), or

1,630 miles (2,623km) with an 8,100lb (3,674kg) bomb load. Fully loaded, the Mk. IA had a maximum speed of 265mph (426km/h) at 17,000ft (5,181m). Integral fuel tanks were replaced by the self-sealing type, more suited to combat conditions. Manchester Is undergoing these modifications retrospectively at Avro, Rollaston Aviation Ltd and Tollertons Ltd were redesignated accordingly.

With such updating incorporated, the Manchester with its 90ft 1in (27.46m) wingspan and improved tail unit now possessed some fine flying qualities, but still the Vulture engines continued to prove the type's Achilles' heel, and would remain so until replaced by four Rolls-Royce Merlin engines in the Manchester Mk. III (of which more anon). Avro had earlier given an assurance of the Manchester's ability to fly comfortably on one engine. This proved a fallacy when the power-plant concerned was the Vulture, especially when the propeller feathering control was defective. If one of its Vulture engines failed in flight or suffered combat damage, the Manchester was usually doomed, but not always. An outstanding exception was the case of Pilot Officer Herring and the crew of Manchester L7432/'Z' of No. 207 Squadron. During a raid on Berlin in August 1941 this aircraft had one engine put out of action by enemy flak. By exceptionally skilful handling of the bomber, which included flying precariously below 1,000ft (304.8m) with the crew throwing out everything possible to lose weight, Herring managed to fly the crippled Manchester back to base. This magnificent effort earned him an immediate award for gallantry.

September 1941 saw Manchesters once again operational with Bomber Command, but in reduced numbers owing to persistent engine defects. On the night of 7/8 September, for example, just four Manchesters formed part of a force numbering 198 aircraft which attacked Berlin. Two months later over 400 Bomber

Above: A 1941 head-on study of an unidentified Manchester Ia. (Author's collection)

Command aircraft again raided Berlin, but only fifteen Manchesters were serviceable. Of a force of 100 RAF bombers which attacked Brest on 17 December 1941, nine were Avro Manchesters, and two of these failed to return. It was feared by now that any Manchester failing to return from a bombing mission was just as likely to have been lost through engine failure as to enemy action. Another hazard faced by Manchester crews over enemy territory at night was the Vulture's habit of emitting a continuous stream of sparks from its exhausts. This was a sure giveaway to any Luftwaffe nightfighter on the prowl for RAF bombers.

Despite the Manchester's shortcomings, the RAF was forced to continue using the type until the four-engine Handley Page Halifax and Avro Lancaster heavy bombers became more readily available. As it was imperative that Bomber Command maintained its pressure on Germany with escalating nocturnal bombing, withdrawal of the available Manchester force would have meant reverting to older and less effective Hampdens and Wellingtons. Consequently, Manchesters continued to be delivered to several Bomber Command units and, from 1941 well into the first half of 1942, they formed part of the numerous night attacks against targets in occupied Europe and Germany. By then, Nos. 97 and 207 Squadrons had been joined by other Manchester-equipped squadrons, mostly in No. 5 Group, which included Nos. 9 (which did not use its Manchesters on operations), 44, 49, 50, 61, 83 and 106 Squadrons. Also Nos. 408 and 420 (Canadian) Squadrons received a number of Manchesters, and sufficient machines to form one flight of No. 144 Squadron were scheduled for delivery to Coastal Command. During 1942, as Lancasters arrived to replace them, numbers of Manchesters were sent to training and conversion units, including No. 25 OTU at Finningley, Nos. 1654, 1656, 1660 and 1661 Heavy Conversion Units (HCU), No. 1485 Bombing and Gunnery School (BGS), and Nos. 1, 3 and 8 Air Gunnery Schools (AGS). Some Manchesters were allotted

to specialised units such as the Air Fighting Development Unit (AFDU) at Wittering, the Air Observers School (AOS), A&AEE Boscombe Down and the Torpedo Development Unit (TDU) at Gosport.

Manchesters soldiered on in 1942 as part of the late Air Marshal Sir Arthur 'Bert' Harris's policy of carrying out an increasing number of night raids on German cities and other targets. On the night of 3 March 1942 some 200 RAF bombers, including 25 Manchesters, dropped their bombs on the Renault vehicle works in France. A few nights later, on 8 March, a raid on Essen was carried out by 211 bombers, among which were 21 Manchesters. Twenty nights later, on 28 March, an incendiary attack was made against Lübeck, and among the 234 aircraft participating were twenty Manchesters. This raid resulted in Lübeck being the first German city to be levelled purely by a fire-bomb attack (this form of raid on Dresden later created intense public controversy). Thirteen bombers were lost on the Lübeck mission, including one Manchester.

Among 1,047 aircraft which carried out the RAF's first 1,000-bomber raid, on the night of 30/31 May 1942, were 35 Manchesters. The railway marshalling yards at Cologne were the target, and for one Manchester pilot, Flying Officer L. T. Manser of No. 50 Squadron, this was his fourteenth operational mission. He was piloting L7301 (D for Dog), which had arrived a fortnight earlier from another unit and was not the Manchester usually flown by him. The previous performance of L7301 had not been over-impressive, and its inclusion as part of the Cologne raid was really to help swell the total bombing force to 1,000 aircraft. Carrying a maximum bomb load, L7301 was struggling at 7,000ft (2,133m), which Manser found was this particular aircraft's ceiling when fully loaded. Try as he might, Manser could not gain further altitude, and the vulnerability of his aircraft to enemy flak over the target area was obvious. But he carried on, and once over Cologne flew straight and steady until his bomb aimer had released all of their bombs at the target. Moments later L7301 received a direct hit in the lower fuselage and the controls were torn from Manser's hands. The Manchester immediately went into a dive amid a hail of shells from 20mm ground defences. Some 800ft (243m) from the ground Manser managed to pull out of the dive and regain some control. The rear of the Manchester was ablaze, and both rear bomb bay doors had been ripped off, but somehow Manser coaxed L7301 up to 2,000ft (609m). Then the port engine burst into flames and heat began spreading along the wing towards the fuel tanks. Manser calmly waited, hoping the fire would extinguish itself, which it miraculously did. He then set the bomber on course for home, but the crippled aircraft again started losing height. It was obvious that they would never reach base, and Manser ordered his crew to bale out as he struggled to keep control of the bomber. As the last man was about to leave the stricken Manchester he begged his skipper to take to his parachute, but Manser indicated that the man should jump, as he was having difficulty controlling the aircraft. Moments after this man had left the aircraft, L7301 plunged to the ground near the Belgian and Dutch border. Sadly Flying Officer Manser perished with the aircraft. For selfless devotion to duty and the safety of his crew, this gallant pilot was awarded a posthumous Victoria Cross.

A second 1,000-bomber raid had Essen as its target on the night of 1/2 June 1942, and 27 Manchesters were among the 956 bombers taking part. From this attack one Manchester went missing. During the rest of that month a fairly rapid phasing-out of Manchesters from front-line squadrons began, as Lancasters were now arriving in considerable numbers. Even so, Manchester squadrons retained at least four of the type temporarily for crew conversion training to the larger Lancasters, as the crew positions and fuselage layout of the Manchester were almost identical to those of its new four-engined successor. The last operational mission for Manchesters occurred on the night of 25/26 June 1942, when fifteen machines formed part of a force numbering 1,006 bombers. The third and final 1,000-bomber raid set up by Bomber Command, this was despatched to attack the Focke-Wulf aircraft factories at Bremen. One of No. 50 Squadron's Manchesters (L7289) failed to return from this raid.

All together, 202 Manchesters were produced, including the two prototypes, 157 being turned out by Avro and 43 at Trafford Park by Metrovick. In the event three other Manchester contracts were cancelled: one for 150 machines from Fairey Aviation dated September 1939 (allotted serials R4525–R4554, R4572–R4611, R4630–R4649, R4670–R4694 and R4710–R4744), a 150-machine order from Armstrong

Below: A fine shot of Manchester Ia L7320 with the revised empennage. (Ron Mackay)

Above: In this view of Manchester Ia L7320, the larger and more oval twin fins and rudders are clearly discernible. (MAP)

Whitworth Aircraft, also dated September 1939 (R5273–R5320, R5339-R5380, R5397–R5426 and R5448–R5477), and a further contract for 150 also to have been built at Armstrong Whitworth, dated December 1939 (W1280–W1299, W1319–W1350, W1374–W1410, W1426–W1475, W1488–W1498). Later, AWA would produce 1,328 Avro Lancaster bombers, the Manchester's illustrious successor.

Two derivatives of the Type 679 Manchester originally put forward included one by Avro for a military transport, designed to carry sixteen fully armed troops and their equipment. This project did not materialise. The second scheme, which did not progress beyond the drawing board stage as far as is

Below: Manchester Ia L7486 on a production test flight in 1941.

known, was for an in-flight refuelling tanker. This resulted from an Air Ministry suggestion that a bomber's capability would be improved when carrying a maximum bomb load if it could refuel in mid-air. So keen was the Ministry on this idea that they awarded Flight Refuelling Ltd a contract to provide plans for the conversion of an Avro Manchester from a bomber to a flying tanker. In liaison with Avro the company drew up a layout, and detailed drawings were submitted in December 1940 for both a tanker and a receiving aircraft. The tanker carried a 1,000 Imp gallon (4,546 lit) fuel tank installed in the bomb bay, with a refuelling hose-and-reel unit up front beneath the cockpit, a hose winch above the tank and a contact winch in the rear fuselage underside. The receiving aircraft would take on its fuel via a reception coupling at the extreme tail beneath the rear turret, from where it was pumped equally to the wing tanks by means of port and starboard distribution pipes.

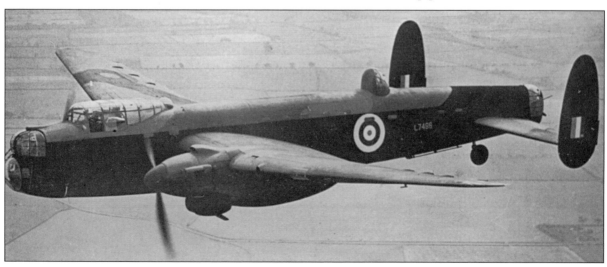

Above: Manchester Ia L7515/EM-S ('S for Sugar') of No. 207 Squadron, November 1941. (Rolls-Royce plc, Derby)

In retrospect, RAF Manchester operations were undertaken by dedicated aircrew, whose faith in and affection for their aircraft was almost nil by comparison with that felt by the crews of some other types of RAF bombers. Manchester crews took off on a mission knowing that their chance of survival relied as much on the aircraft's Vulture engines not failing as on avoiding enemy flak and nightfighters. An assessment of the final figures relating to Manchester operations show that 1,269 missions were flown, during which 1,826 tons (1,855 tonnes) of high-explosive bombs were dropped, plus countless incendiary bombs. In addition, Manchesters flew 221 sea minelaying sorties, usually referred to as 'gardening trips', and on one of these, on 3 May 1942, two Manchesters from eight sent out by No. 206 Squadron failed to return; the only losses on this mission. Of the 200 production Manchesters built, some 40 per cent were lost on operations and 25 per cent written-off in crashes. Many of the remainder were plagued by defective Vulture engines.

Meanwhile, urgent efforts to find a replacement for the offending Vulture had resulted, as mentioned earlier, in proposals for a Manchester II powered by two Napier Sabre or Bristol Centaurus engines. However, E. H. (later Lord) Hives of Rolls-Royce approached the Air Ministry with a scheme for installing four Rolls-Royce Merlin engines in an updated Manchester airframe. A self-contained powerplant, the Merlin X, had recently been developed for the Bristol Beaufighter II, and this could be bolted on to a modified Manchester wing with an increase of some ten feet in span and connected up with minimum design alterations by Avro. This was no problem to Chadwick's team, and they had the modified Manchester layout ready within three weeks towards the end of 1940. Keen to get the modified Manchester built and tested, the Air Ministry

had a Manchester taken off the production line. As BT308/G, this was powered by four 1,145hp (854kW) Rolls-Royce Merlin Xs installed in underslung nacelles. A revised centre section and extended outer wing panels increased the span to 102ft (31m), the 22ft (6.7m) span tailplane and Manchester I central fin being retained. The dorsal turret was deleted. The aircraft was finished in standard camouflage upper surfaces, with yellow undersurfaces as was the practice of the time for new and experimental types.

The first flight of BT308/G, designated Manchester Mk. III, took place at Woodford on 9 January 1941 with Avro test pilot Captain H. A. 'Sam' Brown at the controls. Ensuing trials with this aircraft proved very successful indeed, with superb handling qualities coupled to a performance that exceeded the Avro team's expectations. On 27 January, just eighteen days after its initial flight, the Manchester III flew to the A&AEE, Boscombe Down, where it was to receive a number of accolades and be recognised as a bomber *par excellence*.

By the time another Manchester (DG595/G) had been fitted with four Merlins, the designation Manchester III had been changed to Avro Type 683 Lancaster Mk. I. Thus BT308/G became the first prototype Lancaster and DG595/G the second. Further modifications incorporated in the second prototype included an increase in tailplane span to 33ft (10m), deletion of the central fin and the fitting of large, oval shaped twin fins and rudders as used on the Manchester IA. Power was provided by four uprated 1,280hp (954kW) Rolls-Royce Merlin XX engines, a Frazer-Nash hydraulically-operated dorsal turret was now fitted, housing twin 0.303in (7.7mm) Browning machine-guns, and the Frazer-Nash FN20 rounded tail turret of the Manchester had been replaced by an FN30 of more angular shape, armed with four 0.303in (7.7mm) Brownings. Like the first prototype, the second machine was finished in standard RAF upper-surface camouflage and yellow undersurfaces, while a yellow

Avro Manchester

P within a yellow circle ahead of the fuselage roundel indicated DG595/G's prototype status.

So impressive was the performance of the new Lancaster that it was ordered into immediate full-scale production, and those airframes already partly completed as Manchesters were turned out as Lancaster Is. The last Manchester built, L7526, was followed by the first production Lancaster I, L7527, which first flew at Woodford on 31 October 1941.

Thus ended the story of the Avro Manchester, a fine and innovative aircraft design married to an equally new style of aero engine which, under mitigating circumstances, proved an unsatisfactory match. However, despite an understandable condemnation of the type by its RAF crews, the Manchester was redeemed by its metamorphosis into the four-engined Lancaster, destined to become one of the finest bombers of the Second World War. Without the Manchester it is unlikely that there would have been a Lancaster, which is reason enough for the Manchester to have earned itself a niche in the history of British aviation.

Above: This Manchester III, BT308/G has four Rolls-Royce Merlin XX engines installed. It still has the large central fin, and made its first flight on 9 January 1941. Redesignated Avro Type 683, it became the prototype Lancaster. Note the Blackburn Roc turret fighter in the background. (MAP)

Below: The second prototype Lancaster, DG595, in May 1941. It started on the production line as a Manchester Ia. (MAP)

Blackburn
Botha

The personal observations on lesser-known early Second World War RAF bombers which ex-RAF serviceman Bob Wilcock related to the author included one rather derogatory reference to the Blackburn Botha. Bob's late brother was at Dumfries in 1942 on a bomb-aiming course, flying Bothas. He regarded the type as very unstable: 'As take-off speed increased, the Botha swung about alarmingly at times. A main fault was the type's lack of power, which meant an eternity passing before the aircraft came "unstuck" from the runway; another eternity followed as the crew waited for the Botha to reach anything like the altitude required for their exercises to commence.' Even when airborne, the Botha's unreliability was legendary, and there was a semi-serious joke prevalent among the aircrew at Dumfries that the bottom of the Solway Firth, over which they carried out many of their training flights, was lined with Bothas that had failed to make it back to base.

The Bothas were finally grounded in 1944, when, according to those who had the misfortune to fly in them, their unpopularity and unreliability forced the powers-that-be to acknowledge that whatever other successes the Blackburn Aircraft Company had enjoyed, the Botha was certainly not one of its better creations. Even after relegation to training duties there

were fatal accidents on the type, and some even said that the most suitable Botha deliveries were those made late in 1942, when a number of surviving machines went to RAF Schools of Technical Training as ground instructional airframes.

In its initial planning stage the Botha had great potential. Indeed, in December 1936 a contract was signed for no fewer than 442 machines to be built 'straight off the drawing board'. A further 138 were to be produced later, making a total of 580 machines. However, a contract for another 676 Bothas was cancelled. Why did this promising design become the object of such criticism? To try and produce a balanced account of the Botha's history, it is necessary to revert to the mid-1930s, and torpedo bombers which were all of biplane configuration. Already the RAF was convinced that a modern monoplane design would be a more effective proposition.

The Royal Navy was to use its Fairey Swordfish biplanes with great success in the early years of the Second World War, but the RAF waited anxiously to replace its Vickers Vildebeest biplanes with a more

Below: The first Blackburn Botha built, L6104, ex-works and minus RAF insignia. This machine had inset elevators. (British Aerospace, Brough)

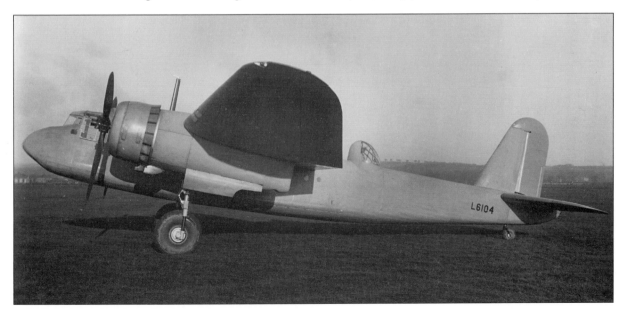

BOTHA

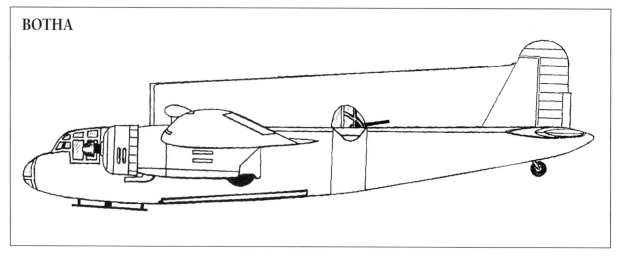

sophisticated design, as one or two RAF Coastal Command units were still operating Vildebeests in 1939. In the Far East, Vildebeest-equipped Nos. 36 and 100 Squadrons flew their biplanes gallantly against Japanese forces at Singapore in 1941, suffering heavy losses. Two machines of No. 36 Squadron fought on in Java until 1942, but were lost trying to reach Burma.

In the meantime, and in spite of the RAF's obvious need for a modern torpedo-bomber, the Air Ministry saw the very specialised role and qualities required for torpedo attack as an expensive undertaking. They insisted that a torpedo bomber specification must include provision for normal bombing and general reconnaissance duties. Obviously these additional roles would reduce the effectiveness of any design intended as a pure torpedo bomber. The result was Specification M.15/35, issued on 27 August 1935 by the Air Staff. This called for a land-based, twin-engine reconnaissance bomber capable of delivering an aerial torpedo. It was to have a three-man crew, and the weapon load of one torpedo, or its equivalent in bombs or depth charges up to 2,000lb (907kg), was to be carried internally.

As the design was based specifically on RAF Coastal Command requirements, the aircraft's maritime duties would necessitate superior range, good slow-flying qualities, good stability and the best possible field of view for the crew. The engines chosen would need to be economical, reliable and able to provide adequate power under attack conditions. It was then decided that a four-man crew would be necessary, and an Air Ministry amendment was issued to that effect.

Tenders had already been received from Blackburn Aircraft and the Bristol Aeroplane Company, the latter

---

BLACKBURN B.6 BOTHA DATA

Manufacturer
Blackburn Aircraft Co Ltd., Brough, East Yorkshire, and Dumbarton, Scotland

Type
Four-seat reconnaissance/torpedo-bomber/advanced trainer

Powerplant
Two 930hp (694kW) Bristol Perseus XA air-cooled sleeve-valve, nine-cylinder radial engines (early Bothas had 880hp (656kW) Perseus Xs)

Performance
Maximum speed, 209mph (336km/h) at sea level; 249mph (401km/h) at 5,500ft (1,675m); 220mph (354km/h) at 15,000ft (4,570m). Cruising speed, 212mph (341km/h) at 15,000ft (4,570m). Initial climb, 985ft

(300m)/min; at 15,000ft (4,570m), 355ft (108m)/min. Service ceiling, 17,500ft (5,335m). Range, 1,270 miles (2,044km)

Weights
Empty, 11,830lb (5,366kg). Loaded (maximum take-off), 18,450lb (8,369kg)

Dimensions
Span, 59ft (17.98m). Length, 51ft 1½in (15.58m). Height, 14ft 7½in (4.46m). Wing area, 518sq ft (48.12sq m)

Armament
One fixed forward-firing 0.303in (7.7mm) Vickers machine-gun in nose; two 0.303in (7.7mm) Lewis machine-guns in FN7 dorsal turret. One 2,000lb (907kg) torpedo or bomb, or equivalent weight of 500lb (227kg), or 250lb (113kg) bombs, mines or depth charges

BLACKBURN BOTHA PRODUCTION

No prototype Bothas built, the first two production machines, L6104 and L6105, acting as such in lieu

Production order for 380 Bothas issued to Specification 10/36. First batch of 242 aircraft (L6104–L6345 inclusive) built at Brough under Contract No. 563935/36 and delivered between March 1939 and March 1941. Second batch of 138 aircraft (W5017–W5056, W5065–W5114, W5118–W5157 and W5162–W5169) built under Contract No. 69254/40

Third production batch of 200 Bothas (L6347–L6546 inclusive) built at Dumbarton works to Specification 10/36.

Above: This Botha, L6250/I-F, carries the identification code of No. 3 School of General Reconnaissance, Squire's Gate. (MAP)

submitting a design resembling the Blenheim but with a longer and deeper centre fuselage aft of a raised cockpit, accommodating a wireless operator, cameras, and a dorsal gun turret. Known as the Beaufort (see next chapter), Bristol's design carried its torpedo in a partly exposed position.

Blackburn's aircraft had a cantilever shoulder-wing layout which provided crews with an advantageous view downward when on convoy protection patrols and general reconnaissance duties. However, despite an excellent forward field of view, visibility sideways and to the rear was blanked off by the engines and nacelles. An all-metal monocoque structure with stressed-skin covering, the fuselage of Blackburn's B-26 Botha (named after South Africa's General Louis Botha), was flush-riveted throughout. The all-metal wings had flush-riveted stressed-skin covering and featured sharply tapered outer panels with pronounced dihedral. The balanced ailerons were fabric covered. Hydraulically-operated split trailing-edge flaps and the engine nacelles were carried by the parallel-chord centre section, which also contained the three main fuel tanks. Two had 146 Imp gal (663lit) capacity, and the third held 132½ Imp gal (602lit). The total capacity of 435¾ Imp gal (1,981lit), which included a 11¾ Imp gal (50lit) distribution tank, could be increased for special purposes to 565¾ Imp gal (2,571lit). Stressed metal skinning covered the all-metal tail unit, but the aerodynamically balanced control surfaces were fabric covered. Each main wheel

Ordered under Contract No. 583994/36, with deliveries between October 1939 and June 1941 An order for a further 676 Bothas was cancelled (L6547–L6590, W5170–W5211, W5216–W5235, W5239–W5288, W5296–W5315, W7247–W7296, W7300–W7339, W7343–W7362, W7368–W7379, W7382–W7409, W9396–W9415, W9434–WW9463, W9469–W9545, W9558–W9597, W9646–W9665, W9702–W9741, W9748–W9772, W9821–W9855, W9880–W9899, W9936–W9975, X1000–X1029)	**RAF BOTHA UNITS** No. 608 Squadron (Thornaby-on-Tees) No. 3 School of General Reconnaissance (Squire's Gate) No. 2 Bombing and Gunnery School (BGS) (Millom) No. 3 Radio School (Prestwick) No. 11 Radio School (Hooton Park) No. 1 OTU (Silloth) No. 2 Electrical and Wireless School (Yatesbury) No. 8 BGS (Evanton) No. 3 Air Observers Navigation School (AONS) (Bobbington) No. 4 Air Observers School/Navigation School (West Freugh) No. 2 AOS (Millom) No. 1 Radio School (Cranwell) No. 10 AOS (Dumfries)	No. 4 AGS (Morpeth) No. 3 (Pilot) Advanced Flying Unit (PAFU) (South Cerney) No. 6 PAFU (Little Rissington) No. 3 AGS (Castle Kennedy, Northern Ireland) No. 1 (Observer) Advanced Flying Unit (OAFU) (Wigtown) No. 3 Radio Direction Finding School Abbotsinch Torpedo Training Unit (TTU) **RAF Schools of Technical Training which received Bothas** No. 1 (Halton) No. 2 (Cosford) No. 3 (Blackpool) No. 4 (St Athan) No. 5 (Locking) No. 6 (Hednesford) No. 7 (Innsworth) No. 9 (Morecambe) No. 10 (Kirkham)

of the rearward retracting landing gear featured a single oleo-pneumatic leg with 'nutcracker'-type retracting struts. The fixed tailwheel had oleo suspension and a castoring action.

Initially, the powerplant for both the Bristol and Blackburn designs had been agreed as two 850hp (634kW) Bristol Perseus sleeve-valve air-cooled radial engines. Both layouts were accepted by the Air Ministry in 1936, but the four-man crew amendment by the Ministry resulted in both designs being updated with enlarged fuselages. These modifications led to the issue of revised Specification 10/36, and inevitably increased the aircraft's weight. The Botha's wireless operator and navigator were accommodated in a cabin amidships, entrance being gained via a door with a built-in ladder, located on the starboard side. This gave access to a gangway by which the navigator could reach the pilot and a prone bomb-aiming position in the nose. The fourth crew member manned a tall, egg-shaped, Frazer-Nash FN7 dorsal gun turret aft of the wing, entrance being from the rear of the midships cabin.

Obviously the performance of both types would be inferior to that envisaged in 1935, but Bristol exchanged the Perseus VI engines in the Beaufort for 1,130hp (843kW) Bristol Taurus radials. Unfortunately for Blackburn this powerplant was in short supply, and none could be spared for the Botha, so the company opted initially for Bristol Aquilas as an alternative. However, it was persuaded by the Chief of Air Staff in October 1937 to install 880hp (656kW) Bristol Perseus X radials, which would supposedly improve the Botha's medium-altitude bombing capability and produce a good performance at 15,000ft (4,572m). The Perseus did not live up to expectations, however,

and although Bristol managed to force a little more power out of the Perseus, resulting in the XA rated at 930hp (694kW), the Botha remained underpowered. Blackburn suggested a revised Botha Mk. II with more powerful Bristol Hercules radials, but the idea was turned down. So the company, having received an order for 442 Botha Is in December 1936, was obliged to fit them with 880hp (656kW) Perseus X radials. These engines, housed in wide-chord cowlings, were fitted with controllable cooling gills and drove de Havilland Hydromatic constant-speed three-bladed propellers.

The Botha's armament consisted of a fixed forward-firing 0.303in (7.7mm) Vickers machine-gun in the nose, fired by the pilot, and two 0.303in (7.7mm) Lewis machine-guns mounted in the dorsal turret. The ordnance load comprised either an 18in (45.7cm) Mk. XII or Mk. XIV torpedo, a 2,000lb (907kg) bomb, or two 500lb (226kg), or four 250lb (113kg) bombs. These weapons were carried in a special compartment within the fuselage, fitted with hydraulically-operated bomb doors, though if a torpedo or 2,000lb (907kg) bomb was to be carried these were removed. Provision was made to fit extra bomb racks beneath the Botha's outer wing panels, and as a maritime aircraft it carried marine gear and a collapsible dinghy with an inflation bottle.

No actual Botha prototype was built, the first production aircraft, L6104, acting as such and making its initial flight on 28 December 1938 at Brough, flown by Blackburn's chief test pilot, Flight Lieutenant H.

Below: Botha L6264 with Bristol Perseus engines and horn-balanced elevators. Note the landing lights in the wing leading edge. (Author's collection)

Above: Botha L6264 with Bristol Perseus engines and horn-balanced elevators. Note the landing lights in the wing leading edge. (Author's collection)

Bailey. The new bomber was sent to the A&AEE at Martlesham Heath in March 1939 for performance and handling trials. Poor elevator control was evident during these tests, and was blamed on the small, inset-type elevator. When the second production Botha, L6105, arrived for further A&AEE trials, it had been fitted with a large horn-balanced elevator and had additional tailplane area, which appeared to cure the problem. The first aircraft was returned to the makers in May 1939, employed as a test aircraft for modifications and equipment, and flown back to the A&AEE (now at Boscombe Down) at the end of the following November. This Botha ended up at RAF St Athan as instructional airframe 2217M in September 1940, joining L6105, which had been sent for the same purpose after finishing armament trials at the A&AEE. The third production Botha, L6106, was sent to the Central Flying School (CFS) at Upavon on 3 Septem-

ber 1939 to allow instructors to gain familiarisation on the type.

In addition to its Brough production lines, Blackburn tooled up for Bothas to be built simultaneously at its Dumbarton site in Scotland, a total of 580 machines being completed by the two factories. Brough produced 380 (L6104–L6345; W5017–W5056; W5065–W5114; W5118–W5157 and W5162–W5169), while Dumbarton built 200 Bothas (L6347–L6546), the first two of which, L6347 and L6348, were delivered to the TDU, Gosport, during October and November 1939, where they joined Brough-built L6107 and L6110. At that stage it was hoped, despite poor performance from the Perseus X engines, that Bothas would be able to fulfil their intended role as torpedo-bombers. Torpedo dropping trials commenced with L6110, but German Luftwaffe activity increased in the Portsmouth area and these were discontinued. Botha L6110 eventually went to No. 3 School of Technical Training (SoTT) at Blackpool as instructional airframe 3374M. Another Botha, L6111, was used at Gosport on minelaying trials, but crashed

Above: The Frazer-Nash FN7 dorsal turret is prominent in this shot of Botha W5065 on a test flight from Brough. (Author's collection)

Below: Taken on 16 August 1941 this view of late-production Botha W5065 shows the non-retractable navigator's window behind the cockpit. The upper surfaces were standard camouflage, and undersurfaces training yellow. Note the partly exposed main wheel. (British Aerospace, Brough)

off Spit Fort on 24 February 1940. Botha L6109 started off at the A&AEE, passed to the RAE at Farnborough, and later went to RNAS Crail, where it served with No. 770 Squadron until being struck off charge on 28 July 1943. Its immediate predecessor, L6108, was not so lucky. After a spell at the TDU it was transferred to No. 2 Ferry Flight, with which it was serving when it overshot in bad weather at Bristol's Filton aerodrome, Gloucestershire (now Avon), on 22 December 1939 and crashed into a house.

The first Botha received by the RAF was L6349, third off the Dumbarton production line, which arrived at No. 5 MU, Kemble, Gloucestershire, on 12 December 1939. It was joined later in the month by L6112 from Brough, both aircraft then going to Gosport for use by the TDU. On 3 June 1940 four Bothas, L6107, L6123, L6124 and L6126, were delivered to Silloth, Cumberland, for use by No. 1 OTU so that Bothas could be introduced into squadron service. By then, peak production was under way at both Blackburn factories, and with 58 Bothas being rolled out in June, No. 1 OTU soon had 25 of the new machines on strength. The first trainee crews arrived at Silloth from No. 608 (North Riding) Squadron, Coastal Command, which operated from Thornaby-on-Tees, carrying out North Sea shipping patrols with Avro Ansons. Three of these Ansons were replaced at the end of June by Bothas L6164–L6166, and in July

seven more of the squadron's Ansons were exchanged for Bothas L6170–L6174, L6188 and L6388. These became the first Blackburn aircraft to equip a land-based RAF unit since No. 246 Squadron flew Kangaroo bombers on maritime reconnaissance in 1918.

Bothas L6170, L6173 and L6190 carried out their first patrol with No. 608 Squadron on 10 August 1940. During the following three months there were only twelve days when Botha operations were prevented by bad weather. Up to five hours were spent in the air on patrol, but no reports were received of any Botha being attacked by the Luftwaffe, although some of the Ansons came under fire. Of thirty Bothas delivered to Thornaby, one machine, L6165, failed to return from its patrol on 31 August 1940, and although a considerable number of hours were clocked up by the squadron's Bothas, the type was gradually replaced, ironically, by reintroduced Ansons! The last operational patrol with Bothas occurred on 6 November 1940, when L6209 and L6198 were piloted by Sergeant Burton and Pilot Officer Keates respectively. In August 1940 No. 502 (County of Ulster) Squadron had started to re-equip with Bothas and three machines (L6228, L6229 and L6231) were delivered, but the plan was cancelled and the three Bothas were transferred to No. 1 OTU. From May 1941 until October 1942 Botha L6128 was allotted to No. 24 Squadron for communications duties. Another, L6156, was on the strength of No. 301 (Polish) Squadron from August 1941 to May 1942, while L6114 was allotted to No. 304 (Polish) Squadron during June 1943.

From its early days the Botha's career was marred by a number of incidents, failures and fatal accidents, some of which were attributed to poor design. The pilot's field of view was excellent, but for the rest of the crew it was far from satisfactory. Stability problems were rife, a factor not helped by the awkwardly shaped tall dorsal turret, which was lacking in aerodynamic qualities. The Botha was not easy to fly, the need for constant adjustments and trimming in flight making the pilot's task strenuous and tiring on lengthy patrols. Also, of course, there were inevitable problems with the underpowered Perseus engines, which at 12,500ft (3,657m) gave a top speed of only 230mph (370km/h), or 200mph (322km/h) at sea level. With a stalling speed of 78mph (125km/h), the Botha's suitability for torpedo launching was marginal.

The first fatal crash of a Botha occurred on 5 March 1940, when L6129 dived into the ground at Flixborough, Lincolnshire, during a routine test flight. Test pilot B. R. Rolfe and his flight test observer both lost their lives. Dumbarton-built Bothas L6377 and L6390 were lost in crashes at Abbotsinch on 26 May and 12 June 1940 respectively, and L6205 suffered a similar fate at Brough on 8 July. Other Botha crashes recorded during the type's time in service between 1940 and 1944 included L6124, L6126, L6136, L6141, L6155, L6160, L6165 (missing on operations with No. 608 Squadron), L6172, L6173 (collision with Fairey Battle P6644), L6178, L6184 (damaged beyond repair at Silloth when it slipped off its jacks), L6186, L6189,

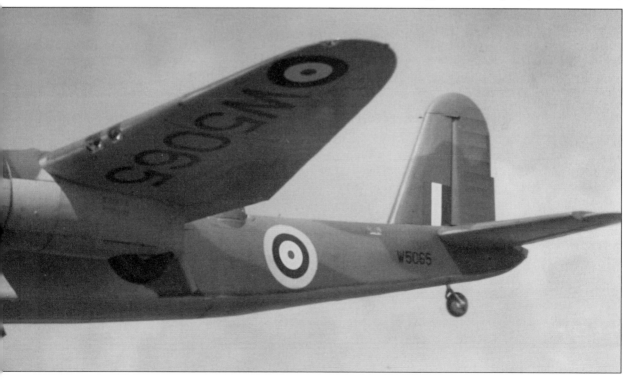

L6193, L6195, L6202, L6203, L6209, L6210, L6211, L6213 (missing on a training flight), L6220, L6223, L6228, L6233, L6237, L6242, L6249 (caught in barrage balloon cables over Cheshire), L6262, L6264 (missing on a training flight), L6265, L6266, L6268, L6274, L6276, L6277, L6283, L6284, L6289, L6290, L6293, L6314, L6315, L6318, L6321, L6326, L6330, L6332, L6341, L6342, L6354, L6355, L6373 (collided with Anson LT528), L6384, L6396, L6404, L6407, L6408, L6414, L6416, L6417, L6418, L6419, L6425, L6426, L6431 (hit by Battle L5785 while parked at Millom), L6432, L6435, L6436, L6438, L6440, L6441, L6442, L6446, L6449, L6451, L6463, L6466, L6471, L6478, L6488, L6498, L6509 (collided with Boulton Paul Defiant N1745 over Blackpool), L6512, L6519, L6528, L6531, L6535, L6539 and L6541. Crashed or written-off Bothas in the 'W' serial range included W5027, W5031, W5042, W5053, W5081, W5121, W5134, W5137 and W5154 (collided with each other mid-air), W5139 (collided with Botha L6339, both destroyed), W5141 (hit at dispersal by Botha L6192), W5146, W5153, W5155 (collided with Westland Lysander T1506), W5156, W5164 (collided with lorry while taking off), W5024 and W5029.

The above casualty list looks pretty grim at first sight, but 112 machines were write-offs out of a total of 580 produced. Records reveal that quite a number of accidents were due to collisions, under- or overshooting on landing and hitting high ground in low cloud and bad weather. At that time maximum wartime effort was being made by all RAF units, so, considering the Botha's fairly high production run and many thousands of hours spent in the air, much of it on gruelling instructional flying over a four-year period, the picture is not quite as black as it might first appear. Under such conditions the percentage of Botha losses was not astronomically high.

The first Botha powered by the uprated Bristol Perseus XA engine was L6155, which went to No. 608 Squadron at Thornaby. Dumbarton-built Botha L6212

was chosen for performance trials with the Perseus XA, and flew to the A&AEE at Boscombe Down on 16 August 1940. This machine had the non-retractable bulged navigator's windows on each side of the fuselage just aft of the cockpit. Other improvements introduced during the ensuing production run included a jettisonable entrance door (first used on L6235), newly designed jacks for the flaps (installed initially on L6378), and a modified system of retraction and locking mechanism for the landing gear (introduced on L6421). At the A&AEE in October 1941 tests were carried out on Botha L6188, which was fitted with 12ft (3.6m) diameter propellers. In December 1942 nocturnal trials went ahead with L6325 fitted with exhaust flame dampeners as used on Bristol Hercules engines. Neither experiment proved successful.

Bothas were withdrawn from operational flying on 6 November 1940, having flown 308 missions. It was decided that recurring faults with the type made it suitable only for second-line duties and, in consequence, an original order for a further 676 Bothas was cancelled and those in service were relegated to training duties. Basically the Botha was a sound design plagued throughout its career by insufficiently powerful engines. Another factor which had some bearing on the Botha's withdrawal from front-line duties was the comparatively short range called for in the original specification. After the collapse of France this no longer applied, as Coastal Command required aircraft with greater range. Thus the Botha became an operational trainer for bomber crews, a role to which it was well suited. Fatal accidents still occurred, however, and the Botha retained its bad reputation. Nevertheless, crews continued to fly in the type until 1944, when 468 Bothas were still in RAF service.

Below: As can be seen here, the Botha pilot's forward field of view was fine, but side and rear vision was very restricted by the engine nacelles. (Author's collection)

Bristol
Beaufort

Probably the most significant aircraft type pro- duced by the Bristol Aeroplane Company for the RAF during the Second World War was the hard- hitting twin-engined Beaufighter, of which some 5,930 examples were produced in Britain and Aus- tralia. They were employed as nightfighters, intruders, long-range escorts, strike fighters and torpedo bombers on many RAF and RAAF operations between 1941 and 1945. However, had it not been for the exis- tence of Bristol's earlier Beaufort torpedo-bomber, swift development, production and introduction into service of the Beaufighter would not have been possi- ble. As it was, the Air Ministry's long-range-fighter requirements were quickly met at Filton by marrying a new fuselage to the existing Beaufort wings, empen- nage and landing gear. The first syllable of the bomber's name was also used for the new Beaufighter.

Although it was a close relative of the Bristol Blenheim bomber, the Beaufort received few accolades despite its yeoman service with RAF Coastal Com- mand in the early years of the Second World War. It was very active in the European theatre of operations until Beaufighters and de Havilland Mosquitoes became available in sufficient numbers, gave valuable service in the Middle East and, in the Pacific, Aus-

tralian-built Beauforts of the RAAF flew operationally from mid-1942 until the war's end.

The Beaufort resulted from Air Ministry require- ments to replace ageing Vickers Vildebeest torpedo- bomber biplanes and Avro Anson reconnaissance- bomber monoplanes as part of its RAF modernisation and expansion programme of the mid-1930s. In the late summer of 1935 the Ministry issued specifications calling for new twin-engined shore-based aircraft to serve in each role. Specification M.15/35 covered a three-seat torpedo-bomber, and G.24/35 a reconnais- sance-bomber with a crew of four, but serious response to these specifications came from only three British manufacturers, Avro, Blackburn and Bristol. Avro submitted its Type 672 as a derivative of the Anson with Armstrong Siddeley Terrier engines to meet G.24/35 requirements, while Blackburn, having produced its Dart, Ripon and Shark torpedo-bomber biplanes, responded to M.15/35 with a high-wing monoplane carrying an internally-stowed torpedo.

Below: The marriage of a Beaufort's wings and empennage to a new fuselage design and Bristol Hercules engines resulted in the famous Beaufighter. This example is X7543, a Mk VIF/C. (Rolls-Royce plc, Bristol)

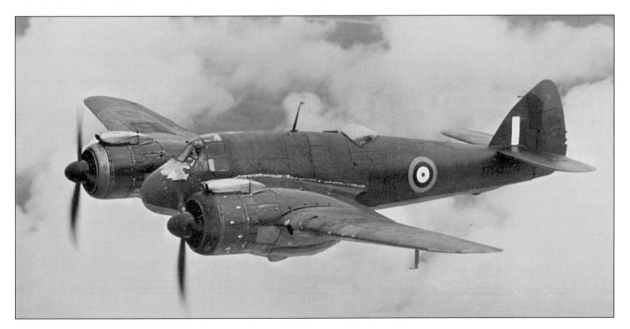

Bristol Beaufort

Bristol, meanwhile, looked to its Blenheim bomber as the basis for two variants covering both specifications. A Type 149 proposal featured a Blenheim I with a widened fuselage to accommodate a pilot, gunner, navigator and radio operator. In response to G.24/35 this revised design included an enlarged dorsal gun turret housing twin 0.303in (7.7mm) Lewis machine-guns and a single wing-mounted 0.303in (7.7mm) Browning gun. Overall dimensions remained the same, a Blenheim-type bomb bay was retained, additional light bomb racks were provided beneath the wing centre-section and power was provided by two Bristol Aquila AE-3M supercharged radial engines. To suit M.15/35, further updating of the standard Blenheim I was necessary in order to house a torpedo in the bomb bay. The pilot's cockpit had to be positioned 54in (1.37m) further forward in this Type 150 project, and the dorsal turret moved further aft to adjust the centre of gravity (CG). The forward fuselage profile remained as in the Blenheim I, and a three-man crew was carried, the radio operator doubling as bomb-aimer for normal bombing. When the aircraft was used as a torpedo-bomber the pilot would be responsible for aiming and launching the torpedo as well as firing the wing gun. Power was to be provided by two 890hp (663kW) Bristol Perseus VI single-row, sleeve-valve, air-cooled radial engines.

Owing to the great similarity between the Types 149 and 150, early in 1936 Bristol's design team considered combining both roles in a single type of aircraft. This necessitated a larger bomb bay in the torpedo-bomber, created by raising the cabin floor but reducing fuselage headroom. A semi-exposed torpedo installation was necessary, and Bristol went ahead with design modifications on what was now the Type 152. A 9in (23cm) increase in nose length allowed a navigator's position to be incorporated, the radio operator, who also worked the camera, being located ahead of the dorsal turret and acting as gunner to maintain a three-man crew. The proposed engines for the Type 152 were either Aquila AE-3Ms or Perseus VIs, the latter being expected to give the aircraft an estimated maximum speed of 288mph (463km/h) at 5,000ft (1,524m).

Impressed by Bristol's one-aircraft, multi-role concept, the Air Ministry issued Specification 10/36 to cover the revised layout but, although the semi-exposed torpedo was acceptable, they insisted on a four-man crew. To comply, Bristol increased the depth of the forward fuselage and joined the cockpit and dorsal turret with a straight roof line. The pilot now sat above the forward part of the torpedo bay, the radio operator immediately aft and the navigator/bomb-aimer at a chart table in the nose, or in a prone

---

BRISTOL BEAUFORT MK. I DATA

Manufacturer

Bristol Aeroplane Co Ltd, Filton, Bristol, and Banwell, Somerset

Type

Four-seat torpedo-bomber, bomber or minelaying aircraft

Powerplant

Two 1,130hp (834kW) Bristol Taurus VI fourteen-cylinder, two-row, sleeve-valve air-cooled radial engines

Performance

Maximum speed, 259mph (416km/h) at 2,000ft (610m); 270mph (434km/h) at 10,000ft (3,050m). Cruising speed, 243mph (391km/h) at 2,000ft (610m); 257mph (414km/h) at 10,000ft (3,050m). Initial climb, 1,450ft (442m)/min. Service ceiling, 19,700ft (6,005m). Range, 1,600 miles (2,574km)

Weights

Empty, 11,739lb (5,350kg). Loaded (carrying torpedo), 14,074lb (6,390kg); maximum take-off, 17,000lb (8,038kg)

Dimensions

Span, 57ft 10in (17.63m). Length, 44ft 2in (13.46m) Height, 15ft 10in (4.83m). Wing area, 451sq ft (41.89sq m). Landing gear track, 18ft (5.49m).

Armament

One/two 0.303in (7.7mm) wing-mounted Browning machine-guns or two 0.303in (7.7mm) gimbal-mounted Vickers guns in nose; two beam-mounted 0.303in (7.7mm) Vickers guns; two 0.303in (7.7mm) Vickers/Browning guns in Bristol B4 Mk. 1/1E or B1 Mk. V dorsal turret respectively. Up to 2,000lb (908kg) bomb load, or one 1,500lb (681kg) mine, or one 18in (45.7cm) Mk. XII torpedo

BRISTOL BEAUFORT PRODUCTION

First production batch = 78 aircraft, L4441–L4518. First five machines non-standard; regarded as prototypes. L4444 with dual controls; L4448 pattern aircraft to Australia; L4441 became instructional airframe 3147M

Second production batch (part 1) = 137 aircraft; L9790–L9838, L9851–L9897 and L9932–L9972 (all Mk. I)

Third production batch = 66 aircraft;

W6467–W6506, W6518–W6543 (all Mk. I)

Fourth production batch = 24 aircraft; X8916–X8939 (all Mk.I)

Fifth production batch = 150 aircraft; AW187–AW221, AW234–AW243 (45 Mk. I), AW244–AW253, AW271–AW315 and AW335–AW384 (105 Mk. II)

Sixth production batch = 120 aircraft; DD870–DD911, DD927–DD944 (60 Mk. II), DD945–DD959, DD974–DD999 and DE108–DE126 (60 Mk. I)

Seventh production batch = 200 aircraft; DW802–DW836, DW851–DW898, DW913–DW962, DW977–DW999 and DX114–DX157 (all Mk. I)

Eighth production batch = 50 aircraft; EK969–EK999, EL123–EL141 (all Mk. I)

Ninth production batch = 111 aircraft; JM431–JM470; JM496–JM517 and JM545–JM593 (all Mk. I)

NB. Some from this batch were transferred to the Royal Navy as trainers

Tenth production batch = 129 aircraft; LR885LR908, LR920–LR963,

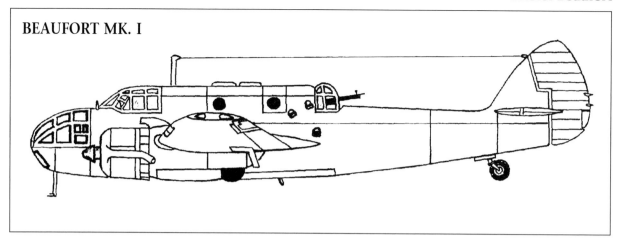

BEAUFORT MK. I

bomb-aiming position. In similar vein, Blackburn updated its three-seat M.15/35 design to satisfy the requirements of Specification 10/36, a fourth crew member being added. Avro also modified its Type 672 to 675 standard for two-role purposes, but after Blackburn and Bristol received 'off-the-drawing-board' contracts for quantity production of their respective designs, Avro abandoned its project.

With permission from the Duke of Beaufort, Bristol's Type 152 was named Beaufort, while Blackburn's

B-26 was named Botha. The intended powerplant for both types was two 850hp (634kW) Bristol Perseus radials. In the light of revised performance estimates for the Beaufort, calculated when weight increases were imposed by essential equipment, it became apparent that a Blenheim would still be faster. Alternative engines in the form of 1,150hp (857kW) Bristol Taurus seemed the answer, but this two-row, sleeve-valve engine had still to be type-tested and, because of Bristol's heavy involvement with other powerplant

---

LR976–LR999, LS113–LS128 (all Mk. I), LS129–LS149 (Mk. II(T) Trainers) Eleventh production batch = 229 aircraft; ML430–ML476, ML489–ML524, ML540–ML586, ML599–ML635, ML649–ML692 and ML705–ML722 (all Mk II(T) Trainers)

AUSTRALIAN PRODUCTION

All Australian-built Beauforts were produced by the Beaufort Division, Department of Aircraft Production, Mascot, New South Wales, and Fishermen's Bend

Beaufort V = 50 aircraft; A9-1 to A9-50 (ex-T9450–T9469 and T9438–T9602)
Beaufort VA = 30 aircraft; A9-151 to A9-180
Beaufort VI = 40 aircraft; A9-51 to A9-90 (ex-T9603–T9618 and T9624–T9647)
Beaufort VII = 60 aircraft; A9-91 to A9-150
Beaufort VIII = 520 aircraft; A9-181 to A9-700
Beaufort IX = 46 aircraft (converted from Mk. VIIIs); A9-701 to A9-746

RAF, RAAF, SAAF, AND RCAF BEAUFORT UNITS

RAF Coastal Command
No. 22 Squadron
No. 39 Squadron
No. 42 Squadron
No. 47 Squadron
No. 86 Squadron
No. 217 Squadron
No. 415 (Canadian) Squadron – non-operational on Beauforts
No. 489 (New Zealand) Squadron – non-operational on Beauforts
Coastal Command OTU (later No. 1 OTU)
Nos. 3, 5, 9, 51 and 54 OTUs
Nos. 301 and 306 Ferry Training Units
No. 12 PAFU
No. 5 Middle East Training Squadron

NB. The Royal Navy received 38 Beauforts as navigational trainers

ROYAL AUSTRALIAN AIR FORCE
No. 1 Squadron
No. 2 Squadron
No. 6 Squadron

No. 7 Squadron
No. 8 Squadron
No. 13 Squadron
No. 14 Squadron
No. 15 Squadron
No. 22 Squadron
No. 100 Squadron
No. 9 Local Air Supply Unit

South African Air Force
Nos. 36 and 37 Coastal Defence Flights; combined to form No. 20 Squadron (later renumbered No. 16 Squadron)

Royal Canadian Air Force
No. 149 Torpedo Bomber Squadron
No. 32 OTU

Turkish Air Force
Received twelve Beaufort Is and twelve Beaufort II(T)s; the units to which these were allocated are not known at the time of writing

Above: Bristol Beaufort prototype L4441 with revised cowling and landing gear fairing plates removed, late 1938. (Author's collection)

production, would have limited availability. A compromise was reached during 1937, when it was agreed that the Beaufort would be Taurus powered while Blackburn's Botha retained the Perseus, with which it proved to be greatly underpowered.

It was intended that the Beaufort's definitive powerplant should be a pair of Taurus Mk. IIs or fully supercharged Mk. IIIs, driving de Havilland three-bladed constant-speed metal propellers. The Bristol Engine Division's designer, Roy Fedden (later Sir Roy) had at the same time produced a low-drag, long-chord, close-fitting cowling of which the exhaust collector ring formed the leading edge. Cooling air was ejected via controllable slots in each side of the nacelle beneath the wing and, as the main landing gear retracted rearwards into the nacelles, oblong fairings fitted to the front legs closed the nacelle bottoms. The maximum power expected from the early Taurus was 1,010hp (753kW) for take-off and 1,065hp (794kW) at 5,000ft (1,524m).

Structurally, the Beaufort had an all-metal monocoque fuselage of oval section with channel and 'Z'-section Alclad transverse frames, extruded Hiduminium angle-section stringers and flush-riveted, Alclad stressed-skin covering. The wings were built in three sections, the centre one passing through the fuselage to which it was bolted and also carrying the engine nacelles. Two outer panels bolted to the centre section completed the wing, which had two main spars of high-tensile steel and light alloy with alloy ribs and was covered by a flush-riveted Alclad stressed

skin. Split trailing-edge flaps fitted to the centre section and inner portion of the outer wing panels were hydraulically operated, and fabric-covered Bristol-Frise ailerons with duralumin tubular spars and Alclad ribs were fitted. The rudder and elevators were similarly built, the rest of the tail unit being covered with flush-riveted Alclad. Each landing gear main wheel was carried between twin Vickers oleo-pneumatic shock absorbing legs and retracted hydraulically rearwards into the engine nacelles. Dunlop wheels, tyres and pneumatic brakes were fitted. On early Beauforts the tailwheel was fixed, but later machines had a fully retracting Lockheed type which was raised forwards into the fuselage. Total fuel capacity was 570 Imp gal (2,591lit), contained in four main tanks; two of 194gal capacity (882lit) in the centre section and two outer wing tanks holding 91gal (414lit). An auxiliary 138 Imp gal (827lit) capacity tank could be accommodated in the bomb bay.

The Beaufort's armament underwent a number of changes as a result of Service experience and weapon development. Initially a single pilot-operated 0.303in (7.7mm) Browning gun was installed in the port wing. Rear defence was to be provided by a Bristol B4 Mk. I/Ie dorsal turret housing twin Browning guns, but limited availability of this weapon resulted in a single magazine-fed Vickers 'K' gun (two later) being fitted. Also a G.42B camera gun was installed. In due course forward firepower was improved by fitting a 0.303in (7.7mm) Browning gun in the starboard wing to complement the port wing gun. In place of the wing guns, twin 0.303in (7.7mm) Vickers GO guns could be installed in the nose on gimbal mountings and fired by the navigator/bomb aimer. Further optional defence was provided on some Beauforts by

Above: The second Beaufort, L4442, in contemporary bomber camouflage with black undersurfaces and large white serials beneath the wings. This aircraft remained with Bristol, crashing on test in May 1940. (MAP)

a 0.303in (7.7mm) Browning gun remotely controlled to fire backwards from an undernose blister, after the fashion of a similar installation in the Blenheim IV. This weapon was often removed, however, in favour of extra Vickers guns mounted in the rear fuselage, one each side ahead of the dorsal turret, and fired by the radio operator as a means of beam defence. Later an improved Bristol B1 Mk. V dorsal turret with twin belt-fed Brownings was fitted. Another update involved the camera gun installation, the original G.22 or G.42B type, normally carried externally on the forward starboard fuselage, being superseded by a G.45 fitted in the port outer wing. If a torpedo was carried, however, an F.46 camera was located in the nose, focused through the bomb-aiming window, and provision was made for an F.24 camera to be mounted in the centre fuselage to take oblique or ventral photographs. A later asset added for the Beaufort's offensive role was ASV Mk. II radar, for which aerials were fitted under the nose and beneath the outer wing panels.

When the Beaufort first entered service its normal offensive load was described as four 250lb (113.5kg) bombs or two 500lb (227kg) bombs, which could relate to general-purpose (GP), semi-armour-piercing (SAP) or anti-submarine (AS) types. Maximum bomb load was normally recorded as 1,650lb (749kg), which allowed the carriage of a standard British Mk. XII aerial torpedo or a 1,500lb (681kg) Mk. I mine. The Beaufort's maximum load was actually 2,000lb (908kg),

and in May 1940, during an attack on a German warship, a Beaufort became the first British aircraft to drop a bomb of that weight. For short-range sorties provision was made to carry additional bombs on underwing Universal No. 1 bomb carriers. An early change to Beauforts involved replacement of the original curved bomb-aiming window by a flat type.

The Air Ministry awarded the first Beaufort production contract to Bristol on 22 August 1936. This 'off-the-drawing-board' order was for 78 aircraft, L4441 to L4518, and it was agreed that, as the first five machines would be non-standard, they could be regarded as prototypes. Two years later the first Beaufort, L4441, emerged at Filton and began ground running tests, which soon made it apparent that there was a serious cooling problem. Fedden's close-fitting cowlings would require further time-consuming development to overcome this, and it was decided to fit stylised cowlings with normal circumferential cooling gills.

Bristol test pilot Cyril Uwins took the prototype Beaufort for its maiden flight on 15 October 1938. In due course an unacceptable amount of yawing occurred, caused by the rectangular landing-gear doors which, being fixed to the legs, presented an obstructive surface to the airflow. When the gear was retracted or lowered and the legs moved out of unison (as often happened with contemporary hydraulic systems), excessive yawing developed. Consequently the doors were removed from L4441 and it flew without them until conventional hinged doors forming part of the nacelle had been introduced. This aircraft flew to the A&AEE at Martlesham Heath on 17 April 1939 for initial handling trials. By early May these had been completed and L4441 returned to Filton, where it served primarily as a test-bed for the Taurus engine, to which modifications were being made in the wake of teething troubles, mainly overheating. Eventually L4441 went to No. 5 OTU, crashed at Ternhill on 12 October 1941 and was repaired to become ground instructional airframe 3147M. The second Beaufort prototype, L4442, first flew in October 1939 and remained at Filton for development flying, but crashed during a test flight on 21 May 1940. The third, L4443, also flew from Filton, mostly on Taurus cooling tests, but it too was lost when it plunged to earth at South Hinksey, Berkshire, on 12 June 1940. For the type's evaluation by the CFS, Beaufort L4444 was fitted with dual controls, later going to No. 5 OTU before being written off on 10 April 1942 when it stalled on approach to Kemble. The fifth Beaufort, L4445, was delivered to the TDU, later flew at the A&AEE and finally went to No. 5 OTU. It ditched off the North Devon coast near Chivenor on 1 March 1942.

The first production-standard Beaufort, L4446, came off the line during November 1939, and several of the initial number built went to No. 22 Squadron, RAF, Thorney Island, for concentrated flying and Ser-

vice trials. By the end of January L4446 and L4447 had ditched and crashed respectively, fortunately without loss of life. These early production Beauforts had fully-supercharged Taurus III engines on delivery, but installation of the lower-supercharged Taurus II proved beneficial for the Beaufort's comparatively low-altitude duties. Indeed, this powerplant was chosen as standard for the Beaufort shortly after production deliveries began. Taurus III engines, modified with smaller impellers, became Taurus IIAs, and during 1940 all Beauforts were returned to Filton for this change to be made. Newly-built Beauforts received updated Taurus VI engines, similar to the Mk. II but with added improvements aimed at mitigating earlier Beaufort/Taurus combination problems.

At the end of 1939 Air Ministry policy decreed that Beaufort mark numbers should be in accord with engine installations. Thus the Beaufort Mk. I had Taurus IIIs and Beaufort IIs the Taurus II, but when the Taurus IIIs were so quickly deleted from the Beaufort schedule it was decided that the name Beaufort I should apply to all Taurus powered machines, while Beaufort II would relate to a version with American

Pratt & Whitney Twin Wasp engines. Hence when Taurus XII or Taurus XVI radials with better crankshafts and other improvements were installed in Beauforts, the aircraft were still referred to as Mk. Is. A projected Mk. III with Rolls-Royce Merlin XX engines and additional wing tanks came to nothing, but plans for a Mk. IV powered by Taurus XXs using 100-octane fuel and armed with a four-gun Bristol B11 dorsal turret nearly did. In 1942 500 Beaufort IVs were ordered, but these were cancelled, although one Beaufort II was to be built and flown as a prototype Mk. IV, with its new engines in longer nacelles, Hydromatic feathering propellers and larger oil-cooler intakes incorporated in the wing leading edges. The following Beauforts Mk. V to IX were Australian-built machines, of which more anon.

For its torpedo-bombing role the Beaufort was for a time fitted with Youngman pneumatically-operated dive brakes. These were intended as an aid to improv-

Below: Beaufort I L4449 served with Nos. 22, 217 and 86 Squadrons before passing to various training units. It was struck off charge on 19 June 1945. (Author's collection)

ing stability and control while approaching the target immediately before launching a torpedo. They were located and opened on the upper and lower surfaces of the outer wing panels, inboard of the ailerons. Operation was by means of air pressure supplied via a venturi tube situated beneath the starboard wing root. These dive brakes proved unsuccessful and were ordered to be locked shut, being replaced by fixed skinning in later production aircraft. Another Beaufort role envisaged by Bristol's design team was that of a twin-float seaplane for use by the Canadian and/or Australian Governments. The design was not built, but its concept proved practicable in tests with a Bolingbroke floatplane in Canada.

Beaufort production had ended at Filton by the end of 1943, the last batch of 250 Mk. IIs powered by Pratt & Whitney Twin Wasps being completed from subcontract assemblies at Bristol's satellite factory, Banwell, during 1943/44. The majority of these machines were produced as dual-control Beaufort II(T) trainers, the dorsal turret and operational equipment being deleted as the aircraft were destined for RAF Coastal Command OCUs. The last Beaufort II(T)s arrived with the RAF on 25 November 1944, bringing the total of all marks built in Britain to 1,429.

Meanwhile, early in 1939 the Australian Government received a British Air Mission intent on strengthening Australian aerial defence. Also discussed was the extent to which Commonwealth aviation concerns would be able to produce specific types of aircraft. A favourite for Australian manufacture was the Bristol Beaufort, intended for RAF and RAAF service. The Beaufort's layout made it ideal for the dispersal of component manufacture in several industries, and it also ideally met the Australian need for a coastal defence aircraft. Consequently a Beaufort Division was established by the Department of Aircraft Production (DAP) for the construction of an initial batch of 180 aircraft, for which a contract was placed on 1 July 1939. Two plants shared final assembly, the Commonwealth Aircraft Corporation of Fisherman's Bend, Melbourne, and a new DAP works at Mascot, New South Wales. It was agreed that the first 90 Australian Beauforts would be built to RAF requirements to enable the ageing Vildebeests of Nos. 36 and 100 Squadrons at Singapore to be replaced as quickly as possible. The remaining half of the order would provide Beauforts of similar standard for the RAAF.

The Bristol Aeroplane Company at Filton supplied the Australians with the necessary drawings, jigs and tools, and it was intended that Taurus engines, gun turrets, instruments and certain main structural parts would be exported from Britain. Bristol's eighth Beaufort, L4448, was shipped to Australia in October 1939 as a pattern airframe, with twenty complete kits of components following for assembly of Australia's first Beauforts. However, Australian officials, worried that supplies from Britain would be erratic because of ship-

Above: A production test flight by Beaufort L4449, later delivered to No. 22 Squadron, RAF Coastal Command. (Author's collection)

ping hold-ups and losses en route through enemy action, decided late in 1939 to replace the Taurus engines with American 1,200hp (895kW) Pratt & Whitney R-1830-S3C4G Twin Wasps, although an importation order for Taurus engines to be installed in the 90 RAF Beauforts was retained. But in addition to supply problems, in May 1940 an embargo was placed on the export of all war materials and equipment from Britain. This necessitated installation of the Pratt & Whitney Twin Wasps in those Australian-built machines destined for the RAF, by which time Twin Wasp powered Beauforts had been designated Mk. IIs by the Air Ministry. An equivalent version for the RAAF was to be designated Beaufort Mk. V.

Once the pattern aircraft had been assembled at Mascot it was fitted with Twin Wasps, making its first flight as a Mk. II on 5 May 1941. (A trial installation of Twin Wasps had already been made at Filton on Beaufort I N1110, which in November 1940 became the first Mk. II to fly.) Deliveries of Australian Beaufort IIs started in August 1941, the initial 90 machines being allotted to the RAF with British serial numbers. Six of these aircraft had reached the RAF in Singapore by December 1941, one going to Malaya (Kota Bharu) for special reconnaissance duties with Allied Headquarters Singapore. This Beaufort was wrecked after a mission over Thailand, and the remaining RAF machines could not be used because crews were untrained and the aircraft lacked full equipment. These Beauforts were returned to Australia and later became part of Beaufort contracts for the RAAF. A dozen or more original Beaufort IIs flew with their RAF serials (T9540–T9552 confirmed), later being given RAAF serials in the A9 series and becoming Beaufort Vs.

The first 50 Australian Beaufort Vs were powered by Twin Wasps produced by General Motors-Holden Ltd of Australia, driving Curtiss Electric propellers. Then, owing to a temporary shortage of these engines, 100

Beauforts were built with American imported R-1830-S1C3G Twin Wasps, 40 being Beaufort VIs with Curtiss propellers and 60 Mk. VIIs with Hamilton Standard propellers. The Mk. VA which followed reverted to Australian-built Twin Wasps, but with Hamilton Standard propellers. A further batch of 30 Mk. VAs completed the original order for 180 Australian Beauforts. Following contracts were for 520 Australian Beaufort VIIIs, the definitive version with Twin Wasp engines driving Curtiss Electric propellers. British or American bombs/torpedoes could be carried by this variant, which was fitted with British ASV radar, twin nose guns on gimbal mountings and extra fuel tanks in the wings. The majority of Mk. VIIIs had the Bristol B1 Mk. V dorsal gun turret with twin 0.303in (7.7mm) Brownings, but the last 140 machines were fitted with an Australian-built Mk. VE turret housing two 0.50in (12.7mm) guns. Beaufort VIII production lasted from November 1942 until August 1944, a peak of 30 aircraft per month being reached during this period, a figure which equalled Bristol's maximum Beaufort production at Filton.

Towards the end of the war 46 Australian Beauforts were converted as freight and passenger transports, the dorsal gun turret being replaced by a streamlined fairing. These machines, designated Mk. IXs, were allotted new serial numbers, and one aircraft, A9-201, was tested with a cargo pannier contained in a deeper fuselage, but reverted later to Mk. IX configuration. One feature of the Australian Beaufort was increased fin area to improve single-engine handling, a critical condition on Beauforts. This was introduced on the 91st production machine, earlier aircraft having the revised fin fitted retrospectively.

In the meantime, as already mentioned, the first British-built Beauforts went to No. 22 Squadron for concentrated trials. It was found that the type tended to swing on take-off, had very poor single-engine performance, was prone to catch fire in a crash landing and lacked sufficient power from its unreliable Taurus engines. When launching a torpedo a low-altitude, level run-in was preferred to diving if the torpedo was to follow its true course a little below the water surface. The Beaufort also proved unstable when bombing from high altitude, even 10,000ft (3,050m) at 238mph (383km/h) revealing it to be 'an exceptionally poor bombing platform' according to a report from the A&AEE. However, at lower altitudes bombing presented few problems. For minelaying, No. 22 Squadron practised drops at 200mph (322km/h) from 500ft (152m) carrying the 1,500lb (680kg) Mk. I mine. This was the weapon with which the squadron went to war, making its first operational mission at night on 15/16 April 1940, when nine Beauforts flew from North Coates to lay mines in the Schillig Roads near Wilhelmshaven. One aircraft was lost on this operation. Two nights later No. 22 Squadron sent its Beauforts on their first bombing mission, and for several months conventional bombing became the unit's forte in day and night attacks.

April 1940 saw No. 42 Squadron, Coastal Command, replacing its old Vickers Vildebeest biplanes with Beauforts at Bircham Newton before moving to Thorney Island at the end of the month. A move to Wick, Scotland, followed, to prepare for operations across the North Sea. But Taurus engine problems still plagued the Beaufort, and until Bristol could overcome them it was necessary to ground the aircraft. However, on 21 June, after the German cruiser

Scharnhorst had been subjected to earlier attacks by other Coastal Command aircraft and Skua dive-bombers of the Fleet Air Arm (FAA) in Norway's Trondheim Fjord, she was sighted at sea eight miles west of the Utyoer lighthouse, steaming south at 25kt escorted by destroyers. She was hit and damaged by torpedoes from the RN submarine HMS Clyde and attacked by FAA Swordfish. Then, although the Beauforts were grounded, No. 42 Squadron's crews volunteered to fly their aircraft, despite risks of engine failure, in an attack on the cruiser. Official sanction was given and the Beauforts, loaded with 500lb (227kg) armour-piercing bombs, took off on their hazardous mission. It was apparent that the German naval personnel thought that the Beauforts, like the previous Swordfish, were making a torpedo attack, for the destroyer escort deployed as though it intended to intercept any torpedoes running against the Scharnhorst. But the Beauforts carried out a diving attack, three bombs hitting the stern, another amidships and a third forward on the port side. A swarm of about 50 Messerschmitt Bf 109 fighters from Norway then attacked the Beauforts, shooting three down. The remainder returned to base. There were no engine failures!

As the Taurus engine problems lessened and Beauforts were updated, the type was once again released for operations. After German advances into the Low Countries Coastal Command was active over the occupied areas, and Beauforts joined Lockheed Hudsons in night raids on oil tanks in Rotterdam. In an attack by seven Beauforts on an oil storage depot at Ghent during June 1940, the aircraft flew in at 400ft (122m) after dropping their bombs and machine-gunned any tanks not hit by bombs. Huge fires were started in this raid, one navigator reporting: 'I saw Germans round the oil containers running about like confused hens. They were the first enemy I had seen.

Below: An ex-works shot of Beaufort I L4449 at Filton in 1939. (Rolls-Royce plc, Bristol)

Bristol Beaufort

We used armour-piercing bullets followed by incendiary, and the tanks flared up like torches.'

Lorient on the coast of Brittany was another prime target, as it was a major German U-Boat base and had a large power station. Beauforts joined Blenheim bombers and Swordfish torpedo-bombers in attacks on Lorient during November, and on 8 and 13 December, following the discovery of U-Boats further south in the Gironde, near Bordeaux, Beauforts made successive raids with landmines, causing several heavy explosions and numerous fires. On 13 January 1941 Beauforts took part in a raid on Brest, one of their pilots stating: 'The bombs caused an enormous explosion which shook the aircraft so violently that the crew thought they had received a direct hit from anti-aircraft fire. Showers of sparks accompanied the explosion, which sent up a column of smoke to the height at which we were flying – 10,000ft (3,048m).' The Beaufort was admirably suited to low-altitude attacks; in a mission against the docks at Nantes on the night of 26/27 October 1941, for example, a formation of Beauforts crossed the stormy sea at 100ft (30m) and, on reaching the French coast, climbed sharply to avoid sand dunes and leapfrogged trees. The docks were bombed from 300ft (90m), the Beauforts turning for home just above the rooftops of the town in bright moonlight.

Meanwhile, No. 22 Squadron had turned to torpedo attacks, its first being made on 11 September 1940, when five Beauforts flew against three ships in convoy off Ostend, one strike being made on a 6,000-ton (6,096-tonne) vessel. Six nights later history was made when the first night drop of a torpedo against an enemy target was carried out. Six Beauforts in two flights of three attacked enemy shipping in Cherbourg harbour. Blenheims bombed the area to divert German anti-aircraft guns from the Beauforts, but even so their crews reported that the enemy gunfire was the fiercest experienced to date. One Beaufort failed to return from this attack, carried out in bright moonlight. Other attacks on enemy shipping were often made by 'Rover' patrols, two or three Beauforts looking for a suitable target. During a typical roving patrol on an early autumn afternoon in 1940, two Beauforts ignored two German destroyers and six escort ships off the Dutch coast at Ijmuiden. Instead they continued on into the

Right: Beaufort I L9878/MW-R) of No. 217 Squadron, RAF Coastal Command. It passed to No. 42 Squadron and was struck off charge in May 1943. (Aviation Photo News)

Below: Beaufort L4456 was intended as an experimental transport version, but was completed in standard configuration. It was employed at the A&AEE before passing to Nos. 5 and 51 OTUs. (MAP)

harbour and tried to torpedo a 2,000-ton (2,032-tonne) minelayer surrounded by four flak ships. Both aircraft returned to base, although one was damaged and some of its crew wounded. In another instance, on 23 October 1940, an enemy convoy off Schiermonnikoog comprising nine merchant ships and three flak ships was attacked by two Beauforts. Despite intense anti-aircraft fire, the largest merchant ship was sunk and another was left listing heavily to port. A fortnight later three Beauforts attacked a German merchant ship off Norderney and, although all torpedoes missed the target, the enemy vessel ran aground while trying to take avoiding action and was wrecked.

Torpedo attacks by Beauforts increased during 1941, and in April, after the battlecruiser *Gneisenau* had been forced to leave Brest dry dock by Bomber Command raids, No. 22 Squadron was ordered to make a torpedo attack against the German warship. Six Beauforts moved from North Coates to St Eval to undertake the mission, scheduled for the morning of 6 April, but two became bogged down on the airfield and of the other four only one found the *Gneisenau*. This aircraft was piloted by Flying Officer K. Campbell, who, in the face of very heavy and accurate defensive fire, pressed home his attack to launch the torpedo from a distance of only 1,500ft (457m) before the Beaufort was shot down. Its crew perished. The torpedo hit *Gneisenau* below the waterline and she was *hors de combat* for several months while repairs were carried out. For their gallantry, Flying Officer Campbell was awarded a posthumous VC and his navigator/observer the DFM.

Beauforts made their torpedo attacks not only off the Dutch, Belgian and Danish coasts but along the coast of Norway, an example occurring on 9 February 1941, when three Beauforts hit two out of six German destroyers they attacked off Norway. Just under a month later a large enemy merchant ship was struck and left burning off the Danish coast, while on 12 March a German destroyer was sunk in moonlight off the Norwegian coast. Then early in September near Stavanger Beauforts made two torpedo hits on a large tanker and one against an escort vessel. They then engaged in a running fight with Messerschmitt Bf 109s which appeared on the scene, one Bf 109 being shot down for the loss of one Beaufort. Another Beaufort sortie made during June 1941 was a torpedo attack against the German pocket battleship *Lutzow*, two hits being scored which caused her to turn about and put into a German base for repairs.

During February 1942 Beauforts were engaged in the unsuccessful operations against the German warships *Scharnhorst*, *Gneisenau* and *Prinz Eugen* when they made their dash from the English Channel into the North Sea. In these attacks the British aircraft were subjected to very fierce anti-aircraft fire and severe fighter opposition; none more so than the gallant FAA Swordfish, all of which were shot down, only five of the eighteen crew members surviving.

Beauforts tangled once more with the *Prinz Eugen* on 17 May 1942, when she was discovered steaming south off the southern tip of Norway. Again the Beauforts carried torpedoes and, together with Hudson bombers and escorting Beaufighter and Blenheim fighters, pressed home their attack with great courage and determination against ferocious anti-aircraft fire and fighters. One Beaufort dorsal gunner fought off a series of attacks on his aircraft which lasted 35 minutes, despite a gun jamming and wounds to his face, hands, legs and head. During this action five enemy fighters were shot down for the loss of nine RAF aircraft.

By this time there were four British-based Beaufort units, Nos. 22 and 42 Squadrons having been joined by No. 217, which operated from Thorney Island and Cornwall to cover the English Channel and Western Approaches, and No. 86, which was to replace No. 22 at North Coates when the latter unit was ordered to prepare for service abroad. Towards the end of 1941 No. 415 (Canadian) Squadron at Thorney Island began training on Beauforts, as did No. 489 (New Zealand) Squadron at Leuchars, but before they became operational these units were re-equipped with Handley Page Hampdens and Bristol Blenheim IVs respectively.

All four UK Beaufort squadrons were ordered overseas during 1942, No. 22 initially being destined for Singapore, then for India and Ceylon, but eventually being held en route to assist with air attacks on Rommel's forces in North Africa. By then, No. 39

Above: A pair of Beaufort Is of No. 42 Squadron, Coastal Command, in 1941. The nearest aircraft is N1172. (Aviation Photo News)

Squadron, a long-standing overseas unit, was Beaufort-equipped and employed on anti-shipping strikes in the Mediterranean. The Beauforts of No. 22 Squadron flew detachments from Luqa, Malta, as backup on some of these missions before carrying on to India, No. 217 Squadron following it into its Maltese base. This unit, also bound for the Far East, was in turn retained temporarily to assist in the air offensive against enemy shipping in the Mediterranean until July. In the meantime, No. 42 Squadron had also been ordered to the Far East, but it too was diverted to Middle East operations and joined No. 47 Squadron, which, having previously flown its Vickers Wellesley bombers from Shandur and several satellite landing grounds, was now a Beaufort unit. In July 1942 No. 86 Squadron was sent to Malta, from where it operated together with No. 39 Squadron and a detachment of No. 217.

Losses among the Malta-based units were heavy at this time and, following the departure of No. 217 Squadron's remaining Beauforts, the aircraft of No. 86 Squadron (which became a Liberator IIIA unit that October) were absorbed by No. 39 Squadron, which formed a twosome with No. 47 as the Middle East Beaufort force until replacement Beaufighter Xs arrived in June 1943. Numbers 22, 42 and 217 Squadrons all arrived later at Ratmalana, Ceylon, from where their Beauforts patrolled the Indian Ocean on the lookout for enemy submarines or warships which might threaten Allied shipping. During mid-1944 the Beauforts in Ceylon were replaced by Beaufighter Xs (Nos. 22. and 217. Squadrons) and Blenheim Vs (No. 42 Squadron).

In Britain, meanwhile, Beauforts served usefully as trainers until the war's end, the last 121 of the final Bristol-built batch of 250 being produced as dual-control trainers. These had the rear turret position faired over for OTU duties, while a number of earlier Beauforts were retrospectively modified in this manner by RAF workshops. The Coastal Command OTU formed at Silloth in 1940 (later No. 1 OTU) flew Beauforts, as did Nos. 3, 5 and 9 OTUs and No. 5 Middle East Training School. In addition, Nos. 1 and 2 Torpedo Training Units (TTUs) and Nos. 301 and 306 Ferry Training Units flew the type (FTUs). Specialised training for nightfighter observers was undertaken by Nos. 51 and 54 OTUs, this being carried out for a period in Beauforts purposely fitted with airborne interception (AI) radar. Training units used various marks of Beaufort, the dual-control Mk.

Below: Beaufort production at Filton in March 1941. Nearest the camera, a Beaufighter is under construction. (British Aerospace, Filton)

II(T) machines, for example, being used by No. 12 (Pilot) Advanced Flying Unit during 1945. That year the Royal Navy is recorded as acquiring 38 Beaufort II(T) trainers for navigational training. The RAF declared its Beaufort Is obsolete in 1944, and its Mk. IIs in July 1945.

In Australia the first Beaufort unit, No. 100 Squadron (named in honour of 100 Squadron RAF, decimated with its Vildebeests at Singapore) had been formed by March 1942. Based in Northern Australia and New Guinea, its first operation on 25 June was carried out by five Beauforts against Japanese shipping off New Guinea, while two other machines bombed the enemy at Lae. The squadron made its first torpedo attack on 7 September, striking at Japanese warships shelling Milne Bay. No hits were recorded but, on 6 January 1943 a night torpedo attack succeeded in sinking two Japanese transport vessels and damaging a destroyer escort. Two Beauforts failed to return from this strike. By the spring of 1943 No. 100 Squadron was receiving Beaufort VIIIs, subsequent deliveries being made to Nos. 6 and 8 Squadrons which, after training, were in action later that year. Some Beauforts joined Lockheed Hudsons on Australian home-defence duties with Nos. 7 and 14 Squadrons, while No. 100 continued to harass the enemy until September 1943, despite a number of losses.

Above: Coastal Command Beauforts of Nos. 22 and 86 Squadrons on a sortie in 1940. (Ron Mackay)

Below: Beaufort W6498/AW-K of No. 42 Squadron. (MAP)

Right: Powered by Pratt & Whitney Twin Wasp radial engines, this Beaufort II, AW245, is destined for Coastal Command. (MAP)

Then, as Nos. 6 and 8 Squadrons joined the battle, all three units began systematic close-support attacks against Japanese forces on land, rather than offshore strikes. These ground-attack missions formed a continuing pattern for the RAAF Beauforts as they pounded enemy ground targets. The fitting of 0.50in (12.7mm) guns and the carrying of offensive loads including antipersonnel fragmentation bombs and incendiaries made the Beaufort attacks more lethal. By 1945 No. 7 Beaufort Squadron had entered the arena, while in Australia Nos. 1 and 2 Squadrons were now Beaufort-equipped and No. 15 Squadron was operational on Beauforts before the war's end. Numbers 13 and 32 Squadrons, RAAF, also flew Beauforts, as did some specialist units such as No. 9 Local Air Supply Unit.

Beauforts also saw service on a much smaller scale with the Royal Canadian Air Force (RCAF), South African Air Force (SAAF) and Turkish Air Force. The eighteen aircraft supplied to the SAAF were delivered late in 1941 for use by Nos. 36 and 37 Coastal Defence Flights (combined to become No. 20 Squadron, later renumbered No. 16 Squadron). The RCAF received fifteen Beauforts in August 1941, these going to No. 149 Torpedo Bomber Squadron for coastal defence purposes off Western Canada. Some machines went to the RCAF's No. 32 OTU at Patricia Bay, but by October 1944 Canadian Beauforts had been withdrawn as an active type. Twelve Beaufort Is were delivered to the Turkish Air Force when Turkey cut off diplomatic relations with Germany. These Beauforts, drawn from Middle East storage and flown to Turkey via Iraq, saw little use, but twelve Beaufort II(T)s delivered to Turkey in 1945 continued to fly as trainers until 1947.

Above: A number of Beauforts with dorsal turret removed were used for training. This one, ML625, was later transferred to the Royal Navy as a navigational trainer. (MAP)

Below: Australian-built Beaufort V T9540, the first of a batch of 100 produced for RAF and RAAF service, powered by Pratt & Whitney Twin Wasp engines. (Author's collection)

Bristol
Blenheim

Probably the least forgotten of the RAF bombers covered in this volume is the Bristol Blenheim. On the whole it has received more attention from aviation historians than the other types in this book, and in recent years, with two restored to flying condition (the first of which sadly crashed) it has gained increased publicity. None the less, the Blenheim has never won public acclaim to the extent of more famous types, despite the fact that in the early years of the Second World War it was a mainstay of RAF Bomber Command.

The Blenheim's ancestry can be traced back to the 1934 Salon International de l'Aeronautique in Paris, where the fuselage mock-up of a new twin-engine commercial monoplane was displayed by the Bristol Aeroplane Company. Known as the Type 135 and the brainchild of Bristol chief designer Captain Frank Barnwell, this low-wing cabin monoplane was to accommodate up to eight passengers, and to have a top speed of 240mph (386km/h) at 6,500ft (1,980m) and a cruising speed of 180mph (289.7km/h). Of all-metal, stressed-skin construction, it was to be powered by Bristol Engine Division's new 350hp (261kW) Aquila single-row, sleeve-valve air-cooled radial.

At that time Lord Rothermere, proprietor of the *Daily Mail* newspaper, was convinced that Britain needed to develop greatly advanced commercial aircraft designs if it were not to lose out to aircraft such as America's Boeing 247 and Douglas DC-2. His Lordship was very impressed with Barnwell's project, and informed Bristol that he would purchase a similar aeroplane if it could operate non-stop between European cities and the UK. Thus no prototype 135 was built, Frank Barnwell designing instead the Type 142, which would have the necessary range. Two 650hp (484kW) Bristol Mercury VI.S2 radials superseded the Aquilas, initially driving fixed-pitch four-bladed wooden propellers (replaced before June 1935 by variable-pitch three-bladed Hamilton-Standard units). The wing design of the Type 135 was retained, but the fuselage cross-section was reduced, though there was

Below: The Blenheim's progenitor, the Bristol Type 142 transport which first flew in April 1935. Later donated to the RAF later by Lord Rothermere, it was named *Britain First* and serialled K7557. It is seen here flying at the A&AEE Martlesham Heath in 1936. (MAP)

Bristol Blenheim

BRISTOL TYPE 142M BLENHEIM MK. I DATA

Manufacturers
The Bristol Aeroplane Co Ltd, Filton, Bristol. Rootes Securities Ltd, Speke, Liverpool. A. V. Roe & Co Ltd, Chadderton, Lancs. Valtion Lentokonetehdas, Tampere, Finland. Ikarus A. D., Zemun, Beograd, Yugoslavia

Type
Three-seat, twin-engine light bomber

Powerplant
Two 840hp (626kW) Bristol Mercury VIII nine-cylinder air-cooled radial engines

Performance
Maximum speed, 265mph (426km/h) at 15,000ft (4,575m). Maximum cruising speed, 230mph (370km/h) at 15,000ft (4,575m). Initial climb, 1,540ft (469m)/min; to 15,000ft (4,575m), 9.96min. Service ceiling, 25,500ft (7,772m). Range (with 1,000lb (454kg) bomb load) at 230mph (370km/h) at 15,000ft (4,575m), 678 miles (1,091km); at economical cruising speed of 165mph (265km/h), 920 miles (1,480km). Endurance, 5.65 hours

Weights
Empty, 8,839lb (4,013kg). Loaded (maximum take-off), 13,100lb (5,947kg)

Dimensions
Span, 56ft 4in (17.17m). Length, 39ft 9in (12.12m). Height, 12ft 9in (3.89m). Wing area, 469sq ft (43.57sq m). Landing gear track, 15ft 6in (4.72m)

Armament

One 0.303in (7.7mm) Vickers GO 'K' machine-gun fixed to fire forward from port wing, with 400 rounds. One 0.303in (7.7mm) Lewis machine-gun mounted in a Bristol B.1 Mk. I or Mk. II dorsal turret with seven magazines. Bomb load up to 1,000lb (454kg) carried within internal bomb bay.

BRISTOL TYPE 142M BLENHEIM MK. IV DATA

Manufacturers
The Bristol Aeroplane Co Ltd, Filton, Bristol. Rootes Securities Ltd, Speke, Liverpool. A. V. Roe & Co Ltd, Chadderton, Lancs.
NB. Built as Bolingbroke in Canada by Fairchild Aircraft Ltd, Longueuil, Quebec, with various engine installations (Bristol Mercury, Pratt & Whitney Twin Wasp and Wright Cyclone)

Powerplant
Two 905hp (675kW) (take-off) Bristol Mercury XV nine-cylinder air-cooled radial engines

Performance
Maximum speed, 266mph (428km/h) at 11,800ft (3,597m). Maximum cruising speed, 225mph (362km/h) at 15,000ft (4,575m). Initial climb, 1,500ft (457m)/min; to 15,000ft (4,575m), 17min. Service ceiling, 22,000ft (6,706m). Range (with 1,000lb (454kg) bomb load) at 225mph (363km/h), 1,160 miles 1,866km). Endurance, 8.65hrs

Weights

Empty, 9,790lb (4,445kg). Loaded (normal take-off), 14,400lb (6,538kg); maximum overload, 15,682lb (7,120kg)

Dimensions
Span, 56ft 4in (17.17m). Length, 42ft 9in (13.03m). Height, 12ft 9in (3.89m). Wing area, 469sq ft (43.57sq m). Landing gear track, 15ft 6in (4.72m)

Armament
One 0.303in (7.7mm) Browning machine-gun fixed to fire forward from the port wing, with 400 rounds. One (optional) gimbal-mounted 0.303in (7.7mm) Vickers GO machine-gun in nose. One 0.303in (7.7mm) Lewis or Vickers 'K' gun, or two 0.303in (7.7mm) Browning machine-guns in dorsal-mounted Bristol B.1 turret. One fixed rearward-firing 0.303in (7.7mm) Browning gun in cupola under nose or two controllable rearward-firing Browning guns in Frazer-Nash FN54 housing beneath nose. Bomb load up to 1,000lb (454kg) within internal bomb bay, plus 320lb (145kg) bomb load on external racks

BRISTOL BLENHEIM PRODUCTION (ALL MARKS)

Original Type 142, R-12/G-ADCZ, built for Lord Rothermere and presented to the nation as *Britain First* (K7557)
First production batch of 150 Blenheim Is by Bristol (K7033–K7182); K7033/K7034 served as prototypes for test purposes. K7072 converted to

BLENHEIM MK. I

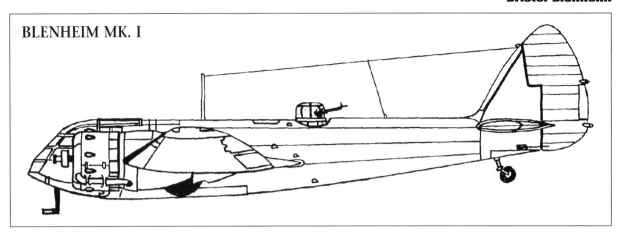

Left: A private venture by Bristol was the Type 143 (R-14) of 1935. Intended as a military derivative of the Type 142, it had Bristol Aquila engines and an orthodox stepped cockpit. Only one Type 143 was completed. (MAP)

long-nose Bolingbroke; later to Fairchild, Canada, as pattern aircraft for Bolingbroke (Blenheim IV) production. K7034–K7036, K7041–K7042 and K7167 fitted with dual controls. Later 34 became instructional airframes (Mk. IAs).

Second production batch of 450 Blenheim Is by Bristol (L1097–L1546). L1483, L1485, L1488, L1489, L1493, L1497 sold to Turkey. L1222 modified to one-off Mk. II. L1242 experimentally fitted with tricycle landing gear. L1424 became prototype Mk. IF. L1348 updated to one-off PR variant. L1345, L1347, L1354 and L1362 sold to Finland. Later 57 became Mk. IAs

Third production batch of 118 Blenheims I/IV by Bristol (L4817–L4934). L4823-L4906 (84 aircraft) Mk. IVs; remaining 34 aircraft Mk. Is. Turkey purchased L4821, L4824, L4826 and L4828. L4822 had dual controls. Eleven later became Mk. IAs

Fourth production batch of 100 Blenheim IVs by Bristol (N6140–N6174, N6176–N6220, N6223–N6242). N6156 to Royal Navy, N6152 and N6209 became Mk. IAs 1649M and 1636M respectively

Fifth production batch of 70 Blenheim IVs by Bristol (P4825–P4864, P4898–P4927). P4910, P4911, P4915, P4916, P4921 and P4922 to Greek Air Force. P4829, P4831 and P4847 became Mk. IAs 4172M,

3992M and 3980M respectively.

Sixth production batch of 62 Blenheim IVs by Bristol (P6885–P6934, P6950–P6961). P6891, P6892, P6897, P6898, P6903 and P6904 to Greek Air Force. P6960 to Royal Navy. P6907 and P6921 became Mk. IAs 2514M and 3438M respectively

First production batch of 250 Blenheims (Mk. Is) by Avro (L6594–L6843). L6696–L6708 and L6713–L6718 to Romania. L6813, L6814, L6817–L6819 and L6821–L6834 to Yugoslavia. Twenty became Mk.IAs

Second production batch of 100 Blenheims (Mk. IVs) by Avro (N3522–N3545, N3551–N3575, N3578–N3604 and N3608–N3631). N3544 and N3600 to Portugal. N3582 and N3622–N3624 to Free French Air Force. N3523 and N3527 to RN. N3566 and N3603 became Mk. IAs 2120M and 4442M

Third production batch of 230 Blenheims (Mk. IV) ordered from Avro (R2770–R3144), of which only 30 built (R2770–R2799), the remaining 200 being cancelled. R2775 and R2781 to Portugal. R2782 to RN. R2778 became Mk. IA 4027M

Fourth production batch of 420 Blenheims (Mk. IVs) by Avro (Z5721–Z5770, Z5794–Z5818, Z5860–Z5909, Z5947–Z5991, Z6021–Z6050, Z6070–Z6104, Z6144–Z6193, Z6239–Z6283, Z6333–Z6382 and Z6416–Z6455).

Twenty to RN, six to Portugal, five to Free French Air Force. Eight became Mk. IAs

Fifth production batch of 280 Blenheims (Mk. IVs) ordered from Avro (Z9533–Z9978), of which 200 were built (Z9533–Z9552, Z9572–Z9621, Z9647–Z9681, Z9706–Z9755 and Z9792–Z9836). Remaining 80 cancelled. A further order for 120 Blenheim IVs to be built by Avro (AA100–AA144, AA178–AA202 and AA224–AA273) was also cancelled, but Avro did produce five replacement Blenheim IVs (AE449–AE453)

First production batch of 380 Blenheims by Rootes Securities; 250 Mk. I (L8362–L8407, L8433–L8482, L8500–L8549, L8597–L8632, L8652–L8701 and L8714–L8731), plus 130 Mk. IV (L8732–L8761, L8776–L8800, L8827–L8876 and L9020–L9044). L8384 and L8385 to Greek Air Force. L8603-8608, L8619, L8620, L8622, L8624-L8630, L8632 and L8652-L8654 to Romania. L9025, L9026 and L9028 to Finland. Twenty became Mk.IAs

Second production batch of 220 Blenheims by Rootes Securities; 86 Mk. I (L9170–L9218 and L9237–L9273), all modified to Mk. IVs. 134 Mk. IV (L9294–L9342, L9375–L9422 and L9446–L9482). L9195–L9203 to Finland. L9309, L9311, L9312, L9376, L9377, L9380 and L9384 to Canada. L9192 had

still comfortable accommodation for up to five passengers and a crew of two.

The first flight of the Type 142 was made from Filton on 12 April 1935 by Bristol chief test pilot Captain Cyril Uwins, and during this and subsequent test flights the new monoplane exceeded all expectations. At the A&AEE, Martlesham Heath, Air Ministry test pilots were very impressed indeed to discover that the Type 142 had a top speed of 307mph (494km/h) at 14,000ft (4,267m), and could achieve 285mph (459km/h) at its gross weight of 9,357lb (4,248kg). This was considerably faster than the RAF's new Gloster Gladiator fighter, and led to great interest being shown in the new transport by the Air Ministry. Consequently Lord Rothermere's permission was sought for the Type 142 to undergo an extended test

programme. His Lordship did better than that; he presented the aircraft to the nation and named it *Britain First*. Initially flown under B conditions as R-12 (it never carried its official civil registration, G-ADCZ) the Type 142 continued trials at Martlesham, receiving the military serial K7557. In July it returned to Filton for repairs after losing a cowling panel, then returned to the A&AEE before passing to the RAE at Farnborough, where it was used for experimental purposes and on transport duties until 1942. It then became instructional airframe 2211M at No. 10 School of Technical Training, and was finally scrapped in 1944.

Meanwhile, in 1935 Bristol had developed a variant known as the Type 143, powered by a pair of 600hp (447kW) Aquila IV engines. This aircraft employed a similar wing profile and tail unit, but its fuselage was

---

long-range tanks. L9171, L9209, L9306 and L9478 became Mk. IAs 2161M, 4007M, 3431M and 3981M respectively

Third production batch of 250 Blenheims (Mk. IV) by Rootes Securities (R3590–R3639, R3660–R3709, R3730–R3779, R3800–R3849 and R3870–R3919). R3877 to Free French Air Force. R3830 to Portugal. R3601, R3695, R3871 and R3888 to RN

Fourth production batch of 400 Blenheims (Mk. IV) by Rootes Securities (T1793–T1832, T1848–T1898, T1921–T1960, T1985–T2004, T2031–T2080, T2112–T2141, T2161–T2190, T2216–T2255, T2273–T2292, T2318–T2357, T2381–T2400, T2425–T2444). T1876, T2004, T2129, T2224, T2322, T2325, T2351 and T2444 to RN. T1817, T1819, T1855, T1857, T1867, T1975, T1935, T2077, T2079 and T2340 to Free French Air Force. T2431 and T2434 to Portugal. T1996 to Turkey. T1800, T1948, T1952, T2131, T2284, T2287, T2425 and T2438 became Mk. IAs 4124M, 4016M, 2363M, 3977M, 4006M, 2538M, 4015M and 4008M respectively

Fifth production batch of 800 Blenheims (Mk. IV) by Rootes Securities (V5370–V5399, V5420–V5469, V5490–V5539, V5560–V5599, V5620–V5659, V5680–V5699, V5720–V5769, V5790–V5829, V5850–V5899, V5920–V5969, V5990–V6039, V6060–V6099, V6120–V6149, V6170–V6199, V6220–V6269, V6290–V6339,

V6360–V6399, V6420–V6469, V6490–V6529). Twenty to RN. V5429, V5434, V5501, V5729, V5883 and V6395 to Portugal. Ten became Mk. IAs

Sixth production batch of 600 Blenheims (Mk. IV) ordered from Rootes Securities (Z7271–Z8323), of which 430 built (Z7271–Z7320, Z7340–Z7374, Z7406–Z7455, Z7483–Z7522, Z7577–Z7596, Z7610–Z7654, Z7678–Z7712, Z7754–Z7803, Z7841–Z7860, Z7879–Z7928, Z7958–Z7992). Z7373, Z7779, Z7842, Z7885 and Z7970 to Free French Air Force. Z7492 to Portugal (Z7585 and Z7678 interned). Z7986 to Turkey. Z7351, Z7354, Z7414, Z7761 and Z7961 to RN. Remaining 170 aircraft (Z7993-Z8323) cancelled

Two prototype Blenheim Mk. Vs (Bisleys) built by Bristol (AD657 and AD661) as ground-attack aircraft and high-altitude day-bomber respectively

First production batch of 780 Blenheim Mk. V (Bisley) by Rootes Securities (AZ861–AZ905, AZ922–AZ971, AZ984–AZ999, BA100–BA118, BA133–BA172, BA191–BA215, BA228–BA262, BA287–BA336, BA365–BA409, BA424–BA458, BA471–BA505, BA522–BA546, BA575–BA624, BA647–BA691, BA708–BA757, BA780–BA829, BA844–BA888, BA907–BA951, BA978–BA999, BB100–BB102, BB135–BB184). BA306, BA326, BA394, BA525, BA596 and BA849 to Free French Air Force. AZ986, AZ987

and BA826 to Portugal. BA137, BA292, BA395, BA495, BA591, BA613, BA614, BA713, BA854, BA855, BA887, BA910, BA922 and BA925 to Turkey. BA106, BA746 and BA856 became Mk. IAs 4387M, 4444M and 4386M respectively

Two Bristol Type 160HA Blenheim Mk. V (Bisley) prototypes built by Rootes Securities (DJ702 and DJ707). DJ707 became Mk. IA 3298M

Second production batch of 415 Blenheim Mk. Vs (Bisleys) ordered from Rootes Securities (EH310–EH872), of which 160 were built (EH310–EH355, EH371–EH420, EH438–EH474 and EH491–EH517). EH320, EH326, EH341 and EH372 to Turkey. EH347, EH443 and EH458 to USAAF. Remaining 255 aircraft cancelled

NB. One Blenheim I (L1431) went to South African Air Force, later returning to RAF service as AX683

RAF BRISTOL BLENHEIM UNITS

Bomber Command (Mk. I) Great Britain

No. 18 Squadron (Upper Heyford)
No. 21 Squadron (Eastchurch/Watton)
No. 34 Squadron (Upper Heyford/Watton)
No. 44 Squadron (Waddington)
No. 57 Squadron (Upper Heyford)
No. 61 Squadron (Hemswell)
No. 62 Squadron (Cranfield)
No. 82 Squadron (Cranfield/Watton)
No. 90 Squadron (Bicester)

Above: The prototype Bristol Type 142M Blenheim, K7033, in its overall metal finish. Note the redesigned glazed nose, the dorsal turret and the propeller spinners (the spinners were deleted on production Blenheims). The serials were black, and the roundels were RAF 'A' type. (Author's collection)

No. 101 Squadron (Bicester)
No. 104 Squadron (Bassingbourn/Bicester)
No. 107 Squadron (Harwell/Wattisham)
No. 108 Squadron (Bassingbourn/Bicester)
No. 110 Squadron (Waddington/Wattisham)
No. 114 Squadron (Wyton)
No. 139 Squadron (Wyton)
No. 144 Squadron (Hemswell)

Overseas (Mk. I bomber)
No. 8 Squadron (Aden)
No. 11 Squadron (Far East/Middle East)
No. 30 Squadron (Middle East)
No. 34 Squadron (Far East)
No. 39 Squadron (Far East)
No. 45 Squadron (Middle East)
No. 55 Squadron (Middle East)
No. 60 Squadron (India)
No. 62 Squadron (Far East)
No. 84 Squadron (Middle East)
No. 113 Squadron (Middle East)
No. 211 Squadron (Middle East)
No. 223 Squadron/OTU (Middle East)

NB. Blenheim IF fighters operated in Great Britain with Nos. 23, 25, 29, 64, 68, 92, 141, 145, 219, 222, 229, 234, 235, 236, 245, 248, 600, 601 and 604 Squadrons of RAF Fighter Command. Overseas they flew with Nos. 27, 30 and 203 Squadrons

Bomber Command (Mk. IV) Great Britain
Nos. 15, 18, 21, 34, 35, 40, 57, 82, 88, 90, 101, 104, 105, 107, 108, 110, 114, 139, 218 and 226 Squadrons

Coastal Command (Mk. IV) Great Britain
Nos. 53, 59, 86, 143, 235, 236, 248, 252, 254, 272, 404, 500 and 608 Squadrons

Army Co-operation Command (Mk. IV)
Nos. 13, 53, 59 and 614 Squadrons

RAF Middle East (Mk. IV bomber)
Nos. 11, 14, 39, 45, 55, 84, 104, 105, 107, 113, 162, 203 and 244 Squadrons

Aden
No.8 Squadron

The Sudan
Nos. 14, 45 and 113 Squadrons

RAF Far East (Mk. IV Bomber)
Nos. 11, 34, 39, 45, 60, 84, 113 and 211 Squadrons

NB. Blenheim IVF fighters operated in Great Britain with No. 600 Squadron (AAF), and with No. 203 Squadron in the Middle East

RAF Blenheim V (Bisley) units

Great Britain
Nos. 13, 18, 114, 139 and 614 Squadrons

Middle East
Nos. 13, 18, 114, 162, 203, 244, 454 and 614 Squadrons

Aden
No. 8 Squadron

Far East
Nos. 34, 42 and 113 Squadrons

Operational Training Units
OTUs using Blenheims included Nos. 1, 2, 5, 6, 12, 13, 15, 42, 51, 54, 55, 56, 60, 70, 72, 75, 132 and 152

Blenheims also flew with numerous other RAF training and auxiliary units, including No. 1 Ferry Pilots Pool (FPP), No. 1 Air Armament School (AAS), No. 1 Middle East Training School, No. 2 School of Army Co-operation, No. 3 Radio School, Nos. 5 and 9 AOS, No. 5 BGS, No. 8 FTS, No. 9 FTS, No. 9 Observers Advanced Flying Unit (OAFU), No. 12 PAFU, No. 17 Service Flying Training School (SFTS), No. 301 Ferry Training Unit (FTU), the Training Unit and Reserve Pool, the Special Duties (SD) Flight, the Air Transport Auxiliary (ATA), the CFS, the Central Gunnery School (CGS), the FIU, the FTU, the School of General Reconnaissance and the Telecommunications Flying Unit (TFU). Blenheims were also used at the A&AEE and RAE.

Blenheim Mk. Vs (Bisleys) were issued to Nos. 17 and 60 OTUs, No. 60 OTU later becoming No. 132 OTU for any Coastal Command units still operating Blenheim Vs

Above: Blenheim I K7170 of No. 61 Squadron, RAF Hemswell, 1938. (Ron Mackay)

longer, with a cabin accommodating up to eight passengers. The cockpit had a conventional stepped profile, as opposed to the well glazed streamlined frontage of the Type 142. Finland's Government showed considerable interest in the Type 143 as a military type, and negotiated with Bristol for nine machines designated Type 143F. This variant was to have Mercury VI engines, and was to be convertible from the transport to fighter-bomber role by changing the nose and rear fuselage sections for units in which a nose-mounted 20mm Madsen cannon and a dorsal 0.303in (7.7mm) Lewis machine-gun could be installed. In the event no Type 143F was built, but the Finnish Government would later transfer its interest to the Type 142M military version of the original transport.

The Type 143 was registered G-ADEK on 22 March 1935, but never carried these markings. Instead, as an Aquila engine test-bed, the B conditions identity R-14 was applied and, owing to delays in delivery of its engines, the aircraft did not fly until 20 January 1936. Development was further retarded by the lack of variable-pitch propellers suited to the Aquila. Imperial Airways showed considerable interest in the aircraft and made tentative enquiries during 1937, but by then Bristol was heavily committed to producing its bomber version of the Type 142. Any plans to build the Types 142 or 143 at Filton for the commercial market were abandoned, and further development of the Aquila engine was stopped in 1938. The Type 143 was then stored minus its engines until it was scrapped early in the Second World War.

In the meantime Air Ministry officials had become convinced of the superiority of the Type 142's basic design after receiving the 1935 test results for K7557. Bristol was requested by the Air Staff to submit proposals for a medium bomber based on the Type 142 which could be produced in reasonable quantity. In response, at the end of May 1935 Barnwell came up with the Type 142M powered initially by super-charged Aquila engines. With a 1,000lb (454kg) bomb load its estimated top speed was 262mph (422km/h) at 15,000ft (4,572m), but the following month it was suggested that the installation of Mercury engines, despite a weight increase, would result in an estimated maximum speed of 278mph (447km/h). This proved more acceptable to the Air Ministry, and by July a Mercury-powered Type 142M was in the offing. The military version differed in having its wing raised from low to mid position, allowing the bomb bay to be located beneath the wing spars. Changes to the tail surfaces included an increase in tailplane span and elevator chord, the addition of elevator trim tabs, and repositioning the tailplane higher up the fuselage. A retractable tailwheel was introduced and the airframe was strengthened throughout. The three-man crew consisted of pilot, navigator/bomb-aimer and wireless-operator/gunner, the bomb-aiming position being in the nose. Armament was to include an 0.303in (7.7mm) Lewis machine-gun in a hydraulically operated, partly-retractable Bristol B.Mk. I gun turret in a

Above: Blenheim I L1295 served initially with No. 107 Squadron, RAF Harwell, in August 1938. (MAP)

dorsal position, an 0.303in (7.7mm) Browning machine-gun mounted in the port wing, and a 1,000lb (454kg) internal bomb load.

Air Ministry approval resulted in Specification 28/35 being issued in August 1935 to cover the Type 142M, and a contract was placed that month for 150 production aircraft to be delivered 'straight off the drawing board'. There was no prototype as such, the first two machines off Filton's production line serving as test aircraft. The initial flight of the first, K7033, took place on 25 June 1936, by which time the Bristol Type 142M had been officially named Blenheim. Acceptance trials of K7033 at Martlesham Heath revealed the need for some modifications to production Blenheims. These included controllable cooling gills for the engine cowlings, improvements to the carburettor air intakes and the fitting of a fixed tailwheel in place of the retractable type, which had been deemed unnecessary. Thus the retractable tailwheel of early production Blenheim Is was superseded on all subsequent machines by a fixed unit. Blenheim Is began leaving Filton's production lines early in 1937 at the rate of six per month, but within a year the figure had risen to 24 a month.

The Blenheim had a monocoque oval-section fuselage built in three portions, with 'Z'-section transverse frames, 'top hat'-section stringers and flush-riveted Alclad stressed-skin covering. The centre section was bolted and riveted to the fuselage and carried the engine nacelles, the outer wing panels being attached to its extremities. Spars and ribs built round two main spars, with overall Alclad stressed-skin covering, formed the wing structure, and Alclad-covered split trailing-edge flaps and fabric-covered ailerons were fitted. The empennage was of light alloy, the fixed surfaces being Alclad covered and the moveable ones fabric-covered. A servo-action trim tab was included in the rudder. The main landing gear had twin oleo legs which retracted rearwards into the engine nacelles, the wheels remaining partly exposed when retracted. As already mentioned, most Blenheims had a fixed tailwheel. Power for production Blenheim Is was provided by two 840hp (627kW) Bristol Mercury VIII nine-cylinder air-cooled radials driving de Havilland three-bladed variable-pitch propellers.

Following the initial production batch of 150 Blenheim Is (K7033–K7182), in accordance with Scheme 'C' of the RAF expansion programme a contract for a further 450 machines, L1097–L1546, was signed on 11 July 1936 under Scheme 'F'. Another 118 Blenheims (L4817–L4934) were added to this order, of which only 34 emerged as Mk. Is, the remaining 84 aircraft being long-nose Blenheim IVs.

The Blenheim IV resulted from complaints about the cramped conditions for the navigator/bomb-aimer and radio-operator/dorsal gunner in Mk. Is. In fact an updated Blenheim was already in the pipeline for service with Coastal Command as a general reconnaissance (GR) type, pending availability of the Bristol Type 152 Beaufort then under development. Designated Type 149 and named Bolingbroke, this interim design was produced in response to Specification 11/36. It incorporated a 3ft (0.91m) extension at the front to accommodate the navigation and radio positions. Increased range was provided by installing extra wing-mounted fuel tanks outboard of the engine nacelles. Piloted by Cyril Uwins, the Type 149, a converted early production Blenheim I K7072, made its first flight on 24 September 1937. Immediate criticism followed regarding the distance between pilot and windscreen, the Bolingbroke's nose profile being identical to that of the Blenheim I. Consequently the windscreen was restored to its original position and the front extension lowered below the pilot's forward view. This still left something to be desired, however, and the port side of the revised nose was further modified by scalloping, a feature which became characteristic of the Blenheim IV and won Air Ministry approval.

Blenheim Is were considered one of the best bombers to have entered RAF service, and were reputed to be the fastest of their class in the world. Certainly the performance was good by 1937/38 standards, the 840hp (626kW) Bristol Mercury VIII engines giving a top speed of 285mph (459km/h) at 15,000ft (4,575m) at a normal loaded weight of 12,330lb (5,600kg). The Blenheim I climbed to 15,000ft (4,575m) in 9.2 minutes, its service ceiling was 30,600ft (9,327m) and its range 900 miles (1,448km) at 200mph (322km/h) or 975 miles (1,569km) at 165mph (265km/h). However, when Service and military equipment had been added the top speed was reduced by over 20mph (32km/h). Thus, if

reports about Germany's latest aircraft, including Junkers' new Ju 88 bomber, were true, the Blenheim with its relatively small bomb load would quickly be outclassed. Moreover, comparison between the Blenheim's performance and that of the RAF's biplane fighters was now irrelevant owing to the appearance of the Hurricane and Spitfire monoplanes. Indeed, the 1938 Air Exercises showed that the Blenheim was too slow and vulnerable to 'enemy' fighters, and the inadequacy of its defensive armament became all too obvious.

An attempt was made to improve the Blenheim's potential by increasing the range and bomb load in modified Mk. I, L1222, in which long-range outer wing tanks added an extra 187 Imp gal (850lit) to the standard 278 Imp gal (1,264lit) carried. Landing weight could be reduced if necessary by means of fuel jettison pipes located under the wings, while two additional 250lb (113kg) bombs could be carried beneath the wings, inboard of the nacelles. A stronger landing gear to cope with a maximum take-off weight of 14,000lb (6,350kg) was also fitted. However, as the Mercury VIII engines were not changed, this Blenheim, known as the Mk. II, only managed a top speed of 236mph (380km/h) and the project was abandoned. There was no Mk. III Blenheim, this being a proposed long-nose, short-range variant without

Below: Blenheim Is of Nos. 44 and 139 Squadrons lined up at RAF Wyton in 1938. The nearest aircraft is L1100 of No. 139 Squadron, and the next in line is K7136 of No. 44 Squadron. (Ron Mackay)

long-range tanks. As it was, the Mk. IV contained extra wing tanks and, as Bristol had been ordered to change rapidly to Blenheim IV production using existing Blenheim I contracts, the revised nose section and extra wing tanks were simultaneously introduced on the production line and the Mk. III was discarded.

When American Lockheed Hudsons ordered for the RAF in 1938 went to Coastal Command for GR duties, plans to produce Type 149 Bolingbrokes for RAF use were abandoned, and the supply of Blenheim Is was ordered by the Air Ministry to continue in their place. However, Fairchild Aircraft Ltd in Canada undertook licensed production of Blenheim IVs at Longueuil, Quebec, for RCAF service, and the name Bolingbroke was retained for these machines. After the original Bolingbroke prototype, K7072, had arrived in Canada, eighteen were built according to Bristol plans and, powered by Mercury VIII engines, became Bolingbroke Is. An updated Canadian Mk. IV was built to North American standards, powered by Mercury XV engines, and 125 of this variant were built. One Bolingbroke I that crashed was rebuilt as a Mk. II to Mk IV standard, while another Mk. I, 717, was fitted with Edo twin floats and powered by Mercury XVs to become the Mk. III. A Bolingbroke IV with 990hp (738kW) Wright Cyclone R-1820-G3B radials was des-

ignated Mk. IVC, and fifteen machines with 1,200hp (895kW) Pratt & Whitney Twin Wasp radials were known as Bolingbroke IVWs.

Meanwhile, Scheme 'F' of the RAF expansion programme had also introduced the shadow production plan, which entailed manufacturers outside the aircraft industry constructing aircraft to help meet Air Ministry production targets. One company, motor car manufacturer Rootes Securities Ltd, received an initial contract at the end of 1936 for 600 Blenheims to be built at Speke, Liverpool. Of these, six batches were Mk. Is and nine batches Mk. IVs, some Blenheim Is being converted to Mk. IV standard on the line. At the same time A. V. Roe & Co Ltd (Avro) was taking over a new factory under the shadow scheme at Chadderton, near Manchester, and was awarded a contract to produce 250 Blenheim Is. This was followed by contracts for Blenheim IVs in batches of 100; 230 (only 30 built, the rest were cancelled); 420; 280 (200 built, the rest cancelled); 120 (all cancelled); and five replacement aircraft. Bristol at Filton produced a substantial number of Blenheim Is and IVs, the first batch of 150 being followed by orders for 450; 118; 100; 70; and 62. Thus before the outbreak of war Blenheim IVs were rolling out of all three factories, and by September 1939 the combined production effort had reached 100 aircraft per month. Not surprisingly the Blenheim had been one of five key types of aircraft chosen by the Air Ministry for priority production for the expanding RAF.

On its introduction the Blenheim IV featured the same poor defensive armament as the Mk. I, but this

Below: These Blenheim Is on a North African airfield in 1940 are with No. 45 Squadron. The unit code letters (OB) are grey, and the individual aircraft letters are red. The nearest machine is 'W'. In the background are Westland Lysanders. (Ron Mackay)

was somewhat improved in accordance with Service requirements and normal updating, a Bristol B.Mk. II turret replacing the Mk. I which had only partial rotation (it also superseded the earlier turret on some Blenheim Is). Next came a Mk. III turret housing a Vickers 0.303in (7.7mm) 'K' gun, followed by a Mk. IIIA with a pair of these guns and, finally, the Mk. IV turret containing twin belt-fed 0.303in (7.7mm) Brownings. To ward off attacks from astern a fixed single Browning machine-gun was mounted to fire aft from a transparent cupola beneath the nose. This was later replaced on many Blenheim IVs by a Frazer-Nash FN54 in which two controllable rear-firing Browning machine-guns were installed.

The first Avro-built Blenheim I, L6594, was at one stage experimentally armed with a 37mm Coventry Ordnance Works (COW) gun mounted to fire vertically downwards, mainly for the anti-submarine role. This machine later became instructional airframe 1805M. Two other Blenheim I experiments are worth mentioning. A fixed tricycle landing gear was fitted to L1242 (ex-No. 34 Squadron) to enable Bristol to gain familiarity with this type of undercarriage. The aircraft

Left: The cockpit interior of a Blenheim I, showing the pilot's field of view forward, the compass below and left of the instrument panel and the gun firing button on the control column. (Ron Mackay)

Below: Based at Ambala, India, these Blenheim Is of No. 60 Squadron are fitted with Vokes air filters under the engine cowlings. This unit later moved to Mingaladon, Burma, just before the Japanese attacked in December 1941. (Ron Mackay)

remained at Filton, being struck off charge on 9 April 1941. In the second experiment, Blenheim I L1348 was modified by the RAE to photo-reconnaissance configuration by having a glossy low-drag finish applied, the dorsal turret removed, part of the nose faired in, the wingtips clipped, the bomb bay doors and joints filled in or covered with special tape and Rotol constant-speed propellers fitted. Trials indicated a 22mph (35.4km/h) speed increase at 8,000ft

(2,438m) which, together with other unimpressive figures, resulted in abandonment of the project. After reconversion to normal Mk. I form, this Blenheim went to No. 88 Squadron and was struck off charge on 12 June 1941.

During 1938 the Blenheim IF long-range fighter was introduced, a number of Blenheim Is being released for this purpose as Blenheim IVs joined Bomber Command in increasing numbers. Conver-

Above: Blenheim I L1348 at Staverton in 1940, a one-off photo-reconnaissance version minus dorsal turret and with blunt wingtips, covered lower nose glazing, a low-drag gloss finish and Rotol constant-speed propellers. (Author's collection)

Below: The four-gun belly pack of four machine-guns is prominent on Blenheim IF fighter L6680/YN-A of No. 601 Squadron, which flew Mk. IFs from Biggin Hill and Tangmere between January 1939 and February 1940, when Hurricane replacements arrived. (MAP)

Above: In all-black finish, Blenheim IF K7159/YX-N is with No. 54 OTU in September 1940. Note the Mk. III AI radar antennae above and below the port wing and on the nose. (Author's collection)

sion of Blenheim I bombers to IF fighter configuration was fairly straightforward, a gun pack containing a battery of four forward-firing belt-fed 0.303in (7.7mm) Browning machine-guns and 2,000 rounds of ammunition being fitted flush beneath the bomb bay. The Southern Railway workshops at Ashford, Kent, manufactured 1,375 of these gun packs from 1938 until 1940, and 200 Blenheim Is were converted to Mk. IFs. A number of similar conversions to Blenheim IVs later created the IVF, all these Blenheim conversions being undertaken by RAF Maintenance Units.

The availability of Blenheim IFs allowed the RAF to replace its ageing Hawker Demon two-seat biplane fighters, the first of the new Blenheim IFs going to No. 600 Squadron (Auxiliary Air Force (AAF)) at Hendon during September 1938. By the end of the year Nos. 23, 25, 29 and 604 Squadrons had all switched to Blenheim IFs, and by September Nos. 64 and 601 Squadrons were flying the type. Abroad, No. 27 Squadron (India) and No. 30 Squadron (Middle East) also received IFs. In the UK, Fighter Command employed its Blenheim IFs as day fighters until 1940, but the type proved inadequate as a day fighter across the Channel and was no match for the heavily escorted Luftwaffe daylight raids on Britain during 1940. But with their fuselages able to accommodate the new AI Mk. III radar equipment and an operator, Blenheim IFs made useful nightfighters. External devices forming part of the IF's radar system included a nose-mounted transmitter aerial, azimuth receiver aerials on the engine nacelles just ahead of the wing leading edge and elevation receiver aerials on the upper and lower port wing. This special equipment

was provided by Pye and Metropolitan Vickers, installation being carried out by RAE Farnborough.

Delivery of radar-equipped IFs started in 1939, the first machines going to No. 25 Squadron, and within a year more than 30 Blenheim IFs had been supplied to RAF units. Three went to No. 600 Squadron at Manston, Kent, for training and evaluation, initially fitted with AI Mk. II radar sets and later with Mk. III equipment. These Blenheim IFs were joined by another three radar-equipped machines and, on 10 April 1940, formed the Fighter Interception Unit (FIU) at Tangmere. The first success came on the night of 22/23 July 1940, when a Blenheim IF closed in on a formation of six German bombers and destroyed a Dornier Do 17. This was the first recorded successful night interception by an RAF radar-equipped fighter. Further 'kills' by Blenheim nightfighters were sparse, but three enemy bombers were shot down by No. 29 Squadron on three nights in August, and three by No. 25 Squadron in September. The same month saw a Junkers Ju 88 shot down by a Blenheim IF of No. 600 Squadron.

Once the more efficient Beaufighters with their standard AI Mk. IV radar had superseded the Blenheim nightfighters, the RAF switched its Blenheim IFs to the night intruder role, attacks being launched against Luftwaffe bomber bases from which raids on Britain were made. Overseas, Blenheim IFs operated with No. 27 Squadron against the Japanese at Singapore in

Above: The Blenheim IVF's deeper belly gun pack is discernible on this Blenheim IVF. The Vokes filters under the cowlings suggest it was one of those allotted to No. 203 Squadron in Aden. Bomb racks are still attached beneath the fuselage. (Ron Mackay)

December 1941 before being overwhelmed. In the Middle East No. 30 Squadron flew its Blenheim IFs against the Italians as they attacked British shipping at Alexandria in June 1940, and later flew its IFs in Greece and over Crete.

Long-nose Blenheim IVF fighters, armed with an identical four-gun belly pack to the IF, replaced only a small number of IFs in Fighter Command, but No. 600 Squadron was fully equipped with IVFs until Beaufighters were received during September 1940. In the Middle East No. 203 Squadron operated Blenheim IVFs with some success in North Africa, Greece, Crete and Egypt. However, the principal employer of Blenheim IVFs was Coastal Command, which operated eleven squadrons of the type alongside its Blenheim IV bombers. Most sorties were flown across the Channel from 1940 to 1941, priority being given to attacks on German invasion barges massed in the Channel ports ready for Hitler's planned assault on Britain. Coastal Command Blenheim IVFs also carried out patrols along the South Coast during the Battle of Britain, sometimes engaging German bomber formations.

In its main function as a bomber the Blenheim began its RAF career at the end of 1936, when No. 114 Squadron at Wyton, Huntingdonshire, was chosen to become the first Blenheim unit. On 10 March 1937 the fourth production Blenheim I, K7036, was the first

to arrive at Wyton, but unfortunately the brakes were applied too hard on landing, it ended up on its back, and the squadron's first Blenheim was a write-off. Further Blenheim Is continued to fly in, and within a month the squadron was fully equipped with the type. By January 1938 Blenheim Is from the first production batch had been delivered to Nos. 90, 139, 144, 110 and 61 Squadrons, and by the end of 1938 home-based Nos. 21, 34, 57, 62, 82, 101, 104, 107 and 108 Squadrons were flying them. The type also entered service with overseas squadrons in 1938, including Nos. 30 (Middle East) and Nos. 34 and 62 (Far East).

At the time of the 1938 Munich Crisis sixteen home-based RAF squadrons were flying Blenheim Is with Nos. 1, 2 and 5 Groups of Bomber Command. During May 1939 No. 18 Squadron became Blenheim I equipped at Upper Heyford and, before the outbreak of war, Blenheim Is were operating overseas with Nos. 8, 30, 45, 55, 84, 113 and 211 Squadrons in the Middle East and Nos. 11, 34, 39, 62 Squadrons in the Far East. The first unit to fly Blenheim Is in India was No. 60 Squadron at Ambala, which began replacing its Westland Wapiti biplanes during March 1939, although a year earlier Blenheim I L1097 had been delivered from No. 30 Squadron (Middle East) to No. 60 Squadron at Ambala as a dual-control aircraft for converting No. 60 Squadron crews to their new aircraft. These were shipped to Karachi Aircraft Depot for assembly and ferried to Ambala by No. 60 Squadron crews who had delivered their redundant Wapitis to Karachi. Later, from June 1941 until January 1942, No. 223 Squadron/OTU (an ex-Vickers Wellesley unit from East Africa) flew Blenheim Is alongside its Martin Marylands and Douglas Boston IIIs.

42M/275

By the time Britain declared war, on 3 September 1939, most home-based Blenheim bomber units had switched to Blenheim IVs, only Nos. 18 and 57 Squadrons remaining fully equipped with Blenheim Is. On 24 September these two units arrived in France as part of the British Expeditionary Force (BEF) Air Component, operating their Blenheims alongside the Mk. IVs of Nos. 53 and 54 Squadrons. At the end of 1939 Nos. 114 and 139 Squadrons flew to France to replace two Fairey Battle units (Nos. 15 and 40 Squadrons) of the Advanced Air Striking Force (AASF) which were returning to Britain for conversion to Blenheim IVs. The French-based Blenheim IV squadrons flew mostly reconnaissance missions during what was known as the 'phoney war', but when Germany invaded Norway and Denmark in April 1940 Nos. 107 and 110 Squadrons flew their Blenheims across the North Sea from Scotland to bomb German targets in Norway. When Germany's forces began their assault on France and the Low Countries on 10

Above: Blenheim IVF fighters of No. 235 Squadron, RAF Coastal Command, in starboard echelon. This unit received its first IVFs in the autumn of 1940. (British Aerospace, Filton)

May 1940, the French-based Blenheim IV units went into action immediately, backed up by No. 2 Group's British-based Blenheims, but suffered heavy losses owing to poor defensive armament and hazardous low-level missions. On 17 May, for example, eleven out of twelve Blenheims of No. 82 Squadron failed to return from a sortie. Three months later this squadron attacked Aalborg in Denmark and suffered similar heavy losses. At the fall of France Blenheim losses amounted to 37 (AASF), 41 (BEF Air Component) and 97 (No. 2 Group UK). A further 59 were lost during July and August.

Like their fighter counterparts, Blenheim IV bombers attacked large concentrations of invasion barges in Channel ports and enemy shipping in the North Sea. Towards the end of 1940 they raided Luftwaffe bomber airfields in an effort to reduce German night bombing over England. In the meantime, Nos. 88, 105, 218 and 226 Squadrons converted from Fairey Battles to Blenheim IVs and No. 101 Squadron (reserve) became operational, although it soon converted to Wellington ICs. At the same time Nos. 86, 500 and 608 Squadrons of Coastal Command were flying Blenheim IVs on anti-shipping strikes, while the aircraft of Nos. 13 and 614 Squadrons superseded Lysanders in Army Co-operation Command (ACC) in the ground-attack role. Some No. 2 Group units also flew anti-shipping sorties over the North Sea, but by mid-1941 this had become the forte of Coastal Command.

Blenheims began anti-shipping strikes in March 1941, approaching in formation at low level over the sea until the enemy vessels were visible. They then split up and attacked selected targets from practically zero feet, running the gauntlet of lethal flak barrages and risking collision with the masts of the target vessels. For these operations the Blenheims carried delayed-action bombs, their loads usually comprising either four 250lb (113kg) or two 500lb (226kg) weapons and four 25lb (11kg) incendiaries.

On 31 March 1941 six Blenheim IVs of No. 82 Squadron attacked two enemy tankers with escorting flak ships off Le Havre. One tanker was set ablaze by a direct hit from the squadron CO, Wing Commander S. C. Elworthy (later Air Chief Marshal Sir Charles Elworthy), and the second tanker, hit by bombs from another Blenheim, was left blazing. Despite heavy flak, all six aircraft returned safely to base with superficial damage. That same day No. 21 Squadron attacked an enemy convoy off the Frisian Islands, a

direct hit on an enemy destroyer being scored by Sergeant Pilot I. Overheu, RNZAF. Two weeks later, in an attack by the same unit on a German convoy, the New Zealander scored damaging hits on a large merchant ship. Other Blenheims claimed hits on a second merchant ship and an escort, but two of the six aircraft sent out failed to return. Sadly, in June, during yet another low-level shipping strike, Overheu's Blenheim hit a mast of the target ship, dived into the sea, and sank.

With Coastal Command now responsible for anti-shipping duties, Bomber Command's Blenheims continued raiding targets in the North Sea, the Channel ports and occupied Europe. Most attacks were made by small formations operating at high altitude, but some raids employed more aircraft or operated at low level. An outstanding low-level attack was made against the docks at Bremen on 4 July 1941, when fifteen Blenheims of Nos. 105 and 107 Squadrons made a daring approach to the target between barrage balloons, under high-tension cables and at chimney-pot height. (One aircraft returned with telephone wires hanging from its tailwheel.) Concentrated heavy flak claimed four of the Blenheims, and serious damage was inflicted on most of the others. For his gallant leadership of this raid the CO of No. 105 Squadron, Wing Commander H. I. 'Hughie' Edwards, who flew Blenheim IV V6028/'D-Dog', was awarded the Victoria Cross.

Blenheims also participated in operations codenamed Circus, in which No. 2 Group's aircraft, heavily escorted by fighters, operated over Germany during 1941 in efforts to draw Luftwaffe fighters into the air. It was hoped that a series of these raids would restrict the release of German fighters to the Eastern Front following Hitler's invasion of Russia. A notable Circus operation occurred on 12 August 1941, when 54

Below: Blenheim I L6655 of No. 8 Squadron is seen in Aden, where it arrived in July 1939. (MAP)

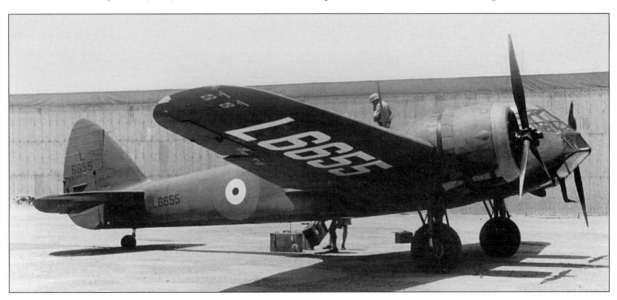

Blenheims from Nos. 18, 21, 82, 107, 114, 139 and 226 Squadrons set out to attack the two power stations at Knapsack and Quadrath, near Cologne. On their outward flight the Blenheims flew at 100ft (30m) or less, and the sky overhead was thick with escorting RAF fighters. But flak was fierce, and although opposition from enemy fighters was greatly reduced by the escort, twelve Blenheims failed to return after hitting their targets. A week later, during a similar raid on Gosnay power station, Blenheim IV R3843 of No. 18 Squadron passed over St Omer to drop a pair of artificial legs for legless fighter ace Wing Commander Douglas Bader, who had recently been shot down and

Above: Blenheim I L6670/UQ of No. 211 Squadron RAF landing in Greece after a mission in 1940. This machine was transferred the Royal Hellenic Air Force on 1 April 1941. (MAP)

captured. Just over a week later, on 28 August, eighteen Blenheims from Nos. 21, 88, 110 and 226 Squadrons, escorted by two Spitfire squadrons, attacked enemy shipping at Rotterdam. They were subjected to heavy flak and, despite the Spitfires, encountered some German fighter opposition, and only six Blenheims returned.

Lockheed Hudsons re-equipped the Blenheim IV squadrons in Coastal Command, while Douglas

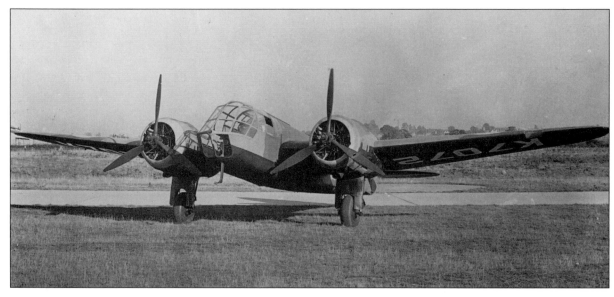

Bostons and an increasing number of de Havilland Mosquitoes began replacing Blenheims in Bomber Command's No. 2 Group. Thus by spring 1942 only four Blenheim IV units were operating from Britain; Nos. 18 and 114 Squadrons with No 2 Group and Nos. 13 and 614 Squadrons of ACC. On 19 August 1942 the two ACC squadrons were in action during the Dieppe raid, assisting Canadian troops and the Commando force by laying smoke-screens. Both Nos. 13 and 614 Squadrons then switched to updated Blenheim Vs and left to join other Blenheim units fighting in North Africa and the Middle East. As for Nos. 18 and 114 Squadrons of No. 2 Group, they too re-equipped with Blenheim Vs and moved to the Middle East.

The Blenheim V evolved from a design developed by L. G. Frise and his team at Filton early in 1940, when it had been decided that low-level ground attack and dive-bombing would be ideal for the support of ground troops. Specification B.6/40 was issued by the Air Ministry, and Bristol responded with the Type 149CS, with a 'solid' nose housing four 0.303in (7.7mm) machine-guns. Extensive armour protection was planned for the cockpit, engines and fuel tanks, and power was to be provided by uprated 950hp (708kW) Mercury XVI radials. After the fall of France B.6/40 was revised to include high-altitude bombing as an alternative role,

Opposite page, bottom: Blenheim I K7072 was converted to the original Type 149 Bolingbroke, as seen here. The longer nose section was unacceptable and was redesigned to stepped configuration, resulting in the Blenheim IV prototype. (Author's collection)

Below: Here, Type 149 K7072 is seen in its modified form with a new lowered front section. The name Bolingbroke was dropped, the aircraft being recognised as the Blenheim IV prototype. (Author's collection)

and to provide a Blenheim IV replacement. Bristol produced the Type 149HA, incorporating a new half-glazed nose section housing the navigator/bomb-aimer and a Blenheim IV-type rear-firing FN undernose gun mounting located at the end of a long fairing which served as a foot-well for the navigator.

Despite a Ministry of Aircraft Production (MAP) suggestion that Rootes should take full responsibility for the Blenheim V, Bristol insisted on undertaking the design and development work. Type No. 160 was allotted, the name Bisley adopted, and the first proto-type, AD657, with a 'solid' ground-attack nose, made its initial flight from Filton on 24 February 1941. A crew of two (pilot and gunner) was accommodated, and rear defence comprised a Bristol B.10 dorsal turret housing two 0.303in (7.7mm) Browning guns and having a full 360° traverse. The Bisley was of similar structure to the Blenheim IV, but some strengthening of the airframe was necessary owing to an increase in gross weight to 17,000lb (7,718kg). Consideration was given to making the nose sections of Types 149CS and HA interchangeable, but the idea was found impracticable as high-level bombing would need extra oxygen and radio equipment and require removal of the protective armour.

Enthusiasm for the ground-attack variant quickly waned and it was abandoned, but the second proto-type Bisley, AD661, flew later in 1941 as a day bomber with the half-glazed nose housing a third crew member. Engines were 840hp (626kW) Mercury 25s, Mercury 30s being fitted later. Two Type 160HA Blenheim Vs were built, DJ702 and '707, the latter eventually becoming instructional airframe 3289M. Rootes received an initial contract for two pre-production and 780 Bisley Is (AZ861–AZ999 and BA100–BB184). A second contract followed in August 1941 for a further 415 Bisleys (EH310–EH872) but 255 (EH518–EH872)

were cancelled from this order, leaving 160 completed. By then the name Bisley had been officially dropped, but as it had been used for some time it continued to be applied on a par with Blenheim V during the type's service. Variants included the Mks. VA (Type 160), VB (Type 160CS), VC (dual controls) and VD (Type 160D). Of these, 940 Mk. VDs were built as the tropicalised version, their operational debut being with Operation Torch in November 1942, at the time of the North African landings.

Squadrons involved in Torch, Nos. 13, 18, 114 and 614, were part of a Tactical Bomber Force based initially at Blida, near Algiers. Daylight attacks were made on enemy docks and aerodromes at Tunis and Bizerta but, like its Mk. IV predecessor, the Blenheim V was no match for German Messerschmitts. In North Africa some of the Blenheim Vs, designed to carry the same 1,000lb (454kg) bomb load plus 350lb (159kg) externally as a Blenheim IV, were loaded with up to 2,100lb (953kg) of bombs, which reduced the top speed even further to between 220 and 240mph (354 and 386km/h). In any event Blenheim V losses became unacceptable by day, and night operations began, but still with a high loss rate.

In November 1942 the Bisley units were ordered to operate from an advanced landing ground at Souk-el-Arba in support of the First Army, which was engaged in a bitter struggle with the enemy at Chouigui. RAF fighter cover was almost non-existent over the area and the Blenheim Vs were badly mauled. Indeed, on 4 December No. 18 Squadron was decimated. In the morning two attacks were made against an enemy landing ground near Chouigui, and a further raid against the same target was carried out during the afternoon. Nine Bisleys led by the squadron CO, Wing

Commander H. G. Malcolm, flew in at 1,000ft (304m) but were intercepted by a large formation of Messerschmitt Bf 109s, and all the British bombers were shot down (four crews survived). For his courage and determination in leading his squadron to their target against overwhelming odds, Malcolm was awarded a posthumous Victoria Cross. After that tragic daylight raid, Bisleys were switched to night interdiction duties to some effect, as enemy road transport heading for Sfax and Tunis was attacked by moonlight with good results. Bisley losses were comparatively low on these nocturnal forays.

Meanwhile, Blenheims had been making their mark in the Middle East from the early days of the Second World War. Number 30 Squadron had started to receive Blenheim Is in Egypt during 1938, and by June 1940, when Italy joined forces with Germany, had been joined by Nos. 45, 55 and 211 Squadrons with Blenheim Is and No. 113 flying Blenheim IVs. Number 84 Squadron was in Iraq with Blenheim Is, while No. 8 Squadron had one flight in Aden and was joined by Nos. 11 and 39 Squadrons, which transferred from Singapore and India respectively with their Blenheim Is. On 11 June a mixed force of 26 Blenheim Is and IVs from Nos. 45, 55 and 113 Squadrons carried out the first attack of the war against an Italian target when they raided El Adem airfield in Libya. The following day Nos. 8 and 39 Squadrons' Blenheims were in action over East Africa. It was a similar story throughout much of 1940, the Blenheim units operating over

Below: Canada adopted the Blenheim IV, and it was built by Fairchild under licence, the name Bolingbroke being reverted to for Canadian (RCAF) service. This was the thirteenth Bolingbroke (No. 714) built by Fairchild. (Ron Mackay)

Above: Bolingbroke 717 fitted with twin Edo floats as the proto-type of an intended Mk. III floatplane version. After one other Bolingbroke was so converted, the project was abandoned. (Ron Mackay

North and East Africa, Nos. 45 and 113 Squadrons for a period over the Sudan, and No. 14 Squadron (Port Sudan) exchanging its Wellesleys for Blenheim IVs in September 1940.

At the end of October Italy invaded Greece and Nos. 84, 211, 113 and 11 Blenheim Squadrons were sent there in that order and saw considerable action. This intensified when Germany attacked Greece and Yugoslavia in April 1941. After Greece fell, the RAF Blenheim units returned to Egypt and Palestine, most having re-equipped with Blenheim IVs, and their main operations for the rest of 1941 were in support of Allied forces in the Western Desert. However, before No. 84 Squadron returned to Egypt it took part in the Iraqi revolt, the invasion of Syria and the occupation of Iran, the last also involving Blenheims of No. 11 Squadron.

Inevitably, losses by the Blenheim units were quite heavy, but protective armour installed in a number of Blenheim IVs proved effective. For instance, despite continuous operations in the winter of 1941, No. 84 Squadron lost only one Blenheim, due to a severe sandstorm. During a two-day concentrated effort operating from Gambut, 25 missions were flown by No. 84 Squadron without loss. The Free French Lor-raine unit, Groupe Reserve de Bombardment (GRB) 1, also joined the RAF Western Desert force, flying Blenheim IVs against enemy targets. However, Blenheim operations in the Middle East became increasingly limited towards the end of 1941, and

Nos. 45, 84, 113 and 211 Squadrons were transferred to the Far East. In fact No. 211 Squadron had been absorbed into No. 72 OTU during November, but re-formed again with its Blenheim IVs a month later before moving to Java (Kalidjati), only to be disbanded in February 1942 and absorbed by No. 84 Squadron (No. 211 was to re-form with Beaufighter Xs at Phaphamau, India, in August/October 1943). Number 11 Squadron transferred to the Far East (Colombo) with its Blenheim IVs in March 1942, and No. 8 Squadron moved to Aden, exchanging its Mk. IVs for Mk. Vs in September 1942, these being retained until January 1944 and flying alongside the unit's Lockheed Hudson VIs during 1943 and the Wellington XIIIs which followed. The Blenheim IVs of No. 14 Squadron were replaced by Martin Baltimore IIs in August 1942, these giving way the same month to Martin Marauder Is. In the meantime, No. 55 Squadron carried on night bombing North African targets with its Blenheim IVs until Baltimores arrived as replacements at Luxor in May 1942.

In the Far East much of the RAF's operational capacity was made up of Blenheim Is and IVs when, on 8 December 1941, Japan attacked Malaya. The Blenheim Is of Nos. 60 and 62 Squadron were based in Burma (Mingaladon) and Malaya (Butterworth) respectively, and No. 34 Squadron at Singapore (Ten-gah) had Blenheim IVs. During the first 24 hours of the Japanese attack many Blenheims were destroyed on the ground, and any survivors managing to get air-borne made little impression on an enemy who far outnumbered them. A Blenheim pilot of No. 62 Squadron, Squadron Leader A. S. K. Scarf, won a posthumous Victoria Cross for his gallantry in attack-ing alone a Japanese air base at Singora, Thailand. All

Above: In overall yellow finish, Bolingbroke IV-T (9896) was an RCAF crew trainer, one of 50 built in 1942. (Ron Mackay)

serviceable aircraft at Butterworth were ordered to make the raid, but Scarf had just taken off when a force of enemy aircraft strafed and dive-bombed the RAF machines, destroying or damaging every one. Rather than abort the mission, Scarf decided to press on alone. Running the gauntlet of patrolling Japanese fighters en route to the target, Scarf managed to drop his bombs on the enemy airfield while his dorsal gunner, Flight Sergeant Cyril Rich, machine-gunned a number of Japanese fighters lined up on the ground. On turning for home Scarf ran into a dozen Japanese fighters and, despite evasive action, received mortal wounds. Enemy fighters continued to attack the Blenheim until it reached the Malayan border, and Scarf knew he could not reach his base. Despite a shattered arm and great loss of blood he made it to Alor Star, where he made a successful forced landing, his crew escaping unscathed. Scarf was rushed to a nearby hospital, but died from his wounds shortly afterwards. Squadron Leader Scarf's bravery did not come to light until after the war, and the Victoria Cross was received by his widow at an investiture in Buckingham Palace on 30 July 1946.

By the end of 1941 only nineteen of over sixty Blenheims originally operational in Malaya remained serviceable for regrouping at Singapore. During January 1942 Nos. 84 and 211 Squadrons arrived in Sumatra with Blenheim IVs, and fought alongside No. 34 Squadron's Blenheims until March, when Japanese forces occupied the whole area. In February 1942 No. 45 Squadron joined No. 113 Squadron at Mingaladon in Burma, where they reinforced a detachment of Blenheim Is from No. 60 Squadron, while Indian Air Force Blenheims patrolled the Bay of Bengal. By June 1942, after the Allied withdrawal from Burma to India, Nos. 34, 60 and 113 Squadrons were flying their Blenheim IVs from Indian bases against Japanese targets in the south Arakan. By the end of the year Nos. 34 and 113 Squadrons were flying Blenheim Vs, but No. 60 Squadron did not relinquish its Blenheim IVs until August 1943, when they were replaced by Hawker Hurricane IICs.

Overseas interest in the Blenheim was shown right from the start, Finland ordering eighteen Mk. Is from Filton and obtaining licences for Valtion Lentokonete-hdas to produce Blenheim Is and IVs at Tampere. The Bristol-built Mk. Is were modified to carry Swedish bombs, and deliveries to Finland started in July 1937. During the Russo-Finnish War, from November 1939 to March 1940, British-built Blenheims were in action with Lentolaivue (LeLv – Flying Squadron) 42, LeLv 44 and LeLv 46 of the Finnish Air Force. The Tampere production line had not by then delivered any Finnish-built Blenheims, so twelve Blenheim Is and twelve Mk. IVs were sent from Britain (ex-RAF stock) to reinforce Finnish Air Force units attempting to stop the advance of Russian forces. Tampere began deliver-

Above: Early production Blenheim IV L4842 was one of a batch of 84 delivered during 1939. It went to No. 53 Squadron (ACC) and to France with the AASF, but it was reported missing on 18 May 1940. (British Aerospace, Filton)

ing its Blenheims in 1941, starting with fifteen Mk. Is, another 30 following during 1943 and finally ten Mk. IVs in 1944. The Blenheims continued flying with the above three Finnish squadrons, plus LeLv 48 and training unit T-LeLv 17. In the Continuation War from 1941 until 1944 the Finnish Air Force, having this time joined the Axis powers, once again opposed Russian forces, using its Blenheims in the day-bomber, ground-attack, anti-submarine and photo-reconnaissance roles. Some Finnish Blenheims had retractable ski undercarriages.

Twelve Blenheim Is were ordered from Filton by the Turkish Government in April 1936, the first two being shipped out in October 1937 and ten flown out between March and June 1938. A second order for twelve Blenheim Is was increased to eighteen aircraft, and all had been delivered by February 1939. Another ten Blenheim Is arrived in Turkey during 1940, and in 1943 three Blenheim IVs and seventeen Mk. Vs were delivered. The Blenheims operated in Turkey with the four units of 3ncu Alay (Regiment) of the 2nci Hava Tumen (Air Division) at Gaziemir, and many remained in service until 1948.

Romania received 34 Blenheim Is during 1939 as part of a deal to persuade that country to support the

Allied cause, but it was to no avail. Romania joined the Axis powers mainly against Russia, the Blenheims serving with three bomber flotile, two being part of the Royal Air Force of Romania (FARR) which flew in support of the 3rd and 4th armies under the command of Luftflotte 4. By 1942 the Blenheims had been switched to reconnaissance duties with the 1st Air Corps (Corpul 1 Aerian).

Yugoslavia had ordered two pattern Blenheim Is in July 1936 in readiness for licensed production of 50 aircraft at the Ikarus works at Zemun. Both Filton-built machines were delivered in November 1936, and the first Zemun-built Blenheim made its initial flight in March 1939. Forty had been produced by the time Germany invaded Yugoslavia, and twenty Blenheim IVs had been diverted from RAF contracts in Britain. The Blenheims operated with the 1st and 8th Bomber Regiments and the 11th Independent Group of the Royal Yugoslav Air Force. They were used to attack German armour advancing from Bulgaria, and against targets in Hungary and Austria. A few survived to join the Croat Air Force, but any Blenheims still on the Zemun production line were destroyed to avoid them falling into enemy hands.

The Greek Government placed a contract with Filton for twelve Blenheim IVs, and these were ferried out to Greece between October 1939 and February 1940. Unarmed, these aircraft carried the British civil registrations G-AFXD to G-AFXO, and were part of an order for 232 Blenheims placed in 1938, intended

Above: Banking sharply to port here is one of the early-production Blenheim IVs delivered in the spring of 1939. (Author's collection)

Below: Blenheim IV L4842, showing clearly the scalloping effect on the port nose glazing. Flying the aircraft is Bristol test pilot A. J. (Bill) Pegg. (Author's collection)

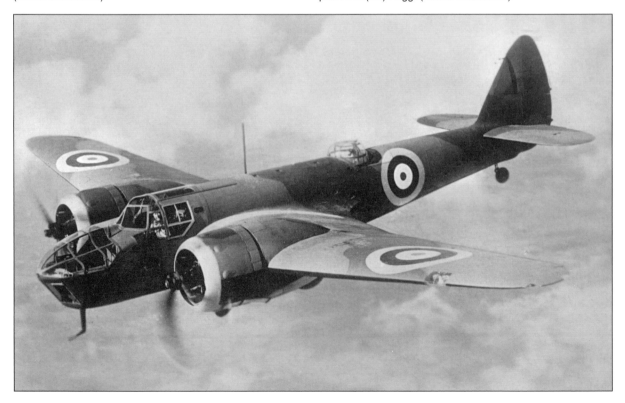

Above: Avro-built Blenheim IV Z5860, fitted with a Frazer-Nash FN54 early-type remote-control chin turret and Vokes air filters beneath the cowlings for tropical operations. (Ron Mackay)

Below: Blenheim IV A-OB of No. 45 Squadron over the Western Desert in 1941. Its bomb bay doors have been removed, the offensive load comprising 40lb (18.1kg) high-explosive and 4lb (1.8kg) incendiary bombs in small bomb containers. (Ron Mackay)

Bristol Blenheim

Above: Blenheim IV bombers of No. 14 Squadron over the Middle East in March 1942. The nearest aircraft is Avro-built Z5893/W. (Ron Mackay)

Below: Blenheim IVL V6083/FV-B, built by Rootes, is an ex-86 Squadron machine, here seen serving with No. 13 OTU. It has the Frazer-Nash NF54A chin turret with a solid metal frame. (British Aerospace, Filton)

mainly for RAF service. Italian forces invaded Greece in October 1940, and one of three Greek Air Force units equipped with these Blenheims, No. 32 Mira, was soon in action, bombing Italian targets in Albania. Early in 1941 six RAF Blenheim Is replaced Mk. IVs lost by the Greeks, by which time RAF Blenheim squadrons were operating out of Greece. After the fall of Greece No. 13 Mira (an ex-Anson unit) re-equipped with Blenheims and became No. 13 (Hellenic) Squadron within the RAF, flying anti-submarine and convoy patrol duties until late 1943. That year twelve Blenheim IVF fighters and eight Mk. IV bombers arrived in Portugal, intended for service

with the Aviacao Naval, but in the event they were transferred to BA2 Squadron of the Aeronautica Militar, based at Ota, where they were later joined by three Blenheim Vs.

The Blenheim can justifiably take its place among the great workhorses of the early Second World War period. It is significant that, during the first 34 months of that conflict, Blenheims of RAF Bomber Command alone flew 11,332 missions and dropped 3,028 tons (3,076 tonnes) of bombs. These totals would be greatly surpassed later in the war, when 5,000 tons (5,080 tonnes) of bombs would be dropped on a selected target in one raid by heavy bombers. Taking production figures into account, if the Type 142 and Type 143 prototypes are excluded, total Blenheim production was 6,185 machines of all marks, including 24 Mk. Is destroyed before final completion in Yugoslavia and five Mk. IVs which remained uncompleted in Finland during 1944. All in all, this is not a bad record for an aeroplane that began life as a small executive transport in 1935.

Below: Bristol Type 149CS (later Type 160) Bisley AD657, with four machine-guns mounted in a 'solid' nose, a Bristol BX dorsal turret and Mercury XVI engines. (Author's collection)

Bottom: A head-on view of Bristol Bisley AD657 with provision for a battery of four machine-guns in its 'solid' nose. (Ron Mackay)

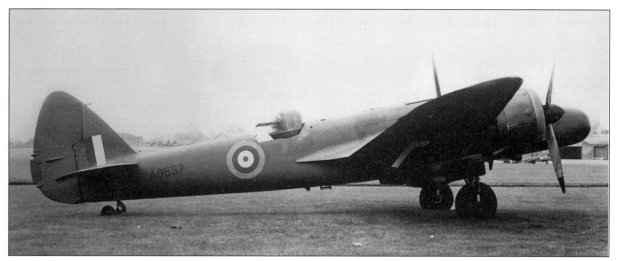

Bristol Blenheim

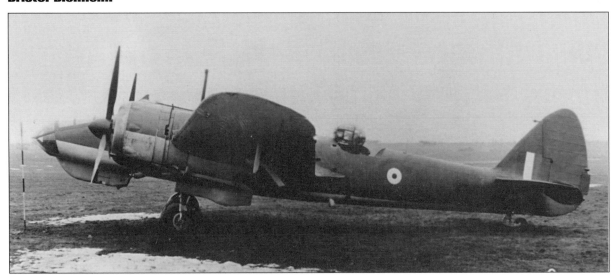

Top left: Early-production Type 160 Blenheim V AZ930 undergoes static tests at the end of 1941. Note the modified nose section with a foot well for the navigator ahead of the chin turret, the cut-away fuselage for the installation of a Bristol BX dorsal turret the and underwing fuel ejection pipes. (MAP)

Centre left: Rootes-built Blenheim V BA614 in the Middle East during 1942.

Its dorsal turret and tyres are covered to protect them from the tropical elements. (MAP)

Bottom left: Among Blenheim exports was this Mk. I, BL-104, of the Finnish Air Force. Note the ski landing gear. (Author's collection)

Above: A Blenheim I of the Turkish Air Force in 1938. The white crescent and

star are on a red rudder, and the wing markings comprise a red square with a white surround. The upper surfaces were overall dark green, and the undersurfaces sky blue. (Author's collection)

Below: Blenheim I BL-183 of the Finnish Air Force in October 1944, showing the revised blue and white roundel which replaced the blue swastika the previous month. (Ron Mackay)

Above: In contemporary camouflage finish, this Blenheim IV carries its ferry flight registration G-AFXG for delivery to Greece. Twelve Blenheim IVs were delivered to the Greek Air Force before Greece surrendered to the Axis powers. (Aviation Photo News)

Below: A preserved Finnish Blenheim on permanent display at Luonetjaervi military base in Finland. Note the propeller spinners to help prevent ice forming in the engines during Finland's severe winters. (Ron Mackay)

Bristol Type 130
Bombay

During the early 1930s the RAF bomber-transport fleet in India and the Middle East consisted mainly of ageing Vickers Valentia biplanes. To provide a more modern replacement, Britain's Air Ministry issued Specification C.26/31, calling for an aeroplane able to function as a troop-carrier with accommodation for up to 24 fully equipped soldiers, an air ambulance carrying ten stretcher cases, a freighter with the capacity to convey heavy spares and components, or a heavy bomber with a crew of four and capable of defending itself against aerial attack.

In response, three prototypes competed in the Air Ministry trials: Armstrong Whitworth AW.23 K3585, from which would evolve the Whitley bomber; Handley Page H.P.51 J9833, progenitor of the Harrow bomber; and Bristol Type 130 K3583, which was the successful contender.

An Air Ministry contract for one prototype had been awarded to Bristol at Filton in March 1933, and chief designer Frank Barnwell decided to employ a multi-spar cantilever wing structure. This method of construction had been developed at Filton after wing twisting caused aileron reversal on the Bristol Type 95 Bagshot. This twin-engine monoplane fighter, J7767, was abandoned following only a few test flights, but its failings were directly responsible for the company's intensive research programme into cantilever wings

which led to the structure used in the successful Type 130.

Frank Barnwell's all-metal wing design for the Type 130 incorporated a large box spar and seven I-section auxiliary spars joined by open and solid (plate) ribs running the whole length of the stressed-skin-covered wing. The wing was fitted with hydraulically-operated, split trailing-edge flaps and Frise statically-balanced ailerons. Built in three units, a centre-section and two outer panels, the wing was located in the top of the fuselage, giving a high-wing configuration, the engine mountings being positioned at the outer extremities of the centre section. To each of these mountings was fixed the upper end of a long-stroke oleo leg for the divided-type landing gear, the main wheels of which were encased in streamline spats with supporting stays extending to the fuselage bottom.

The fuselage was an oval-section, stressed-skin monocoque structure built in five sections consisting of the nose portion, housing a manually-operated Bristol-type gun turret, the flight deck, the centre sec-

Below: The Bristol Type 95 Bagshot experimental three-seat fighter (J7767) which, owing to wing torsion problems, was directly responsible for Bristol's development of the cantilever wing used successfully on the Bombay. (MAP)

tion, the aft section, and the extreme rear section incorporating a tail-gunner's position.

The externally-braced monoplane tail unit carried twin fins and rudders formed from metal frames, with Alclad-covered fixed surfaces and fabric-covered rudders. The tailplane was based on the box-spar principle and had three spars with alloy ribs, the whole being Alclad covered. The elevators were fabric covered.

Power for K3583 was initially provided by two 750hp (559kW) Bristol Pegasus IIM.3 air-cooled radial engines driving two-bladed fixed-pitch metal propellers, but in due course these were replaced by uprated Pegasus XXIIs rated at 1,010hp (753kW), fitted initially with three-bladed Fairey-Reed (later Rotol) metal propellers. The top speed was 192mph (309km/h) at 6,500ft (1,981m); the climb rate was 750ft (219m)/min; the Service ceiling 25,000ft (7,620m) and the normal operating range 880 miles (1,416km). The Type 130 made its maiden flight from Filton on 23 June 1935, with the company's chief test pilot, Cyril F. Uwins, at the controls. It was the largest aeroplane to have been produced at Filton up to that time, and it appeared in the New Types Park at the annual RAF Display at Hendon the same year. Manufacturer's tests were satisfactory, and K3583 was sent to the A&AEE at Martlesham Heath for its official trials, where much of the type's military testing was undertaken by Flight Lieutenant A. J. 'Bill' Pegg, who would later become well known as Bristol's chief test pilot on the Brabazon and Britannia airliners.

Trials with the prototype continued at the A&AEE for some considerable time, during which several improvements were incorporated into the machine. These included the previously mentioned Pegasus XXII engines, a Scarff gun-ring in the tail-gunner's position housed in a glazed cupola, and modifications to the area around the freight loading door in the port side to facilitate the loading of bulky or heavy cargo. This enlarged doorway was complemented by the provision of a built-in gantry to assist with the handling of weighty items such as engines and machinery.

In April 1937 the name Bombay was bestowed upon the Type 130 and the Air Ministry signed a contract with Bristol for 80 production aircraft (later reduced to 50) to revised Specification 47/36. To comply, Bombay Is would have new Bristol-type hydraulically-operated gun turrets installed in nose and tail locations, the front turret containing the bomb sight and being located immediately above a protruding bomb-aimer's panel. To complement the original internal bomb load, racks were fitted beneath the fuselage, bringing the maximum bomb load to 2,000lb (907kg). Defensive armament comprised a Vickers 'K' gun in both nose and tail turrets. On all production Bombays the streamline wheel spats were deleted, the fully castoring tailwheel was retained, slight alterations were made to the rudder profile, a D/F loop and radio masts were located above the fuselage, and three-blade Rotol propellers were fitted.

For bombing operations the Bombay carried a crew of four consisting of the pilot, a navigator/bomb-

Right: Bombay prototype K3583 up from Filton in 1935. Its initial flight was made on 23 June by chief test pilot C. F. Uwins. (British Aerospace, Filton)

BRISTOL TYPE 130 BOMBAY (PRODUCTION) DATA

Manufacturer
Short & Harland Ltd, Belfast

Type
Bomber-transport with four-man crew (bomber). Three-man crew (transport) plus up to 24 fully equipped troops

Powerplant
Two 1,010hp (753kW) Bristol Pegasus XXII nine-cylinder, air-cooled, radial engines

Performance
Maximum speed, 192mph (309km/h) at 6,500ft (1,980m). Cruising speed, 160mph (257km/h) at 10,000ft (3,050m). Service ceiling, 25,000ft (7,620m). Range, 880 miles (1,416km); 2,230 miles (589km) with full fuselage tanks.

Weights
Empty, 13,800lb (6,260kg). Loaded (maximum take-off), 20,000lb (9,072kg)

Dimensions
Span, 95ft 9in (29.18m). Length, 69ft 3in (21.11m). Height, l9ft 6in (5.94m). Wing area, 1,340sq ft (124.49sq m)

Armament
Two 0.303in (7.7mm) Vickers 'K' guns mounted one each in nose and tail turrets. Maximum bomb load 2,000lb (907kg) carried internally and on external racks

BRISTOL BOMBAY PRODUCTION

One prototype, K3583, to Specification C.26/31. Fifty production Bombay Is (L5808 to L5857) built by Short & Harland Ltd, Belfast, to Specification 47/36. Delivered between April 1939 and June 1940. Original order was for 80 aircraft, the 30 cancelled machines having been allotted serials L5858 to L5887

RAF Bombay units

No. 117 Squadron (re-formed from 'C' Flight of No. 216 Squadron), based at Khartoum

No. 216 Squadron, coded SH, based at Heliopolis, El Khanka and Cairo West

No. 267 Squadron, coded KW (1940 to 1942), was the Heliopolis Communication Flight redesignated. It was reported to have numbered a few Bombays among its large assortment of various aircraft types based at Heliopolis

No. 271 Squadron, coded BJ, re-formed at Doncaster on 1 May 1940 from No. 1680 Flight. Flew Bombays until February 1941

aimer, a wireless operator/gunner and a tail gunner. A second pilot was carried if required, but in troop-carrying mode the Bombay needed only three crew members.

When the aircraft was originally ordered into production the parent company was heavily preoccupied with the development and construction of its new Blenheim bomber. There was no apparent urgency for the Bombay, but when it was realised that Great Britain possessed no comparable aircraft to the German Junkers Ju 52/3M bomber-transport, the Bombay suddenly became a part of the RAF expansion programme. However, with Blenheim work absorbing most of the Filton facilities, Bristol entrusted the building of the 50 Bombays ordered (L5808 to L5857) to Short Brothers and Harland of Belfast, Northern Ireland.

BOMBAY

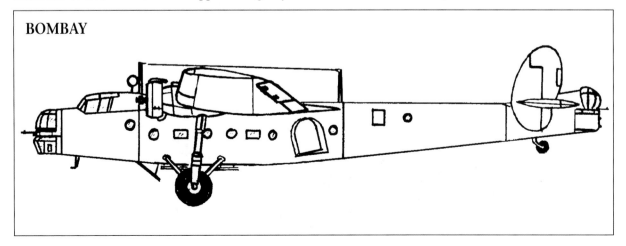

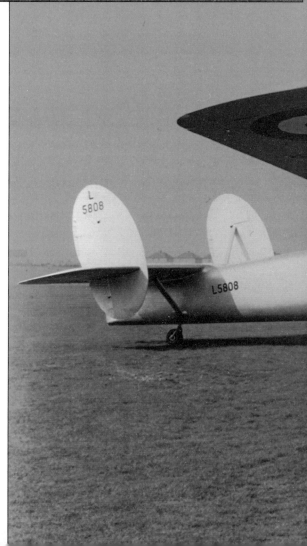

The first production Bombay, L5808, made its initial flight during March 1939 in an all-silver finish with standard RAF markings. A further ten machines followed, painted in a similar scheme, but from L5819 all remaining Bombays were finished in the contemporary RAF camouflage pattern of dark earth and green upper surfaces and sky undersurfaces. Fuselage roundels were of the A1 type (red, white, blue and outer yellow), the wing upper surface roundels were B type (red and blue), the standard red, white and blue vertical fin flashes were applied, and the underwing markings were A-type red, white and blue roundels.

The first production Bombay crashed during flight trials on 23 August 1939 and was written off, but two months later No. 216 Squadron at Heliopolis (El Khanka), Egypt, began to receive their first Bombays. They served alongside the Vickers Valentia biplanes they were intended to replace until September 1941, when the squadron finally became an all-Bombay unit. Before the arrival of replacement Dakotas in May 1943, the squadron had received 37 Bombays, and before using the type on mostly transport duties, operated it as a night bomber along the North African coast. One Bombay carried out an attack against Tobruk on the night of 14/15 June 1940, and further raids were made, including effective night attacks on Benghazi and a sortie by two Bombays against Bardia in January 1941. The price paid for this six-month period of bombing missions by RAF Bombays was four

Right: The first production Bombay, L5808, at Short Bros., Belfast, in March 1939. Note the revised nose turret, the extended bomb-aiming panel, the three-bladed propellers and removal of the wheel spats. (British Aerospace, Filton)

Left: Bombay prototype K3583 at Filton in 1935, No. 9 being its New Type number for that year's RAF Display at Hendon. (MAP)

aircraft lost. During the fighting against Iraq in 1941, No. 216 Squadron transported troops of the Arab Legion and a company of the Essex Regiment from Egypt to Lydda, and for most of May that year a detachment from the squadron remained at Lydda, its Bombays (plus two Valentias still on strength) carrying troops and supplies to British positions.

To allow for the greater distances covered on special missions by Bombays, maximum fuel was carried, with wing tanks and internal centre-section tanks full. Additional fuel was conveyed in standard 4 Imp gal (18lit) petrol cans, a crew member topping up the internal tanks from these. Fuel was transferred from internal to wing tanks by means of a hand pump.

On 30 April 1941 No. 117 Squadron was re-formed from 'C' Flight of No. 216 Squadron at Khartoum. They received Bombays, a collection of other Allied types and a few captured Italian transport aircraft. The Bombays, which included L5811, L5828, L5840 and L5856, flew regular supply missions between Takoradi (Gold Coast) West Africa and Egypt until November, when No. 117 Squadron transferred to Egypt as a support unit for Allied forces fighting Rommel in the Western Desert.

Bombays were among a collection of Allied transport and communications aircraft which flew a West-

Bristol Bombay

Above: In this view of L5808 at Belfast, the Bristol-type rear gun turret can be seen at the extreme tail. (MAP)

Below: The second production Bombay, L5809, takes off from Belfast. It later served with Nos. 271 and 216 Squadrons and was struck off charge in July 1944. (MAP)

Above: Attracting considerable attention here is L5812, the fifth production Bombay. Note the open entrance door and ladder. (MAP)

Below: The ninth production Bombay, L5816, still in an all-silver finish. The RAF type B roundel (red/blue) was introduced on fuselage sides when war was declared in 1939, and the type A/A1 (the latter with an outer yellow ring) was reverted to during and after December 1939. (Author's collection)

Above: Bombay L5827/A of No. 216 Squadron, North Africa (probably at El Khanka), circa 1941–42. Note the external bomb racks and wheel covers. (MAP)

ern Desert mail service, carried VIPs, made regular flights to Malta and supplied specialised Allied ground forces such as the Long Range Desert Group far out in the desert. They were active during the Greek campaign and participated in the evacuation from Crete. Bombays flew out troops and equipment, often operating at an overload weight of some 5,000lb (2,268kg). Thousands of Allied casualties were also evacuated by Bombays, one specialised unit in this field being No. 1 Air Ambulance Unit (AAU) of the RAAF. They airlifted some two thousand casualties from Sicily to North Africa and, following the Allied landings at Anzio, flew in nursing sisters to attend the wounded. Casualties from the Italian campaign were also evacuated by AAU Bombays. During July 1943 two of the Bombays were lost in take-off and landing accidents in Sicily and Tunisia respectively. This Australian unit's Bombays wore desert camouflage on the upper surfaces, had white undersurfaces and carried a large red cross on top of the centre section and red crosses on a white circle aft of the fuselage roundel.

Although the Bombay was flown primarily in the Middle East war zone, one unit flew the type in the UK. This was No. 271 Squadron, which operated eleven Bombays; L5813, L5814, L5817, L5832, L5833, L5840 and L5851 to L5855. Formed on 1 May 1940 at Doncaster, No. 271 Squadron was responsible for the transportation of RAF equipment and personnel as units moved around the UK. Before the French collapse in 1940, the squadron's Bombays carried out a number of sorties flying supplies across the English Channel to Allied forces facing the German onslaught. Soon afterwards, however, most Bombays had departed from the UK, two exceptions being the prototype, K3583, and production machine L5836. For some reason the name *Josephine* was bestowed upon the prototype, which continued as a development aircraft until 1941. As for L5836, it first went to No. 24 Squadron, passed to the FTU, and later transferred to the Airborne Forces Experimental Establishment. This machine was recorded as going to BOAC before withdrawal in September 1943. Earlier, the intention had been to convert three Bombays into civil transports for wartime use by BOAC. The registrations G-AFYM, 'YN and 'YO were reserved for the trio but not taken up, as the plan was apparently abandoned.

By August 1944 the Bombay had been phased out, although it had performed well in its dual role. The type received little recognition for its wartime exploits, which were carried out reliably and without fuss; reason enough for the Bombay to secure a place in RAF history.

Fairey

Battle

Obsolete when the Second World War started, the Fairey Battle was thrown in at the deep end with the AASF in France during the early months of the conflict. Losses among Battle crews, valiantly attempting to stem the German advance on the Low Countries in May 1940, were catastrophic. Hopelessly slow, underarmed and outnumbered, many Battles fell to the guns of marauding Luftwaffe fighters, or to the withering groundfire they faced when attacking their targets at low level. What had promised to be a high-performance light bomber in 1936 was, by the outbreak of war in September 1939, an anachronism.

Not that there was anything fundamentally wrong with the Fairey Battle's design. Indeed, its elegant lines were a great advance over the biplane it was scheduled to replace, the two-seat Hawker Hart day bomber. This biplane had continued a long tradition of RAF single-engine, two-seat, open-cockpit light bombers – the de Havilland D.H.4, D.H.9 and D.H.9A, the Fairey Fawn and Fox, and the Hawker Horsley (day bomber and torpedo bomber) and Hind. In 1932, after the Hart had been in service for two years, the Air Ministry began to consider its replacement, and in April 1933 Specification P.27/32 was issued. This called for a single-engine, two-seat, monoplane day bomber with front and rear armament, capable of carrying a 1,000lb (454kg) bomb load over a distance of 1,000

miles (1,609km) at 200mph (322km/h), and this was exactly what Marcel Lobelle, Fairey Aviation's chief designer, produced.

In the light of subsequent events it is as well, perhaps, to digress and look at the political background that was largely responsible for the vulnerability in 1939 of an aircraft which, at the time of its conception in the mid-1930s, was well in advance of contemporary day bombers. Specification P.27/32 was issued while B.9/32 was calling for a twin-engine monoplane medium bomber to replace the RAF's ageing biplanes. However, at the 1932 Geneva Disarmament Conference Britain had been willing to endorse a proposal restricting the empty weight of bombers to 6,600lb (2,994kg), a decision that could possibly determine whether or not Specification B.9/32 would be acceptable under such an international agreement. (In the event no agreement was reached, and the Handley Page Hampden and Vickers Wellington resulted from B.9/32.) It was decided that the P.27/32 light bomber design would therefore provide insurance should the medium-bomber layout be untenable, while at the same time the Air

Below: Fairey Battle prototype K4303 in its original configuration, flying over Fairey Aviation's Hayes works in 1936. (Author's collection)

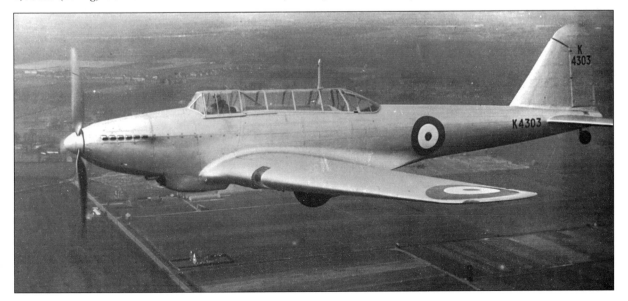

Ministry could compare contemporary single- and twin-engine bomber designs.

Doubt about the feasibility of a suitable high-performance light bomber emerging from P.27/32 was rife among some members of the Air Staff. They knew that no engine available at that time was powerful enough to fulfil all the requirements of the specification. Fairey Aviation realised that the demands of P.27/32 were inadequate for the type's intended purpose, and tried in vain to persuade the Air Ministry that an alternative twin-engine type, or a smaller single-engine design with superior performance but reduced ordnance, would be more suitable. At the time the company was developing its own Prince aero engine which, in twelve-cylinder P.12 form, was expected to produce 850hp (634kW) by 1934. Uprated P.16 and P.24 versions with sixteen and twenty-four cylinders respectively had estimated ratings of up to 2,000hp (1,492kW). Aware that

the Ministry were sticking rigidly to Specification P.27/32, Marcel Lobelle suggested that Fairey's design should be powered by an uprated Prince, and even the original mock-up constructed at Hayes in 1934 portrayed cowling outlines for a Prince engine. It also featured proposed accommodation for the two-man crew in the form of separate enclosed cockpits in tandem. The armament was shown as a 0.303in (7.7mm) Vickers 'K' gun on a swivel in the rear cockpit, and a fixed forward-firing Browning machine-gun of the same calibre in the starboard wing root. As no official backing was forthcoming for Fairey's projected engines, its new light bomber had to comply strictly with the Air Ministry's demands. It was decided that the new Rolls-Royce PV-12 (later named Merlin) would be the most suitable powerplant.

Four manufacturers submitted designs to P.27/32; Armstrong Whitworth Aircraft, the Bristol Aeroplane

---

FAIREY BATTLE MK. I DATA

Manufacturers

Fairey Aviation Co Ltd, Heaton Chapel, Stockport. Subcontracted to Austin Motor Co Ltd, Longbridge, Birmingham

Type

Three-seat light bomber

Powerplant

One 1,030hp (768kW) Rolls-Royce Merlin II twelve-cylinder vee liquid-cooled engine

Performance

Maximum speed, 252mph (406km/h) at 15,000ft (4,575m). Cruising speed, 147mph (237km/h) at 15,000ft (4,575m). Climb to 15,000ft (4,575m), 16.2min. Service ceiling, 26,000ft (7,925m). Range (with 1,420lb (644kg) bomb load), 1,065 miles (1,714km) at 200mph (322km/h) and 1,200 miles (1,931km) at 147mph (237km/h)

Weights

Empty, 7,410lb (3,361kg). Loaded (normal), 10,900lb (4,944kg); maximum take-off, 11,700lb (5,307kg)

Dimensions

Span, 54ft (16.45m). Length, 42ft 5in (12.93m). Height, 15ft 6in (4.72m). Wing area, 422sq ft (39.2sq m). Landing gear track, 9ft 9in (2.97m)

Armament

One fixed forward-firing 0.303in (7.7mm) Browning machine-gun in starboard wing. One pillar-mounted 0.303in (7.7mm) Vickers GO machine-gun in rear cockpit. Bomb load, 1,000lb

(454kg) internally in wings and optional 500lb (227kg) on external racks

FAIREY BATTLE PRODUCTION

Prototype K4304 to Specification P.27/32

Initial production batch at Stockport of 155 Battle Is (K7558–K7712), of which 136 had Merlin I engines and nineteen Merlin IIs. Some later to RCAF, SAAF and RAAF

Second production batch of 500 Battle Is ordered from Stockport (K9176–K9675), of which K9487–K9675 were cancelled, leaving 311 (K9176–K9486) built, all with Merlin II engines except engine test-beds K9222 (Exe), K9240 (Dagger VIII), K9257 (Merlin X), K9331 (Taurus II), K9370 (P.24 Prince) and K9477 (Peregrine). A number transferred to RAAF and SAAF

First production batch of 863 Battles from Austin Motor Co of Longbridge (L4935–L5797), of which L4935–L4937 were non-standard; up to L4993 had Merlin IIs, the rest Merlin IIIs except L5286 (Napier Sabre test-bed). The last 200 from this batch (L5598–L5797) were produced as TT.1 target tugs. From this batch 567 were sent under CATP mainly to the RAAF, RCAF and SAAF, but some went to India, two to SRAF and one to RNZAF

Third production batch of 189 Battle Is

by Fairey at Stockport (N2020–N2258), of which N2042 and N2184 were fitted with fixed landing gear and used as Bristol Hercules test-beds. Sold to Turkey: N2111–N2117, N2120–N2123, N2130–N2131, N2149, N2153–N2155, N2211–N2218, N2220–N2222 and N2224. To Poland: N2219. A further 99 from this batch despatched to RCAF, RAAF and SAAF under CATP. A number became instructional airframes

Fourth production batch of 150 Battles from Fairey at Stockport, (P2155–P2369). Some to RCAF, RAAF and SAAF under CATP. P2353 transferred to Belgian Air Force after a forced landing. Four (P2159, P2243, P2270 and P2272) became instructional airframes 2556M, 2483M, 2143M and 2159M respectively

Fifth production batch of 50 Battle Is from Fairey at Stockport (P5228–P5294), of which 40 went directly to RAAF, RCAF and SAAF under CATP

Sixth production batch of 200 Battle Is from Fairey at Stockport (P6480–P6769), of which the last 100 were built as trainers and sent to CATP units. Two (P6613 and P6615) direct to RHAF; eleven later became instructional airframes

Second production batch of 100 Battle Is by Austin Motor Co of Longbridge (R3922–R4054), all of which were

---

BATTLE

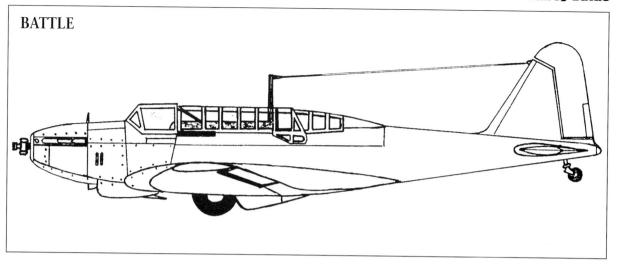

sent direct to RAAF, RCAF and SAAF under CATP

Seventh production batch of 100 Battle (T) trainers from Fairey at Stockport (R7356–R7480), of which 62 went to RCAF, four to SAAF and three to RAAF. R7375 and R7378 became instructional airframes 2485M and 3909M respectively

Third and final production batch of 300 Battle TT.1 target tugs ordered from Austin Motor Co of Longbridge (V1201–V1594), of which only 66 built (V1201–V1280) the rest being cancelled. Under CATP RAAF received 23, SAAF 22 (minus one sunk en route) and SRAF four. V1222 to Eire (IAAC) after landing in error on Irish territory. V1204 became instructional airframe 3908M.

Excluding the prototype, 2,184 production Fairey Battles were built in Britain by Fairey Aviation (1,155) and the Austin Motor Co (1,029)

NB. The above serials include 'blackout' blocks from Battle N2020 onwards. This system, introduced for security reasons, prevented serials on RAF aircraft running in direct sequence. After L7272, a Percival Vega Gull III, and starting with L7276, an Avro Manchester, serial number allocations for production aircraft were divided into blocks ranging from ten to fifty numbers, the unused serials in between being referred to as 'blackout blocks'. This system is retained to this day for RAF aircraft

RAF BATTLE UNITS

Bomber Command (1937-1939)

No. 12 Squadron (Andover)
No. 15 Squadron (Abingdon)
No. 35 Squadron (Cottesmore)
No. 40 Squadron (Abingdon)
No. 52 Squadron (Upwood)
No. 63 Squadron (Upwood)
No. 88 Squadron (Boscombe Down)
No. 98 Squadron (Hucknall)
No. 103 Squadron (Usworth)
No. 105 Squadron (Harwell)
No. 106 Squadron (Thornaby)
No. 142 Squadron (Andover)
No. 150 Squadron (Benson)
No. 185 Squadron (Thornaby)
No. 207 Squadron (Cottesmore)
No. 218 Squadron (Boscombe Down)
No. 226 Squadron (Usworth)

Advanced Air Striking Force, Bomber Command No. 1 Group in France, September 1939

No. 12 Squadron (Berry-au-Bac/Amifontaine/Echemines/Souge)
No. 15 Squadron (Betheniville and Conde/Vraux)
No. 40 Squadron (Betheniville)
No. 88 Squadron (Auberives-sur-Suippes/Mourmelon-le-Grande/Les Grandes-Chappelles/Moisy)
No. 103 Squadron (Challerange/Plivot/Betheniville/St Lucien Ferme/Ozouer-le-Doyen/Souge)
No. 105 Squadron (Reims/Villeneuve/Echemines/Nantes-Chateau Bougon)
No. 142 Squadron (Berry-au-Bac/Plivot/Faux-Villecerf)
No. 150 Squadron (Challerange/Ecury-sur-coole/Pouan/Houssay)
No. 218 Squadron (Auberives-sur-Suippes/St Lucien Ferme/Nantes)
No. 226 Squadron (Reims/Faux-Ville-cerf/Artins)

Other Bomber Command Battle Units, 1940

No. 300 Polish Squadron (Swinderby)
No. 301 Polish Squadron (Swinderby)
No. 304 Polish Squadron (Bramcote)
No. 305 Polish Squadron (Bramcote)
No. 98 Squadron to Coastal Command, Iceland
No. 88 Squadron to Belfast (Sydenham)
No. 226 Squadron to Belfast (Sydenham)

Main RAF Training Units which Flew Battles

Nos. 1, 7, 11, 12 and 16 FTS
Nos. 4, 7, 8 and 10 BGS
Nos. 4, 5 and 10 AOS
No. 3 AGS

Hundreds of Battles flew overseas with many training units of the RCAF, RAAF and SAAF under the CATP

Co, Fairey Aviation and Hawker Aircraft. Two designs were accepted and built in prototype form, Armstrong Whitworth's AW.29 and Fairey Aviation's machine. The AW.29, K4299, powered by a 920hp (686kW) Armstrong Siddeley Tiger VIII radial, was a mid-wing cantilever monoplane. Its two-man crew sat 12ft apart, the pilot in a glazed canopy and the gunner/radio operator/observer/bomb aimer behind him in an AWA manually-operated cupola housing a 0.303in (7.7mm) Lewis machine-gun.

The Fairey prototype, K4303, emerged as an aesthetically pleasing low-wing cantilever monoplane with retractable landing gear, its crew of two accommodated under a lengthy glazed canopy and a Rolls-Royce Merlin 'F' engine (No. 25) driving a Fairey-Reed three-blade, fixed-pitch metal propeller fitted with a streamlined spinner. The original separate cockpits had been replaced by the long 'greenhouse'-type canopy to reduce drag and noise effects, and Lobelle's choice of a Merlin engine appeared to provide sufficient power while its compact frontal area resulted in a clean, streamlined profile and good performance by 1936 standards.

Prototype flight testing was delayed owing to early problems with Merlin development, but eventually Fairey test pilot Chris Staniland took K4303 up for the first time on 10 March 1936 from the Great West Aerodrome near Hayes in Middlesex (now swallowed by London (Heathrow) Airport). The streamlined spinner merged beautifully into the contours of the cowling with its flush exhaust ports, and initial flight tests presented no problems. By July K4043 was at the A&AEE at Martlesham Heath for handling and performance trials which proved that Fairey's new bomber, which had been named Battle on 2 April, outclassed any contemporary day bomber, with a maximum speed of 257mph (414km/h) at 15,000ft (4,575m). Its cruising speed was

Above: A rival to Fairey's Battle in the P.27/32 competition was Armstrong Whitworth A.W.29 K4299, a far less aesthetically pleasing design. (MAP)

200mph (322km/h) carrying a 1,000lb (454kg) bomb load at 14,000ft (4,267m) over a range of 980 miles (1,577km). Even so, although the requirements had been met and no serious criticism was aimed at it during trials, the Battle's performance was considered disappointing for a potential front-line aircraft.

Then, to make matters worse, the Air Ministry decided that a third crew member should be allowed for, as it had been decided that a separate bomb-aimer would be needed to enable the rear gunner to concentrate fully on defence during combat. The bomb-aimer was to sit between the pilot and rear gunner, carrying out his duty from a prone position on the fuselage floor. This extra weight adversely affected the aircraft's performance. The first production Battle, K7558, flew in April 1937 and, when tested in June with a full load including a third crew member, could manage only 241mph (388km/h) at 13,000ft (3,962m).

Structurally, the Fairey Battle comprised a monocoque rear fuselage of light alloy, oval in section and formed from hooped frames, Z-section stringers and a covering of riveted metal panels. The front portion of the fuselage ahead of the cockpit was a tubular construction riveted and bolted together, with a skin of detachable metal panels. The rear of the long glazed canopy had been raised on the prototype, but was contoured more smoothly into the rear fuselage decking on production aircraft and was hinged to allow the gunner maximum movement when operating his Vickers 'K' gun. A sliding section was provided forward for the pilot.

The all-metal wings, tapered in chord and thickness, were built up from a light alloy two-spar struc-

Above: Seen here in its final form, Fairey Battle prototype K4303 has a revised rear canopy, no propeller spinner and a new de Havilland variable-pitch propeller. (MAP)

ture, with alloy ribs and a metal stressed-skin covering. They comprised two outer panels with detachable wingtips, joined to a centre section integral with the fuselage. The skinning was riveted to spanwise Z-section stiffeners, while the light alloy aileron frames were fabric covered. Metal skinned trailing-edge flaps extended from the ailerons to the fuselage sides. The tail unit was a light alloy structure with stressed-skin fixed surfaces and fabric-covered moveable surfaces.

The undercarriage was retractable, each main unit folding rearwards into wing positions which left part of the wheel exposed, supposedly handy in the event of a wheels-up landing! A fixed, castoring tailwheel was fitted beneath the rear fuselage.

Fuel was contained in a 45 Imp gal (205lit) fuselage tank and two 106 Imp gal (482lit) wing tanks. Bombs were housed in four cells incorporated in the wing roots, a normal load consisting of four 250lb (113.5kg) bombs carried on hydraulic crutches which, in a dive-bombing attack, swung the bombs clear of the Battle's fuselage and propeller arc. External underwing racks could carry an additional 500lb (227kg) bomb load. Defensive armament comprised a single fixed 0.303in (7.7mm) Browning machine-gun in the starboard wing root and an 0.303in (7.7mm) Vickers 'K' gun in the rear cockpit.

By 1935 the RAF expansion programme was getting under way, and a growing number of new squadrons needed to be equipped with the latest types of aircraft available. Among these was the Fairey Battle, and, despite an obvious lack of official enthusiasm for the P.27/32 design, it was included in the Air Ministry's 'straight off the drawing board' policy of the time,

under Scheme C of the expansion programme. Thus almost a year before the Battle prototype made its first flight a production order was placed with Fairey Aviation for 155 aircraft (K7558–K7712), production being established at the company's Heaton Chapel, Stockport, factory and flight tests being made at Ringway Airport, Manchester.

The first production Fairey Battles were built to Specification 23/25, which covered a third crew member, a modified cockpit canopy, improved internal equipment, external 'kidney'-type exhaust manifolds on the cowlings and a de Havilland variable-pitch propeller instead of the original Fairey-Reed fixed-pitch type. This last change necessitated removing the streamlined spinner, as the larger spinner necessary to cover the pitch-changing device would have entailed alterations to the engine cowling profile. In the first 136 production Battles power was provided by a 1,030hp (768kW) Rolls-Royce Merlin I twelve-cylinder vee, liquid-cooled engine (a Merlin F with minor changes). The last nineteen aircraft from this first contract had the Merlin II (Merlin G type-tested at 1,030hp (768kW) at 3,000 rpm).

With the introduction of Scheme F during 1936, allowing a substantial increase in the number of military aircraft to be built for RAF service, a large quantity of Fairey Battles was included. A further 500 were ordered from Fairey under Specification 14/36 in the serial range K9176–K9675, but when a progress report of 1937 showed that Fairey would be 189 machines short by the delivery date of 31 March 1939, the last 189 from this contract (K9487–K9675) were cancelled. However, Scheme F also introduced the Shadow Factory programme, and Austin Motors established aircraft production lines at its Longbridge site in Birmingham. It received contracts to produce 863 Fairey Battles to Specification 32/36 in the serial range

Fairey Battle

L4935–L5797, the initial order for 400 machines being received on 17 August 1936 and materials being supplied for constructing another 100. In 1938, when expansion Scheme L was introduced, requiring 12,000 aircraft of all types to be built for the RAF by the end of March 1940, it was decided to reinstate the cancelled order for 189 Battles with Fairey at Stockport (new serials N2020–N2258 were allocated). This resulted in Austin's second contract for 363 Battles, but the Longbridge production schedules began dragging behind and, on 1 November and 15 December 1938, Fairey at Stockport received contracts for a further 150 and 50 Battle bombers respectively (P2155–P2369 and P5228–P5294). On 11 February

Left: The first production Battle, K7558, with camouflaged upper and black lower surfaces and black and white serials respectively.(Author's collection)

Below: The first production Fairey Battle shows off its elegant lines over the English countryside in the spring of 1937, wearing contemporary 'sand and spinach' camouflage. (Fairey Holdings Ltd)

1939 another 200 Battles were ordered (P6480–P6769), albeit to ensure that the Stockport factory workforce remained intact until such time as production hopefully transferred to Avro Manchesters, though when the switch did come it was to Handley Page Halifaxes. Orders for Battles still kept coming, both Austin and Fairey being awarded contracts for 100 airframes each (R3922–R4054 and R7356–R7480) on 27 June and 29 September 1939 respectively. With the outbreak of war in September 1939, Austin received yet another contract for 300 Battles (V1201–V1594), this time for use as target tugs, but only 66 of these were completed (V1201–V1280), the remainder being cancelled.

In July 1938, about a year after Battle deliveries had started from Stockport, the first Austin-built machine, L4935, flew from Northfield, piloted by Squadron Leader T. H. England. The first 59 Battles from Longbridge had Merlin II engines, but subsequent machines had the 1,440hp (1,074kW) at 5,500ft (1,676m) Rolls-Royce Merlin III, this becoming the standard Merlin on both Fairey- and Austin-built Battles. However, a number of Battles were fitted with the uprated Merlin IV or V, the latter engine having higher boost pressures to produce increased power at altitude. To distinguish their various Merlin installations, Battles were eventually referred to as Mks. I, II, III, IV or V. (In 1937 reference had been made to a projected Mk. II Battle of lighter weight with an estimated top speed of 255mph (410km/h) at 15,000ft (4,575m) and a range of over 1,400 miles (2,253km), but nothing came of this proposition.)

Meanwhile, public attention was first drawn to the Fairey Battle at the annual RAF Display at Hendon on 27 June 1936, when the prototype appeared in the New Types Park with an overall silver finish and bearing a large black 'New Type' number '4' ahead of the fuselage roundel. By then the long 'greenhouse' canopy had been modified at both ends and the spinnerless de Havilland variable-pitch propeller fitted. The aircraft remained at Hendon to be exhibited at the Society of British Aircraft Constructors (SBAC) show, held on the same site, before flying to Martlesham for its trials.

The first RAF unit to receive Battles was No. 63 Squadron, based at Upwood, Huntingdon, which had re-formed from 'B' Flight of No. 12 Squadron at Andover on 15 February 1937 to fly Hawker Hinds. In March the squadron had moved to Upwood and exchanged their Hinds for Hawker Audax army co-operation biplanes, and the first Battle, K7559 (the second production machine), arrived on 20 May. This was one of several early-production Battles fitted with dual controls to facilitate conversion of crews to the new monoplane. A further three Battles followed in June, and by the year's end the squadron had fifteen on charge. From 2 July 1937 until 21 March 1938 No. 63 Squadron carried out numerous trials, and became known as the Battle Development Unit. It was also the

first Battle squadron to reach operational status. Other units which began receiving Battles during 1937 were Nos. 105 Squadron at Harwell (ex-Audax), No. 226 Squadron at Harwell (ex-Audax), No. 52 Squadron at Upwood (ex-Hind) and No. 88 Squadron at Boscombe Down (ex-Hind), in that order. One of these units, No. 105 Squadron (disbanded in 1968), later commemorated the Fairey Battle in its crest, which featured a battleaxe and the motto 'Valiant in Battles'.

During 1938 a further twelve squadrons switched to or were formed with Battles in the following order: No. 218 Squadron, Upper Heyford and Boscombe Down (ex-Hind); No. 12 Squadron, Andover and Bicester (ex-Hind); No. 35 Squadron, Worthy Down and Cottesmore (ex-Wellesley); No. 207 Squadron, Cottesmore (ex-Wellesley); No. 98 Squadron, Hucknall, with detachments at Weston Zoyland, Upwood and Bassingbourn (ex-Hind); No. 15 Squadron, Abingdon (ex-Hind); No. 142 Squadron, Andover (ex-Hind); No. 40 Squadron, Abingdon (ex-Hind); No. 103 Squadron, Usworth and Abingdon (ex-Hind); No. 106 Squadron, Abingdon and Thornaby (ex-Hind); No. 150 Squadron, Boscombe Down (re-formed August 1938 with Battles); and No. 185 Squadron, Abingdon and Thornaby (ex-Hind).

By May 1939 Battle bombers were serving with seventeen RAF Bomber Command squadrons, and were allotted as follows. Number 1 Group, all Fairey Battles, comprised Nos. 15 and 40 Squadrons (Abingdon), 103 and 150 Squadrons (Benson), 12 and 142 Squadrons (Bicester), 88 and 218 Squadrons (Boscombe Down), and 105 and 226 Squadrons (Harwell). Battle units with No. 2 Group were Nos. 35 and 207 Squadrons (Cottesmore), 52 and 63 Squadrons (Upwood), and 98 Squadron (Hucknall). Battle units joining No. 5 Group were Nos. 106 and 185 Squadrons (Thornaby). In the

Above: Three crew members can be seen in Battle K7650/M of No. 63 Squadron, Upwood, circa 1937. Note the contemporary RAF A1 roundels, the squadron number ahead of fuselage roundel and the serial number applied to the rear fuselage and rudder. (Author's collection)

event, No. 2 Group's Battle units were transferred to No. 6 (Training) Group of Bomber Command in September 1939, forming Group pool squadrons. Number 98 Squadron became a reserve unit, and in the spring of 1940 a number of OTUs were formed, drawing from No. 6 Group's pool squadrons.

When war was declared on 3 September 1939, the ten Battle squadrons of No. 1 Group had already landed in the Reims area of France the previous day, at selected landing grounds mostly of a primitive nature, the ground crews arriving a few days later. The plan was that, if the Germans started any bombing operations, the Battles would be able to strike back at targets in the Ruhr from a much closer range than bases in Britain. However, at that time neither side seemed prepared to begin a serious bombing offensive and, as the vanguard of the AASF, the Battles became involved in what became known as the 'phoney war', though for some of the aircrews it was real enough.

On 20 September 1939 three Battles from No. 88 Squadron, based at Mourmelon-le-Grand, were on an armed daylight reconnaissance patrol over the Siegfried Line when they were attacked by Messerschmitt Bf 109s. Two of the Battles were shot down, but retaliation came from the other Battle, K9243, when its gunner, Sergeant F. Letchford, shot down one of the Bf 109s, this being the RAF's first aerial combat 'kill' of the Second World War. But on 30 September five of No. 150 Squadron's Battles from Ecury-sur-Coole, en route to carry out a reconnaissance of a strongly defended enemy position in the Saar, were set upon by fifteen Bf 109s. The inevitable result was three Battles shot down and two wrecked in forced landings owing to severe damage caused by the attacking fighters. It was a glaring example of the need for RAF bombers over enemy territory in daylight to have a fighter escort.

To help protect the Battle's belly following this encounter, a semi-fixed, rearward-firing ventral gun was fitted, the presence of this weapon being confirmed in later German reports referring to Battles shot down in their areas. Before the German main assault on the Low Countries, which began on 10 May 1940, AASF Fairey Battles flew mainly weapon training and navigation exercises, both in the daytime and at night, although they did carry out several short-range leaflet dropping raids over towns in the Rhineland. At the same time, Nos. 15 and 40 Squadrons returned to Britain in December 1939 to exchange their Battles for twin-engined Bristol Blenheim bombers. When the German attack began, therefore, some 110 RAF Battles were ready for action and, at midday on 10 May,

Below: A formation of Battle bombers of No. 105 Squadron, Harwell, in 1938. The leading aircraft is K7689, and the one to the right is K7575. This squadron was part of the AASF sent to France on 2 September 1939. (Author's collection)

many of them were ordered to attack enemy troops advancing through Luxembourg.

No fighter escort was available to protect the Battles, and their pilots were instructed to fly in very low, dropping their bombs, fused at eleven seconds delay, from 250ft (76m). Inevitably the Battles faced intense German machine-gun and small-arms fire, and only 23 aircraft returned from a force of 36 sent out that first day. On the following day eight Battles from Nos. 88 and 218 Squadrons were ordered to attack German troops, again in Luxembourg, but only one aircraft returned. On 12 May, in an attempt to stem the German advance on Brussels, five volunteer crews from No. 12 Squadron were asked to make low-level attacks on two road bridges over the Albert Canal in Belgium, one a concrete structure at Vroenhoven and the other a metal bridge at Veldwezelt. The first attack was made by two Battles which dive-bombed the Vroenhoven bridge from 6,000ft (1,828m), causing little damage, but at Veldwezelt one end of the bridge was destroyed when Flying Officer D. E. Garland led the other three Battles on an extremely low bombing run through a storm of flak and machine-gun fire. All five Battles were shot down and four of their gallant crews killed or taken prisoner. Sadly Flying Officer Garland and his observer/gunner, Sergeant T. Gray, perished with their aircraft, both being awarded a posthumous Victoria

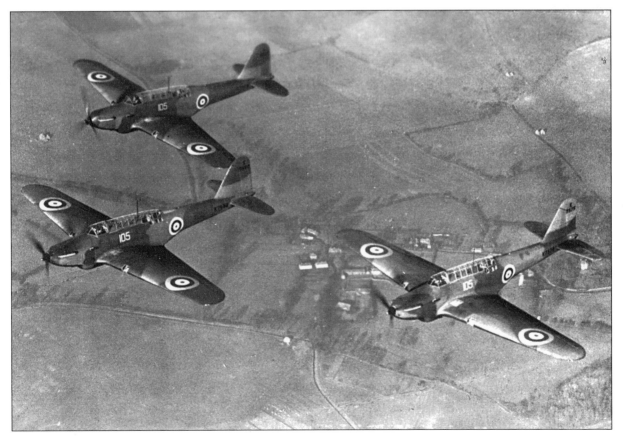

Cross, the first RAF VCs of the war.

During the morning of 14 May 1940 ten Battles from Nos. 103 and 150 Squadrons were sent to attack German pontoon bridges across the river Meuse at Sedan. They did this without loss, as no enemy fighters appeared, a factor which raised the aircrews' spirits a little for a few hours. That afternoon all available Battles from eight squadrons were again sent to attack bridges at Sedan and columns of German troops in that area. But this time the Luftwaffe was up in force, and its Bf 109s came in for the kill. Four Battles out of five from No. 12 Squadron were shot down, four out of eight from No. 142 Squadron, three out of six from No. 226 Squadron, six out of eleven from No. 105 Squadron, all four from No. 150 Squadron, one out of ten from No. 88 Squadron, three out of eight from No. 103 Squadron, and ten out of eleven from No. 218 Squadron. Of a total 63 Battles which took off, only 28 returned, and on the same raid Nos. 114 and 139 Squadrons lost five out of eight Blenheims despatched.

So severe were the losses that Nos. 218 and 105 Squadrons temporarily disbanded owing to an acute shortage of crews and aircraft, re-forming later with Blenheims and Wellingtons respectively. The remaining six Battle units, Nos. 12, 88, 103, 142, 150 and 226 Squadrons, continued to hit back at the enemy despite increasing losses, hurried changes of base and a serious lack of ground support. Between the middle of May and 15 June 1940, as the final withdrawal from

Above: Maintenance crew work on a Fairey Battle of No. 105 Squadron at Harwell in February 1939. (Mrs M. Hunt)

Right: Six Fairey Battles of No. 105 Squadron fly in line-abreast over England in 1938. A year later they would be at war, based at Reims in France with the AASF. (Mrs M. Hunt)

Lower right: Three Battles of No. 226 Squadron up from Harwell in 1939. The nearest, K9176/G, went missing over France on 20 May 1940, K9180/X (centre) was burnt during the BEF's evacuation the same day, and K7709 returned to become instructional airframe 3555M. (Mrs M. Hunt)

France was undertaken, the Battle squadrons flew some 200 nocturnal sorties against German communication targets, during which only one aircraft was lost.

With the return of AASF squadrons to Britain, the operational days of the Fairey Battle were by no means over. Bomber Command's No. 1 Group re-formed, its Battle units comprising No. 12 Squadron (Finningley and Binbrook), No. 103 Squadron (Honington and Newton), No. 142 Squadron (Waddington, Binbrook and Eastchurch) and No. 150 Squadron (Stradishall and Newton). They were joined by four other Battle units, manned by Polish crews, which had formed in the summer of 1940. These comprised Nos. 300 and 301 Squadrons (Swinderby) and Nos. 304 and 305 Squadrons (Bramcote). From their various bases the eight Fairey Battle squadrons carried out attacks by night on concentrations of German barges and troops in French and Dutch ports. This build-up was in preparation for Operation Sea Lion, Hitler's planned invasion of England, which never materialised. The Battles continued these raids until October 1940, the last sortie by No. 1 Group's Battles taking place on the night of 15/16 October, when No. 301 (Polish) Squadron bombed German targets at Boulogne and Nos. 12 and 142 Squadrons attacked enemy forces around Calais.

By November 1940 No. 1 Group's English-based Battle squadrons were converting to Wellingtons, but two of its other units operated until 1941. These were Nos. 88 and 226 Squadrons, which, after returning from France, had been re-mustered at Driffield and Thirsk respectively to receive brand new Battles. In June 1940 both units moved to Sydenham (Belfast), from where they flew continuous dawn and dusk reconnaissance patrols along Northern Ireland's coastline, on the watch for any attempted landings by enemy agents. At Sydenham in February 1941 No. 88 Squadron's Battles were replaced by Douglas Boston and Bristol Blenheim bombers, while No. 226 Squadron returned to Wattisham in May 1941 and exchanged its Battles for Blenheim IVs. The last RAF unit to employ Fairey Battles in an operational role was No. 98 Squadron, the old reserve unit of No. 2

Group. Posted to Iceland in July 1940 and based at Kaldadarnes, near Reykjavik, they flew as part of Coastal Command's No. 15 Group. For nearly a year the squadron's Battles carried out regular reconnaissance sorties, anti-submarine patrols and convoy escort duties.

Before the outbreak of the Second World War a number of countries showed interest in the Fairey Battle, but only one firm order was placed, when the Belgian Government signed a contract for sixteen machines in 1937 (Fairey constructor's numbers F.3258–F.3273). These Belgian Battles were built at Fairey's Heaton Chapel works and deliveries commenced in March 1938. They differed from RAF Battles in having extended radiator and intake cowlings, a smoother finish and minor detail changes. They were powered by the Rolls-Royce Merlin III and had a slight edge in speed over their RAF counterparts. Serving with Nos. 5 and 7 Squadrons of the Belgian Air Force's 3rd Air Regiment at Evere, they flew alongside the RAF's Battles when the German invasion began on 10 May 1940, but they fared no better. That day, five were lost through accidents or enemy action, and on the following day, when three formations of three aircraft made similar attacks to the RAF Battles on bridges over the Albert Canal, only three Belgian Battles sur-

vived. The sixteen Belgian Battles, released from Fairey's Stockport production line by the Air Ministry for export to Belgium, have on occasion been wrongly recorded by some sources as being built by Belgian-based Avions Fairey at Gosselies.

Turkey also received Battles from Fairey's RAF production line, although four machines originally destined for Turkey and finished in Turkish Air Force colours were at first stopped by the British Government. However, in September 1939 Fairey was allowed to release 29 Battles for export to Turkey (N2111–N2117, N2120–N2123, N2130–N2131, N2149, N2153–N2155, N2211–N2218, N2220–N2222 and N2224). Turkish aircrews enjoyed flying the Battle, finding it very manoeuvrable and carrying out numerous low-flying activities, a practice which reportedly accounted for a number of the Battles being written off.

Another temporary cancellation was imposed on an order for nine Fairey Battle bombers for Greece (P6607–P6615), but at the end of 1939 twelve machines were released by the RAF for service with the Royal Hellenic Air Force (one Greek Battle was numbered B282 on the fuselage sides aft of the roundel). They operated with No. 33 Mira, and were in action briefly against the Italians in October 1940, during the invasion of Greece. One Battle, N2219, was shipped to Poland in September 1939, but with the fall of Poland this aircraft was diverted to the Middle East area.

Later, and nearer home, on 24 April 1941 Battle V1222 from No. 4 Air Observer's School, West Freugh, was on a training flight from Northern Ireland when its Polish pilot made a navigational error and landed at Waterford, Eire. After internment this aircraft became No. 92 of the Irish Army Air Corps, and served

as a target tug for several years before being struck off charge on 3 May 1946.

In April 1939 one Battle, L5374, arrived in South Africa for evaluation by the South African Air Force, but on 19 June 1940 it was shot down over Italian Somaliland while being flown by the CO of No. 11 Squadron, SAAF, on a photographic reconnaissance sortie. At the time No. 11 Squadron had a complement of twelve newly arrived Battles, including R3938 and R3845, and was working-up on the type. Their first mission was to attack enemy targets in East Africa on 19 August 1940, after which, joined by No. 12 Squadron, SAAF, which numbered two Battles in its inventory, similar operations continued until June 1941. Number 11 Squadron then transferred its twelve Battles to No. 15 Squadron, SAAF, which flew further operations against the Italians until the middle of August. During 1942 the SAAF received some 150 Battle trainers and target tugs which, after South Africa joined the Commonwealth Air Training Plan (CATP), served with Nos. 41, 42 and 43 Air Schools.

The Fairey Battle trainer, evolved from the original dual-control conversion variant, was introduced in 1940 as an emergency measure to assist in training Hurricane and Spitfire pilots. However, because the long glazed canopy restricted the forward view of the instructor in the rear seat, Fairey decided to revise the design. Two separate cockpit canopies, as featured in the original design for the prototype Battle bomber,

Below: These three Battles, K9353/HA-J, K9324/HA-B and K9325/HA-D, are seen in 1939 with No. 218 Squadron from Boscombe Down before moving to France with the AASF. Aircraft K9325 and K9353 went missing on 12 and 13 May respectively; K9324 was transferred to the RAAF on 19 September 1940. (Author's collection)

were incorporated in the definitive trainer version designated the Battle (T) trainer. This altered layout involved some fairly extensive modifications to the standard Battle, with dual controls as standard and each cockpit having practically identical windscreens, rearward-sliding hoods, controls and instrument panels. Control runs, internal arrangements and part of the fuselage structure also required changing. The prototype Battle (T), P2277, came from Fairey's fourth production batch, and 200 production Battle trainers followed, starting with P6616. A number were retrospectively fitted with a rotatable Bristol Type 1 gun turret incorporating a 'break-out' panel and a redesigned faired canopy aft of the cockpit. A 0.303in (7.7mm) Lewis or Vickers GO machine-gun was mounted in this turret, and the aircraft were dubbed Battle 'turret trainers'. The first two Battles so converted for trials were K9376 and K9382, both Fairey-built machines.

For its target-towing role the Battle target tug retained the 'greenhouse' canopy, but wind-driven winching gear was fitted on the port side of the fuselage, just ahead of the rear cockpit, and worked by a second crewman acting as winch operator in the rear cockpit. A drogue target was carried in a faired container beneath the rear fuselage. The first target-towing equipment was fitted to Battle K7587 in July 1939 for trials. The prototype proper, L5598, emerged in February 1940 and flew to Boscombe Down the following month for its trials with the A&AEE. The last

Above: A quartet of Battles from No. 98 Squadron, Hucknall, in 1938, then classed as a reserve unit. It transferred to Iceland in July 1940 and flew with No. 15 Group, Coastal Command. (Author's collection)

Austin-built Battle, V1280, delivered on 9 September 1940, was a target tug.

Under the CATP, Australia, Canada, India, New Zealand and Southern Rhodesia were to receive Fairey Battles, the largest number (739) going to Canada, where 560 were allotted RCAF serials (1301–1320 and 1601–2140), the remaining 179 retaining their British serials in the K, L, P and R ranges. The first eight RCAF Battles arrived in Canada during August 1939 and were delivered to Camp Borden. A steady supply followed from Britain, Battles making a substantial contribution to the RCAF training programme as dual-control trainers, target tugs and gunnery trainers in various Bombing and Gunnery Schools of the CATP in Canada. As more advanced training aircraft reached Canadian units, the number of Battles dwindled, but some remained in service until the end of the war. Battles were also operational with Nos. 111 and 122 Squadrons of the RCAF. One Canadian Battle 'turret trainer', R7439, had its turret removed and was experimentally powered by an 840hp (626kW) Wright Cyclone GR-1820-G3B air-cooled radial engine. This installation was undertaken by Fairchild at Quebec (which also fitted the Bristol gun turrets to Battles in Canada) as a safeguard against the possible non-avail-

Above: Battle N2031 flew with No. 616 Squadron, Auxiliary Air Force, from May to November 1939. Then based at Doncaster, it is seen visiting RAF Manston, Kent. (Author's collection)

ability of spare Merlins. In the event this never occurred, and R7439 was the only Wright Cyclone powered Battle.

Australia received 366 Battles, the RAAF allotting the prefix A22 to its machines, although all retained their original British serials. The first Battles to arrive in Australia were P2167, P2169, P5239 and P5247, their delivery to No. 1 Aircraft Park at Geelong, near

Below: A trio of Battles from No. 12 Squadron in 1938. The first two RAF VCs of the war were posthumously awarded to Flying Officer Garland and Sergeant Gray of this squadron for their gallantry in attacking a bridge spanning the Albert Canal on 12 May 1940. (MAP)

Melbourne, on 30 April 1940 being followed on 29 June by a test flight of the first Battle assembled there, P5239. Delivery and assembly in Australia continued to increase steadily, the last Australian Battle, V1202, being taken on charge by No. 2 Aircraft Park on 7 December 1943. In all, the RAAF received 32 Battle bombers, 304 dual-control trainers and 30 target tugs, most of which served at Bombing and Gunnery Schools until the end of the war. Indeed, a number of RAAF Battles remained in service until 1949. One British RAF Battle pilot, Pilot Officer R. Givens, while on an exchange posting to Australia as an instructor to RAAF Battle crews, had the odd experience of flying Battle K9297, the same aircraft he had flown over France in 1940 with No. 88 Squadron.

Some Battles went to other Commonwealth countries, but in far smaller numbers, a few going to India during 1942, where they eventually flew as target tugs

with the Anti-Aircraft School at Karachi. Royal Air Force records show that two Battles were sent to the Southern Rhodesian Air Force (SRAF) during 1942/43, while another was delivered to the Royal New Zealand Air Force (RNZAF) in 1942. None of these three Battles is believed to have operated with either air force.

Another excellent use found for the Battle was that of engine test-bed, a number being converted for this purpose because the type was considered to have a robust airframe and excellent handling qualities, and was available in quantity. At least seventeen Battles were used as engine test-beds, and others went to the RAE at Farnborough for various test programmes. As well as the aforementioned Canadian Battle with its Wright Cyclone air-cooled radial engine, radial engines were experimentally fitted to Fairey Battles in Britain. A 1,010hp (753kW) Bristol Taurus T.E.1M was installed in Battle K9331, and

Above: Battle K9264/PM-L of No. 103 Squadron went missing on 10 May 1940 while operating over France with the AASF. (MAP)

flight trials with this engine began in June 1938. This aircraft had its landing gear converted to a fixed type and later flew powered by the uprated Taurus III, with which trials commenced during February 1939. Bristol Hercules radials were fitted to a pair of Battles, N2042 and N2184, which also had fixed landing gear. Both initially had the 1,300hp (969kW) Hercules II engine installed. Trials started in February 1939, and N2042 was later fitted with a fan-cooled Hercules XI, with which it was tested at Farnborough

Below: The prototype Fairey Battle two-seat trainer, P2277, which appeared in 1940. Note the separate cockpits, similar to the original Fairey P.27/32 design of 1934. (MAP)

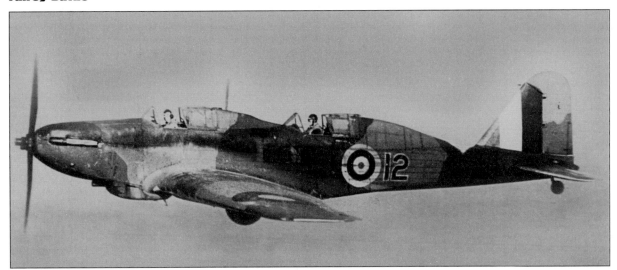

in 1942. This aircraft was scrapped at Filton in February 1945.

Meanwhile, as mentioned earlier, Fairey's aero-engine department had been developing its own P.24 Prince engine since 1936. This very innovative engine comprised two self-contained twelve-cylinder vertically opposed engines using a common crankcase, with side-mounted superchargers and glycol cooling, the separate counter-rotating crankshafts being connected by reduction gears to individual co-axial three-blade Fairey variable-pitch (later constant-speed) propellers. Each half-engine was expected to produce about 1,000hp (746kW), but the P.24 as a unit had a potential output of some 3,000hp (2,238kW). During 1938 each half-engine had to be tested separately at Fairey's Hayes works as the Heenan & Froude equipment installed there was not capable of managing the total 2,200hp (1,7639kW) produced. To flight-test the P.24, Stockport-built Battle K9370 was fitted with a sizeable broad radiator located in a ventral position, and a double row of exhaust stubs protruded from the upper and lower sections of the engine cowling. This P.24 powered Battle made its initial flight on 30 June 1939, with test pilot C. S. Staniland at the controls. In July K9370 was sent to the RAE, Farnborough, where nearly 87 hours of test flying were accumulated.

Authorities in the USA then became interested in the P.24 as a suitable powerplant for the USAAF's Republic P-47 Thunderbolt fighter. To save the time which would be required to prepare another P.24 and adapt an American aircraft to accept it, Battle K9370 with its P.24 Prince was shipped to the USA on 5 December 1941, destined for the USAAF test centre at Wright Field, Ohio. It was still there in September 1942, but returned to Farnborough in 1943 after amassing some 250 hours' flying time at Wright Field.

In all, during its test flying in Britain and the USA, Battle K9370 clocked up 340 hours in the air powered by the P.24. This Fairey engine, designed by Captain A. G. Forsyth, was intended to power carrier-borne aircraft, and would have proved an asset, offering 'double' engine capability in an aircraft taking up no more carrier hangar space than a normal single-engine machine. The engine was also considered for the Hawker Typhoon and, being simpler and less troublesome than the Napier Sabre which retarded the

Top left: Battle Trainer R7365/12. Note the gas warning patch atop the rear fuselage. (MAP)

Centre left: Battle K9382, an ex-226 Squadron machine, was one of two experimentally fitted with a rotatable Bristol Type 1 gun turret. It went to the RCAF in November 1941 as 2109. (MAP)

Left: Austin-built Fairey Battle target-tug L5566, with a winch on the rear port side of the cockpit and painted in overall black and yellow target-tower stripes. (MAP)

Typhoon's progress, might well have proved a better proposition. However, with wartime production in full swing it was necessary to abandon further work on the P.24, and a very promising engine was no more. One that survived has been presented to the Fleet Air Arm Museum at RNAS Yeovilton.

Another 24-cylinder engine fitted to a Fairey Battle was the 1,200hp (895kW) Rolls-Royce Exe, a single-crankshaft 90° 'X' with sleeve-valves and air-pressure cooling. A 1935 design by A. J. Rowledge, the Exe was intended for the Fairey Barracuda naval torpedo and dive-bomber, and its test-bed was Fairey Battle K9222, converted to accept the Exe before the war and test-flown at Hucknall for a considerable time. The first main intake beneath a specially fitted spinner on K9222 proved poor, and a second larger and better profiled design was fitted which incorporated an auxiliary intake below. A 'nostril'-type intake was located each side of the cowling.

In the event, although the Exe was also a potential engine for Fairey's projected FC.1 transport and a Spearfish project, it too was abandoned. Even so, the Exe-powered Battle proved popular with Hucknall's pilots, who flew it as their communications 'hack' aircraft until at least 1943. It was reported that K9222 was scheduled to test-fly a Rolls-Royce Griffon engine, while another Battle, K9477, was test-bed for the Rolls-Royce Peregrine, later used in the Westland Whirlwind twin-engine fighter-bomber. Rolls-Royce employed nine Battle test-beds over a period of time for trials of various Merlin engines, and when Battle K2234 was fitted with a 1,280hp (954kW) Merlin XII, a 'chin' radiator faired back to the centre-section was added.

Extensive use was made of three Fairey Battle test-beds by D. Napier & Sons Ltd, which in 1938 used Battle K9240 for development flying of its 955hp (712kW) Dagger VIII. This aircraft was flown from both Northolt and RAE Farnborough, and underwent experiments including supercharging, cooling systems and water injection. It later became instructional airframe 2213M. Two other Fairey Battles, K9278 and L5286, also served with Napier as test-beds for its very impressive Sabre engine. This powerplant, designed by Major F. B. Halford, had an initial output of 2,200hp (1,641kW), but was to cause many headaches before and after its entry into service in the Hawker Typhoon, albeit in more sophisticated and uprated form. (By 1944 the Sabre weighed 2,540lb (1,152kg) and produced 3,055hp (2,279kW) at 3,850rpm.) Before their Sabres were installed, both Battle test-beds were fitted with a relocated fixed landing gear, a large ventral radiator and an auxiliary air intake. The first flight of Sabre-powered K9278 was made from Northolt on 31 May 1939 and, after moving to Luton, it had clocked up 375 flying hours by June 1942. This Battle was struck off charge on 31 May 1944. Its partner at Napier, L5286, was completed for Sabre test fly-

Above: This Battle Gunnery Trainer, 7384/35 (ex-R7384 RAF), has a Bristol turret and is seen in RCAF service circa 1941–42. (Aviation Photo News)

ing at Luton during March 1941, and logged 33 hours in the air from there before passing to RAE Farnborough for an extension of Sabre air tests. Eventually L5286 was struck off charge on 7 December 1943, but between them the two Sabre-powered Battles accumulated some 700 hours of test flying.

The author has been fortunate in having two personal recollections of the Fairey Battle related to him by ex-RAF members, the first once again from Bob Wilcock, who remembers seeing Battles 'lumbering into the air' at RAF Dumfries, where his late brother was on a bomb-aiming course in 1942. According to Bob's brother, as a Battle prepared for its bombing run the bomb-aimer had to 'shuffle' down from his seat and lie flat on the bottom of the fuselage, where a removable Perspex cover allowed a good sight of the ground below and accommodated the bomb sight. Once he was in that position some quite nasty engine fumes blew into his face, and often when he stood up he was not only dirty faced but could feel quite nauseous.

A more detailed account of flying in a Battle came from ex-Battle observer Don Bruce of East Sussex.

Below: Battle K9331 in use as a test-bed for the Bristol Taurus TE1M radial engine during 1939. A fixed undercarriage has been fitted. (Author's collection)

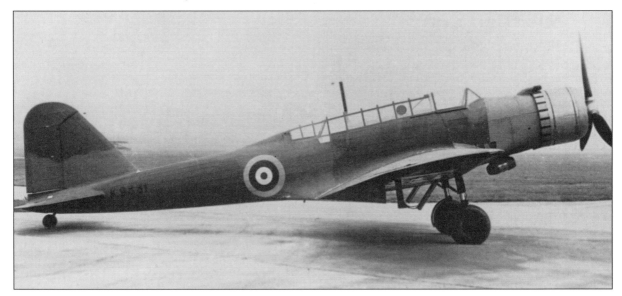

Above: The innovative Fairey P.24 Prince engine powered Battle test-bed K9370, which was shipped to Wright Field in the USA in December 1941 for USAAF tests. It returned to RAE Farnborough in the UK during 1943. (MAP)

Don was sent to Canada for his bombing and gunnery training course, and attended No. 31 BGS at Picton, Ontario, during August/September 1941. The aircraft were Fairey Battles, and Don remembers them as very strong aircraft structurally, underpowered, but quite fast and manoeuvrable when flying light and minus a bomb load compared with the Wellington which he flew in later with No. 115 Squadron. The Battle's observer sat on a small step in a restricted area below the gunner, with feet dangling in a well below which was also the bomb-aiming position. A petrol tank was about a foot in front of one's head and the manufacturer's tab ('Austin Motor Co., Longbridge') on a nearby bulkhead. In this position one could not see outside the aircraft, apart from through the sliding hatch where the course setting bomb sight (CSBS) was situated. Communication with the pilot was via Gosport tubes and, when these had been clipped very short through wear, one had to get right down over the bomb sight to plug the tube in. The pilot's seat was on the other side of a bulkhead that isolated the cockpit, and was well above the bombsight. Don said that sometimes, no matter how much you shouted, little heed seemed to be taken by the pilot of what you were trying to tell him. On practice bombing a shield, operated by the pilot, deflected engine heat away from the CSBS and, if the pilot forgot to activate this shield the bomb-aimer's chinagraph pencil dissolved in a pool of wax on the glass surface of the CSBS, making it impossible to obtain a three-course wind speed and direction.

The Battle's gunner sat on a rotating bicycle-style saddle seat, most pupils finding it more comfortable to stand. The single Vickers GO machine-gun in the rear cockpit was mounted on a collapsible tripod which stowed away flat in a streamlined fairing aft of the cockpit housing. Erection was via a trigger attached to a Bowden cable and, after a heave on the gun, it all 'clicked' into place and could be swung to either side of the cockpit. The nearest thing Don Bruce experienced to 'pure' flying was air firing from a Fairey Battle. He says:

'The rear cockpit hood hinged up to give some protection from the slipstream but, if you stuck your head out far enough over the side, you were clear of the hood and with the roar of the slipstream in your ears and blowing the water out of your eyes (if you weren't wearing goggles), the Vickers gun thudding and bucking away on its free mounting, it was most exhilarating and among the more memorable of my wartime flying experiences.'

On one gunnery exercise Don had to shoot at a towed drogue target below and to port of the Battle's pupil gunner. He had to fire down between the tailplane and fuselage side and, 'as electrical cut-outs were unknown on Vickers GO armed Battles, one only needed to hit a bump at the crucial moment to find a few rounds had gone through your own tailplane'. Don had a few hair-raising experiences on Battles in Canada, the pilots apparently being 'a pretty crazy bunch' who got up to all sorts of antics both as individuals and in formation. But Don says the Battle was strong enough to withstand a lot of rough treatment, and recalls one occasion when one Battle taxied into a building. Although the latter was a sorry mess, the Battle was relatively unmarked! The Battles in which Don Bruce flew were: K7632, K7671, K9194, K9323,

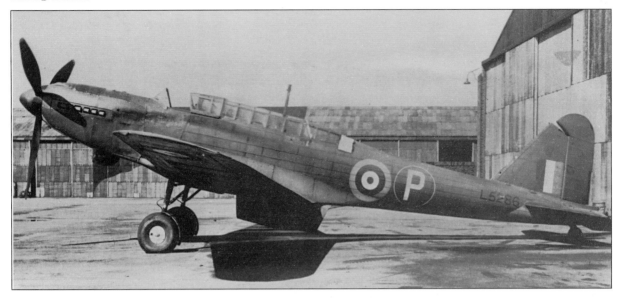

K9399, L5009, L5036, L5205, L5308, L5315, L5510, P2304, P6541, P6564, R3961 (pilot Flying Officer D. J. Locker, ex-615 Squadron during the Battle of Britain), R3992, R3993 and R3998.

A pristine example of a Fairey Battle can be seen today in the RAF Museum at Hendon, in the Bomber Command Hall. This aircraft, L5343/VO-S, is in the markings of No. 98 Squadron, the unit in which it was serving with Coastal Command at Kaldadarnes, southern Iceland, in 1940. On 13 September that year L5343 suffered engine failure on a flight to Akureyri, forced-

Above: Battle test-bed L5286 with a Napier Sabre engine installed. It has a large ventral radiator, an auxiliary air intake and a relocated, fixed landing gear. (MAP)

landed and was abandoned until 1972, when an RAF recovery team brought its remains home for restoration. Many years of frustration and hard work were finally rewarded in May 1990, when L5343 took a well deserved place among the greats of RAF history at Hendon.

The Fairey Battle fought bravely against overwhelming odds in 1940, but advancing technology quickly overtook its potential as a fighting machine. No match for contemporary adversaries, the Battle nevertheless gave yeoman service in second-line duties as a training and auxiliary aircraft for much of the Second World War.

Below: Many RAF crews took their bombing and gunnery courses in Canada on Fairey Battles. The machine shown here, 'Turret Battle' 7384, is preserved and on permanent display at Rockcliffe, Ontario. (Aviation Photo News)

Handley Page
Hampden & Hereford

When RAF Bomber Command began its night bombing offensive against Germany early in the Second World War, one of the main bomber types employed was the Handley Page Hampden. Because of its rather unorthodox appearance this aircraft earned itself nicknames such as 'flying suitcase', 'tadpole' or 'frying pan'.

The Hampden resulted from an Air Ministry specification of 1932, B.9/32, which was issued to the Bristol Aeroplane Co, the Gloster Aircraft Co, Handley Page and Vickers Aviation. This specification was issued in accordance with proposals (backed initially by the British Government) made at the Geneva Disarmament Conference, limiting new bombing aircraft to a tare weight not exceeding 6,600lb (2,994kg). The Air Staff were keen to replace the RAF's Boulton Paul Sidestrand biplanes with a new day bomber capable of carrying a 1,500lb (680kg) bomb load, but the Geneva weight restrictions had to be complied with, at least while the subject was still under discussion.

Requirements were therefore laid down for a twin-engine aircraft with sufficient power to cope with the proposed bomb load, a top speed of 190mph (306km/h), a cruising speed of 125mph (201km/h) at 15,000ft (4,572m), a normal range of 600 miles (966km) and an extended range of 1,250 miles (2,012km) provided for by means of reserve and auxiliary fuel capacity. It was stipulated that a four-man crew be carried, consisting of pilot, navigator, radio operator and gunner. However, at least two gun posi-

tions were required, rear defence being of primary importance, and both gunners were to be afforded adequate protection from the weather. It was envisaged that the navigator and radio operator would double as gunners and bomb aimer.

The designs submitted by Handley Page and Vickers were chosen for prototype construction at the end of May 1933, both being advanced concepts by contemporary standards. They progressed more or less in parallel, their initial flights being made within a week of each other. Vickers' B.9/32 was to earn fame as the Wellington, and, although employed mainly as a night bomber until 1943, it would serve with Coastal Command as general reconnaissance and anti-submarine aircraft until 1945, others serving as transports (Mks. XV and XVI) and as trainers with Air Navigation Schools (converted Mk. Xs), some of the latter flying with Flying Training Command until 1953. No doubt the Wellington owed its comparative success and longevity compared with the Handley Page design to its rugged geodetic construction and much roomier fuselage.

Handley Page's response to B.9/32 was the brainchild of Dr G. V. Lachmann, company chief designer from 1931 to 1935, when his place was taken by G. R. Volkert. Dr Lachmann had pioneered the Handley

Below: This side view shows why the Hampden earned such nicknames as 'frying-pan', 'tadpole' and 'flying suitcase'. (Author's collection)

Handley Page Hampden and Hereford

Page wing slot and had designed the H.P.47 single-engine general-purpose monoplane (K2773) in response to Specification G.4/31. First flown in November 1934, this aircraft was the first Handley Page type to incorporate an all-metal wing with a low drag and weight factor. This tapered wing had full-span flaps with inserted ailerons, together with full-span leading-edge slats, resulting in excellent landing and take-off performance. The H.P.47 also had a very slim, low-drag rear fuselage section, which afforded the gunner in his raised dorsal position a superb field of fire. Many of the H.P.47's features were employed by Lachmann in his twin-engine B.9/32 layout which, designated H.P.52, emerged as an unusual design intended to combine the range and load of a heavy bomber with the speed, manoeuvrability and handling qualities of a light bomber.

Structurally the H.P.52 was quite advanced for its time, with a very slim-section fuselage only 3ft (0.91m) wide, consisting of an all-metal semi-monocoque structure covered with a flush-riveted, stressed skin. It was built in three sections comprising the nose portion, centre-section and a lengthy boom-type extension carrying the empennage. The boom and centre section were constructed in two halves longitudinally. At the junction of the tail boom and main fuselage on the prototype, a Handley Page Heyford-type ventral 'dustbin' turret was located, and an angular flat dorsal turret was provided above. Although a nose turret had been considered, problems arose over a suitable gun mounting and the limited width available.

The all-metal wings, mounted midway on the fuselage, were well tapered and of low-drag profile. They had three main sections, the centre section being adjoined by two outer panels with detachable leading and trailing edges. The centre section carried the two engines, which were located as close to the fuselage as possible allowing for propeller diameter. In keeping with a desired take-off performance in which a height of 50ft (15.2m) was to be cleared after a run of 1,800ft (550m), the inner wing trailing edges incorporated 20 per cent-chord slotted flaps, while Handley Page patented automatic slats were fitted to the leading

---

HANDLEY PAGE HAMPDEN MK. I DATA

Manufacturers
Handley Page Ltd, Cricklewood and Radlett. Subcontractors: English Electric Co, Preston, and Canadian Associated Aircraft Ltd

Type
Four-seat, twin-engine medium bomber

Powerplant
Two 1,000hp (746kW) Bristol Pegasus XVIII nine-cylinder air-cooled radial engines

Performance
Maximum speed, 254mph (409km/h) at 13,800ft (4,206m). Cruising speed, 167mph (269km/h) at 15,000ft (4,572m). Initial climb, 980ft (298m)/min; time to 15,000ft (4,572m), 18.9 minutes. Service ceiling, 19,000ft (5,791m). Range (with 2,000lb (907kg) bomb load), 1,885 miles (3,034km) at 155mph (249km/h); with 4,000lb (1,814kg) bomb load, 1,100miles (1,770km) at 206mph (332km/h)

Weights
Empty, 11,780lb (5,343kg). Loaded (normal), 18,756lb (8,508kg); maximum take-off, 22,500lb (10,206kg)

Dimensions
Span, 69ft 2in (21.08m). Length, 53ft 7in (16.33m). Height, 14ft 11in (4.55m).

Wing area, 668sq ft (62.06sq m). Landing gear track, 17ft 4in (5.28m)

Armament
One fixed and one moveable 0.303in (7.7mm) Vickers 'K' gun in nose; twin 0.303in (7.7mm) Vickers 'K' guns in ventral and dorsal positions. Maximum bomb load, two 2,000lb (907kg) or four 500lb (227kg) bombs in bomb bay; two 500lb (227kg) bombs on underwing racks

HANDLEY PAGE HAMPDEN / HEREFORD PRODUCTION

Prototype H.P.52 Hampden K4240 to Specification B.9/32. Later became instructional airframe 1490M

Prototype H.P.53 Hereford L7271 to Specification 44/36. Later became 2057M

First production batch of 180 Hampden Is by Handley Page (L4032–L4211); L4032 trials with Wright Cyclone engines; L4207 pattern aircraft to English Electric Co; L4208–L4211 pattern aircraft to CAA, Canada, (L4210/'11 returned to RAF); six were converted to TB.I torpedo-bombers

Second production batch of 200 Hampden Is by Handley Page (P1145–P1189, P1194–P1230, P1233–P1261, P1265–P1305 and

P1309–P1356); 44 converted to TB.I torpedo-bombers; P1167, P1200, P1230, P1311 to RCAF in 1943; P1279, P1280, P1324 and P1327 became 1857M, 2108M, 2261M and 2214M respectively

First production batch of 75 Hampden Is by English Electric Co (P2062–P2100, P2110–P2145); thirteen converted to TB.I torpedo-bombers. P2067, P2133 to RCAF in 1943. P2073, P2117 and P2131 became 4384M, 2270M and 2177M respectively

Third production batch of 120 Hampden Is by Handley Page (P4285–P4324, P4335–P4384 and P4389–P4418); ten converted to TB.I torpedo-bombers. P4337, P4349 and P4369 became 2169M, 2157M and 2140M respectively

First production batch of 80 Hampden Is by CAA, Canada, (P5298–P5436); seventeen converted to TB.I torpedo-bombers. P5298, P5336, P5337, P5399, P5400 and P5421-P5436 delivered to RCAF. P5311 became 3075M in UK

Second production batch of 150 Hampden Is by English Electric Co (X2893–X2922, X2959–X3008, X3021–X3030, X3047–X3066 and X3115–X3154); X3115 prototype Mk. II with Wright Cyclones; twenty con-

---

HAMPDEN

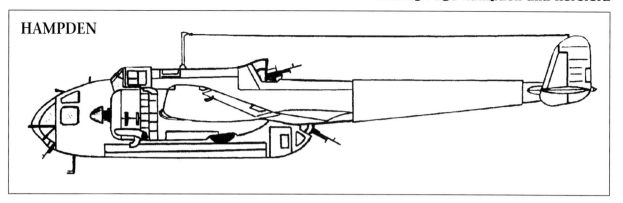

verted to TB.I torpedo-bombers. X3137 and X3149 to RCAF

Third production batch of 125 Hampden Is by English Electric Co (AD719–AD768, AD782–AD806 and AD824–AD873); eighteen converted to TB.I torpedo-bombers.

Fourth production batch of 300 Hampden Is by English Electric Co (AD895–AD939, AD959–AD988, AE115–AE159, AE218–AE267, AE286–AE320, AE352–AE401 and AE418–AE442); 66 converted to TB.I torpedo-bombers; AD908 and '977, AE194, '231, '307, '310 and '363 sent to Russia

Second production batch of twelve Hampden Is by CAA, Canada, (AJ988–AJ999). Majority delivered to No. 32 OTU, RCAF

Third production batch of 68 Hampden Is by CAA, Canada, (AN100–AN167); 22 converted to TB.I torpedo-bombers. From this batch 35 allocated to RCAF

Fifth production batch of 250 Hampden Is (AT109–AT434) ordered from English Electric Co; 120 (AT109–AT260) built and 130 (AT261–AT434) cancelled. 38 converted to TB.I torpedo-bombers

First production batch of 100 Hereford Mk. Is by Short & Harland (L6002–L6101); thirteen converted to Hampden Is

Second production batch of 50 Hereford Mk. Is by Short & Harland (N9055–N9106); eleven converted to Hampden Mk. Is. Three (N9064 and '96 and N9106) became Hampden TB.I torpedo-bombers. Ten (N9055, '57, '58, '68, '75, '79, '89, '93 and N9102 and '04) became 2804M,

2192M, 2805MN, 2913M, 2830M, 2914M, 3019M, 2754M, 2767M and 2781M respectively

Including the H.P.52 and H.P.53 prototypes, 1,582 Hampdens and Herefords were produced, 1,431 as Hampdens. Of the 151 built originally as Herefords, at least 20 were converted to Hampden I configuration with Pegasus engines

RAF HAMPDEN AND HEREFORD UNITS

Bomber Command Hampdens (1938-1942)

No. 7 Squadron (Finningley)
No. 44 Squadron (Waddington)
No. 49 Squadron (Scampton)
No. 50 Squadron (Waddington)
No. 61 Squadron (Hemswell)
No. 76 Squadron (Finningley)
No. 83 Squadron (Scampton)
No. 97 Squadron (Coningsby) July/August 1941 only
No. 106 Squadron Reserve (Evanton/Cottesmore/Coningsby)
No. 144 Squadron (Hemswell, North Luffenham)
No. 185 Squadron Reserve (Cottesmore). To merge as No. 14 OTU
No. 207 Squadron (Waddington) July/August 1941 only
No. 408 Squadron RCAF (Syerston/North Luffenham and Leeming)
No. 420 Squadron RCAF (Waddington)
No. 455 Squadron RAAF (Swinderby)

Coastal Command

No. 144 Squadron ex-Bomber Command (Leuchars and detachments)

No. 415 Squadron RCAF (St Eval, Thorney Island, North Coates, Wick, Leuchars and detachments, Thorney Island)
No. 455 Squadron RAAF ex- Bomber Command (Wigsley, Leuchars and detachments)
No. 489 Squadron RNZAF (Thorney Island/St Eval, Skitten, Wick, Leuchars)

Meteorological Reconnaissance

No. 517 Squadron (St Eval, St Davids)
No. 519 Squadron (Wick)
No. 521 Squadron (Docking)
No. 1403 Flight (Gibraltar)

Test Establishments and other units which flew Hampdens

A&AEE; RAE; CFS; TDU; CGS; Air Transport Auxiliary; Telecommunications Flying Unit; Bombing Trials Unit; Station Flight, Farnborough; No. 5 OTU; No. 14 OTU; No. 16 OTU; No. 25 OTU; No. 5 BGS; No. 10 BGS; No. 1 Air Armament School; No. 1 TTU; No. 5 Group Training Flight; No. 5 AOS; No. 3 OAFU; No. 4 OAFU; No. 3 Overseas Aircraft Preparation Unit; No. 4 FPP; No. 16 FPP; No. 12 MU

Establishments and Units which used Handley Page Herefords

No. 185 Squadron (Cottesmore); A&AEE; RAE; Napier & Sons; CFS; ATA; SD Flight; TDU; No. 3 FPP; No. 1 AAS; No. 5 BGS; No. 5 AOS; No. 5 AGS; No. 5 Signals School; No. 5 OTU; No. 14 OTU; No. 16 OTU (Upper Heyford); No. 25 OTU

Left: Several features of the Handley Page H.P.47 K2773, seen here, were used in the company's twin-engine H.P.52 design. (Author's collection)

Right: The prototype H.P.52, K4240, in overall grey-green gloss and sporting a white number 8 on its tail-boom for the July 1936 SBAC show at Hatfield.

Left: The H.P.52 prototype takes to the air from Radlett in July 1936. It incorporates a modified Heyford biplane-type ventral gun turret. Note the sheet aluminium covering the nose section for security purposes. (MAP)

edge of each outer wing panel. These, like the hinged flaps, were actuated hydraulically. Except for the fabric-covered flaps and ailerons, the wing surfaces had a flush-riveted stressed-skin metal covering.

Twin fins and rudders and a cantilever monoplane tailplane comprised the all-metal empennage, which was fitted at the extreme end of the fuselage boom. The fins and tailplane had a metal stressed skin, while the rudders and elevators were fabric covered. A rearwards-retracting Handley Page landing gear with cross-braced twin oleo legs was installed, the wheels

being fully enclosed in the engine nacelles when retracted. The Dowty tailwheel was also retractable, but part of the wheel remained exposed beneath the extreme rear fuselage boom.

The choice of suitable engines for the new bomber initially put the Handley Page team in a dilemma. Owing to the Geneva tare weight limitations still being under discussion, a favourable solution appeared to be the steam-cooled Rolls-Royce Goshawk powerplant with its acceptable power-to-weight ratio. However, the complex steam condensing apparatus

required by the Goshawk convinced Handley Page that it would do better to consider Bristol air-cooled radial engines such as the Mercury, Perseus or Pegasus. On the other hand, if more powerful engines were fitted in the H.P.52, although the performance required by B.9/32 would be greatly improved, such an installation was bound to exceed the proposed Geneva weight limit. Then, in June 1934, with the Geneva Conference still in stalemate over the issue, Britain scrapped her tare-weight restrictions. This allowed the Air Staff to increase the required maximum range of B.9/32 to 1,500 miles (2,414km). It also meant that Handley Page was now able to accept Bristol's P.E.5-SM Pegasus, a new version of the radial with two-speed supercharging which would later be produced as the Pegasus XVIII.

Although a mock-up H.P.52 had been completed at Cricklewood in the summer of 1933, it was to be three years before the prototype, K4240, was ready to fly. During that time much development and updating of detail design was undertaken, but the aircraft's overall profile was unchanged. It was completed in the spring of 1936 with two early-type P.E.5S(a) Pegasus engines driving three-blade de Havilland variable-pitch propellers. On 21 June 1936 Handley Page chief test pilot Major J. L. H. B. Cordes took K4240 into the air on its maiden flight.

Manufacturer's trials were followed at the end of June by the new bomber's appearance at the annual RAF Display at Hendon, painted a nondescript glossy grey-green with its New Types Park number 8 in white on its nose. The aircraft then flew to Hatfield to appear in the SBAC trade show, the display number 8 having

been transferred to the tail boom, aft of the roundel. For these public appearances the H.P.52's angular glazed nose was covered with sheet aluminium fairings as a security measure to prevent unauthorised persons viewing the interior. On 6 July K4240 was among new types of military aircraft on display at the A&AEE, Martlesham Heath, for a review by HM King Edward VIII, but by 23 July flight trials were under way again at Radlett. A further visit was made to Martlesham at the end of that month for speed trials, by which time the security nose sheeting had been removed, the glazed panels remaining until a suitable turret or gun mounting could be provided. The A&AEE trials proved promising, with a recorded top speed of 265mph (426km/h), although gross weight had risen to 16,000lb (7,258kg). This was well in excess of the original B.9/32 requirements, but on the credit side the bomb load had also increased and would eventually total 4,000lb (1,814kg).

Teething troubles did occur during the flight testing of K4240. For example, on 5 November 1936 the main landing gear collapsed after touchdown owing to an indicator circuit fault. The indicator had shown green, signifying that the main wheels were locked down, but turned red only after K4240 flopped on its belly and dug up some turf. On board with Cordes was flight observer R. S. Stafford, who wittily remarked about a smell of grass permeating the aircraft's interior. Once a smashed main wheel, the starboard engine and a bent propeller had been replaced, K4240 was soon airborne again, but while flying over Elstree on a test flight in January 1937 a second incident occurred. The new starboard engine's reduction gear and propeller broke away, striking the fuselage just aft of the pilot's cockpit and dropping to smoulder in a ploughed field below. Fortunately no one was hurt either in the air or on the ground, and after that no further problems arose. During February K4240 was flown to the RAE at Farnborough for vibration tests, and later, from July to September 1937, handling trials were carried out at Martlesham. The aircraft then returned to Radlett for minor modifications.

Meanwhile, the problem of suitable defensive armament for the Hampden (the name bestowed on the H.P.52 at the end of 1936) still remained. In 1936 it had been planned to fit a Boulton Paul remotely-controlled gun in the rear fuselage, and, indeed, alterations to design of the tail unit were undertaken during construction of the prototype. This involved lengthening the tail boom end and dividing the original one-piece elevator into two halves located each side of the boom. But this idea was abandoned in November 1937 and the single elevator reinstated. It was then decided to install a single Vickers 'K' 0.303in (7.7mm) machine-gun on a moveable mounting, housed within a more rounded and glazed position, in place of the old ventral 'dustbin' turret.

This modified ventral gun housing was introduced on the second prototype, L7271, which appeared in the spring of 1937 as the H.P.53. It was originally designed to meet a Swedish Air Force (Flygvapnet) order for a twin-engine coastal patrol aircraft equipped with an interchangeable landing gear enabling wheel, float or ski operations. The Swedish aircraft differed from the Hampden prototype not only in its landing gear, but in equipment and armament, which included a 20mm nose-mounted Bofors gun and an 8mm Colt machine-gun in the dorsal position as rear defence. An externally carried torpedo was to be the main offensive weapon, and power was to be provided by Bristol Pegasus II radial engines in short-chord Townend-ring cowlings built under licence in Sweden.

An order for two H.P.53s was initially placed by the Flygvapnet, but work was undertaken on only one machine while negotiations regarding the equipment installation took place. In the event Bristol Pegasus XX engines were fitted to facilitate flight trials in England, but early in 1937 Handley Page proposed that Sweden purchase standard production Hampdens, which could then be fitted out to Swedish requirements after delivery. This idea was accepted by the Swedish authorities and, instead of the H.P.53, they took delivery of the fifth production Hampden powered by Bristol Pegasus XXIV engines but not, as requested, fitted with dual controls. It underwent load tests at Heston in September 1938, weighing 18,000lb (8,164kg) gross, and on 24 September, with the serial I-90, flew to Sweden wearing that country's triple-crown national markings. It flew with the Flygvapnet as a P.5 until 1945, when it became an electronics equipment test-bed with SAAB as SE-APD, finally being withdrawn on 17 November 1947. This was the only Hampden used in Sweden, an updated financial agreement between the Swedish Government and Handley Page having cancelled the second aircraft originally ordered.

Meanwhile, Britain's Air Ministry agreed to purchase the H.P.53 on 28 May 1937 so that it could be used as the Dagger-Hampden prototype. This engine/airframe combination resulted from Air Min-

Below: Handley Page chief test pilot Major Cordes runs up the Pegasus engines of the first production Hampden, L4032, before a test flight in June 1936. (Author's collection)

istry concern that Bristol might not be able to fulfil the demand for Pegasus XVIII engines in the specified time. It was therefore decided that, as an alternative, 1,000hp (746kW) sixteen-cylinder H-type Napier Dagger VIII in-line engines would be installed in Hampdens produced by Short & Harland in a new shadow factory on Queen's Island, Belfast.

Thus the one-off H.P.53 became the Dagger-Hampden prototype, L7271, which first flew from Radlett on 1 July 1937, powered by two Bristol Pegasus XX radial engines and piloted by Cordes. This aircraft, resplendent in an overall polished natural metal finish, differed from the Hampden prototype in a number of details. The glazed nose was wider, with a slightly smoother and more rounded profile (it had been intended to install a Frazer-Nash turret in this position), the pitot head was transferred from a mounting above and aft of the cockpit to a location beneath the fuselage, and a streamlined ventral gun position, similar that of production Hampdens, was incorporated. However, the dorsal gun position retained the shallow sliding canopy originally designed for a Swedish gun mounting. After flying over the SBAC trade exhibition on its initial flight, L7271 completed its handling trials on 6 July at a gross weight of 11,412lb (5,176kg). It underwent a short spell of performance trials at RAE Farnborough before flying to Short & Harland at Belfast for conversion into the prototype Dagger-Hampden. This lengthy mouthful was dropped in February 1938 when the name Hereford Mk. I was officially adopted, only the prototype Hereford retaining the H.P.53 designation of the original Swedish prototype. Subsequent pro-

duction Herefords would be akin to Hampdens, being designated H.P.52s.

Despite the poor defensive armament of the Hampden, which could not be fitted with any available design of powered gun turret, the Air Ministry was satisfied that the aircraft's low-drag fuselage greatly enhanced its manoeuvrability and performance. So much so that within six weeks of the successful initial trials of Hampden prototype K4240, a production contract was awarded to Handley Page for 180 of the new bombers to be built in accordance with updated Specification B.30/36. At the same time a Ministry instruction was sent to Short & Harland for the production of 100 H.P.52 bombers to Specification B.44/36, in which alternative power units in the form of 24-cylinder H-type Napier Daggers were to be installed. The revised specifications resulted in production Hampdens and Herefords differing in a number of respects from the two prototypes. Two 1,000hp (746kW) Bristol Pegasus XVIII radials with two-speed superchargers were installed in the Hampden, while in both types the nose glazing featured a revised and nicely curved Perspex moulding incorporating an optically flat bomb aiming panel. Detail improvements were made to the ventral gun location, and a new raised dorsal gun position of semicircular shape included a hinged cupola which pushed back over the gunner's head when the gun was to be fired.

A rapid and cost-effective method of construction was used by Handley Page, following studies of assembly lines in the USA. Developed as the split-assembly technique, all components were sub-assembled and arrived for integration on the final production line, a system which greatly speeded up the roll-out of completed aircraft. In the case of the Hampden, each fuselage side was completed in its jig before being moved

Below: The second production Hampden, L4033, at the A&AEE in 1939. (MAP)

to stands where installation of internal equipment took place. At this stage the standard offensive and defensive armament for the Hampden I comprised two forward-firing 0.303in (7.7mm) Vickers 'K' machine-guns, one hand-operated from the nose and stowable when not in use, and one fixed to fire from port ahead of the cockpit, this gun being operated fighter fashion by a firing button on the control column. Rear defence consisted of two 0.303in (7.7mm) Vickers 'K' guns, one each in the ventral and dorsal positions. A maximum bomb load of 4,000lb (1,814kg) was carried in a bay stretching from below the cockpit to a point just ahead of the ventral gun position. Two 2,000lb (907kg) or four 500lb (226kg) bombs could be carried, and there was provision for two extra 500lb (226kg) bombs on underwing racks outboard of the engine nacelles, these reducing the cruising speed by 8mph (13km/h). Inevitably the aircraft's gross weight had risen, and now totalled 21,000lb (9,526kg), which in turn necessitated the fitting of larger wheels to obviate problems in operating from RAF grass airfields. Thus the Hampden's tare weight of 11,780lb (5,343kg) was nearly twice the original Geneva weight limitation associated with Specification B.9/32.

The first two production Hampdens, L4032 and L4033, were ready for their initial flights in mid-June 1938. There was a noted increase in wing dihedral to 6.5°, as opposed to 2.75° on the prototype, to improve lateral stability. On 21 June the first production Hampden made its initial flight from Radlett, piloted by Major Cordes. Three days later it was officially named

Right: The first production Hampden with Major Cordes at the controls in June 1936. Note the improved crew positions and increased outer dihedral compared with the prototype. (Author's collection)

Below: The Hampden production line at Radlett in 1939. The nearest aircraft is L4075, which went first to No. 50 Squadron, then Nos. 16 and 14 OTUs before being struck off charge on 7 March 1944. (MAP)

Hampden by Viscountess Hampden in a ceremony at Radlett, after which it flew a series of manufacturer's trials at Radlett until August. It was joined by the second production Hampden, L4033, and delivered to the A&AEE at Martlesham for acceptance trials. Recorded performance figures included a speed of 265mph (426km/h) at 15,000ft (4,724m), a cruising speed of 167mph (269km/h), a range of 1,990 miles (3,203km) with a 2,000lb (907kg) bomb load, and 870 miles (1,400km) carrying a maximum bomb load. The incorporation of advanced slat gear allowed a landing speed of only 73mph (117km/h), enhancing the Hampden's handling qualities, while the Hampden's 980ft (298m)/min initial climb rate was better than that of its contemporaries.

The third production Hampden, L4034, was delivered to the CFS at Upavon on 8 August 1938 for handling trials. It was transferred to No. 49 Squadron at RAF Scampton on 20 September, where it was joined by Hampdens L4039 and L4046. By November this unit, part of the newly formed No. 5 Group of RAF Bomber Command, was fully Hampden equipped. In the following month No. 83 Squadron, also at Scampton, became an all-Hampden unit, and No. 50 Squadron was fully equipped with the type by the end of December. Two Hampdens, L4035 and L4037, joined L4033 at Martlesham for Service trials, which included developing Lorenz blind-flying equipment for use in the type.

In 1938 the important decision was made to subcontract some Hampden production to comply with the RAF's re-equipment and expansion programme. English Electric of Preston, which had not built an aeroplane since its Kingston flying boats of 1926, received an initial contract for 75 H.P.52 Hampden bombers in August 1938. A pattern aircraft, L4207, was delivered to the company, and the first Preston-built Hampden, P2062, flew from Samlesbury on 22 February 1940, piloted by J. D. Rose. Four subsequent batches brought the total of Hampdens produced by English Electric to 770, the last, AT260, being delivered on 15 March 1942. Four Hampdens, L4208–L4211, went to Canada as pattern aircraft for Canadian Associated Aircraft Ltd (CAA), which was to produce Hampdens at its two plants in Malton, Ontario, and St Hubert, Quebec Province. An initial contract for 80 Hampdens (P5298–P5436) was split equally between both sites, St Hubert building P5298–P5337 and Malton P5338–P5346, P5386–P5400 and P5421–P5436. A further 80 Hampdens ordered from

Above: A Hampden of No. 44 Squadron, Bomber Command, Waddington, in pre-September 1939 coding. This unit's code was changed from JW to KM to confuse enemy intelligence. (MAP)

CAA (AJ988–AJ999 and AN100–AN167) brought total Canadian production to 160, all completed by mid-1942. Of these Hampdens, 84 were ferried across the Atlantic via Iceland and Aldergrove, Northern Ireland, to RAF Finningley, Yorkshire, where No. 5 Group Bomber Command's Group pool squadrons, Nos. 7 and 76 (later No. 16 OTU) were based. From there, Hampdens were distributed as required among No. 5 Group's squadrons at Waddington (Nos. 44 and 50), Scampton (Nos. 49 and 83), Hemswell (Nos. 61 and 144), Evanton and Cottesmore (No. 106 Reserve), and Cottesmore (No. 185 Reserve). Some also flew with No. 420 Squadron (Waddington) from January to August 1942 before being replaced by Wellington IIIs.

The other 76 CAA-built Hampdens were retained in Canada for use by the RCAF, most being delivered to No. 32 OTU at Patricia Bay, British Columbia. Hampdens at this training establishment underwent a gruelling time, being used for crew training, lengthy day and night navigation exercises over water and torpedo dropping practice. The attrition rate was high, with losses of two or three aircraft per month owing to pilot inexperience, mechanical faults, engine failures, extreme weather conditions on long navigation flights and, sometimes, control problems. The last cause was related to the Hampden's tendency to swing when taking off, combined with an occasional reluctance to 'unstick'. It was also liable to yaw badly during a circuit and, if on a climbing turn at low speed and altitude, one wing would drop and a yawing dive ensue, often too late for recovery. But in the hands of experienced pilots the Hampden generally proved to be reliable and successful in its class. In the event, and to boost numbers at No. 32 OTU, twenty ex-RAF Hampdens were flown across the Atlantic in a reverse ferry

operation. By the end of 1944 Hampdens had ceased flying with No. 32 OTU, all of the remaining 46 machines being sent to Sea Island, Vancouver, for breaking up.

Meanwhile, concern had arisen over the continuity of the supply of Pegasus engines to Canada, owing to the increasing threat from German U-boats in the Atlantic. As a shortage of engines would impede the delivery of Canadian-built Hampdens to Britain, it was decided to test alternative powerplants for the Hampden. Two Hampdens had 1,100hp (820kW) Wright Cyclone GR1820-G102A radials installed, the first production aircraft, L4032, having two fitted at RAE Farnborough and X3115 (English Electric-built) being similarly modified and sent to the A&AEE at Boscombe Down for tests as the H.P.62 Hampden Mk. II. In the event there was no interruption in the supply of Pegasus engines, and X3115 was reconverted into a standard Pegasus-powered Hampden I before serving with No. 408 'Goose' Squadron, RCAF. Hampden L4032 remained with the RAE until May 1941, when it became instructional airframe 2711M.

In the meantime, Short & Harland at Belfast completed its contract for 100 Herefords (L6002–L6101) on 8 June 1940, aircraft L6011, L6018–L6020, L6049, L6055, L6069, L6076, L6080, L6085, L6089, L6090 and L6096 being converted to Hampden Is either before or after leaving the production line. The first production Hereford, L6002, had made its initial flight on 17 May 1939 but, together with the second pro-

Above: Hampden L4135 of No. 144 Squadron, Hemswell, has early 1939 coding, NV being changed that September to PL. The unit later moved to North Luffenham and Leuchars. (MAP)

duction machine, L6003, it did not arrive at the A&AEE at Martlesham Heath until August. The Napier Dagger VIII produced 955hp (712kW) at 4,200rpm at sea level and 1,000hp (746kW) at 4,200rpm at 8,750ft (2,667m). Weighing 11,700lb (5,307kg) empty and 17,800lb (8,074kg) loaded, the Hereford had a slight edge on the Hampden, with a top speed of 265mph (426km/h) at 15,500ft (4,724m) and a cruising speed of 172mph (276km/h). But the Hereford's Achilles' heel proved to be its engines, which constantly over-

heated and were notorious for their excessive noise level, factors which had manifested themselves earlier in H.P.53 prototype L7271. Consequently Herefords did not equip first-line operational units, but nine machines (L6005, '7, '8, '11, '12, '16, '25, '52 and '70) were allocated as a Flight of No. 185 Squadron at Cottesmore in August 1939 to fly alongside their Hampdens. (As already mentioned, Hereford L6011 was converted to a Hampden.) However, this unit merged into No. 14 OTU in April 1940, but not before a lone Hereford had flown the type's only operational mission with No. 185 Squadron's Hampdens (No. 185

Below: Hampden L4129 of No. 144 Squadron visits RAF Harwell late in 1938. (Mrs M. Hunt)

Above: Hampden P1228/ZN-L of No. 106 Squadron, Coningsby, in 1941. It failed to return from a raid on 1 December 1941. (MAP)

Squadron was to re-form as a fighter unit in Malta with Hawker Hurricanes in May 1941).

Despite the Hereford's shortcomings, a further batch of 50 (N9055–N9106) was ordered from Short & Harland in 1940 and delivered between June and July of that year. Of this batch, eleven were converted to Hampdens (N9062, '64, '65, '70, '80, '86, '90, '96, '101, '105 and '106), and several later became instructional airframes. Other Herefords were used by various OTUs, AOSs, BGSs, Air Armament Schools, the AGS, the CFS, the CGS and Special Duty Flight, No. 16 OTU at Upper Heyford receiving its first Hereford on 7 May 1940. Once the Hereford contract had been completed, Short & Harland continued in similar vein by manufacturing a large quantity of Hampden components for the repair of damaged aircraft.

At the war's outbreak on 3 September 1939, No. 5 Group of Bomber Command contained ten Hampden squadrons, of which six were fully operational, two reserve and two Group pool units. The total number of Hampdens then available was 212 (all Radlett-built), and the type was considered suitable for both day and night operations, although the original requirement did not include nocturnal duties. Initial operations comprised daylight armed reconnaissance sorties against German shipping. On 4 September No. 83 Squadron's Hampdens were sent to attack enemy warships in the Schillig Roads, but owing to very poor visibility this mission was aborted.

The futility of sending Hampdens on daylight sorties became apparent on 29 September, when eleven aircraft from Hemswell based No. 144 Squadron were sent to reconnoitre the Heligoland Bight. The bombers flew in two formations of five and six, the first, led by Wing Commander J. C. Cunningham, taking off at 0650, and the second following ten minutes

later under Squadron Leader W. H. J. Lindley. Not one aircraft from Cunningham's formation returned; all five were shot down by Bf 109s of I and III/JG26, but not before two of the German fighters had been hit by the Hampdens' gunners and forced to ditch. Their pilots were picked up by a German patrol boat, as were two British airmen. The Hampdens lost were L4134 (Wing Commander Cunningham), L4126 (Flying Officer R. D. Baugham), L4127 (Flying Officer N. C. Beck), L4132 (Pilot Officer R. M. Coste) and L4121 (Flying Officer J. T. B. Sadler). In the meantime Squadron Leader Lindley's section came upon two German destroyers, the *Bruno Heidemann* and *Paul Jacobi*, steaming in line astern at about 20kt. The six Hampdens prepared to approach their targets at only 300ft (91.4m), but the destroyers' evasive manoeuvres and heavy flak prevented three of the aircraft attacking. The other three managed to drop bombs, but without success. Lindley's Hampden suffered flak damage, and one crew member, Sergeant Baker, was wounded. However, all six Hampdens in Lindley's formation returned safely to base.

By December Bomber Command had decided that its Wellingtons and Hampdens were too vulnerable to Luftwaffe fighters on daylight operations, and they were switched to night operations. Initially the Hampdens joined Whitleys of No. 4 Group on 'security patrols' to help prevent Luftwaffe seaplanes laying magnetic mines near the British coast. As Bomber Command was not allowed to bomb German land targets at that time, No. 5 Group's Hampdens were limited to attacking waterborne flarepaths used for the guidance of German minelaying seaplanes. During 71 of these anti-minelaying sorties flown by the Hampdens no aircraft were lost, and their attacks undoubtedly hampered the minelaying seaplanes' activities.

On 6 March 1940 No. 5 Group was ordered to send its Hampdens on leaflet dropping raids over Germany, accompanying Whitleys from No. 4 Group and some Wellingtons from No. 3 Group. Known as 'Nickels', these missions involved unloading thousands of propaganda pamphlets over German cities and towns. By the end of 1940 Hampdens alone had flown 123 such raids for the cost of one aircraft missing. Another task allotted to Hampdens was the laying of mines at sea. The RAF began its sea-mining operations during the winter of 1939–40, the activity being pioneered by No. 5 Group's Hampdens. Minelaying should have been the province of Coastal Command, but at that time

Hampdens were the only aircraft capable of carrying the Mk. I modified naval mine, Britain's first magnetic type, although Bristol Beauforts and Fairey Albacores would shortly be able to perform the task. Thus Hampdens were instrumental in laying extensive patterns of mines in Baltic, Danish and coastal sea routes, operations calling for very precise targeting accuracy, minelaying from a height of 300ft (91.4m) and the probability of facing heavy flak from flak ships and coastal guns.

British magnetic mines were first 'sown' off the Danish coast on the night of 13/14 April 1940 by Hampdens from Nos. 44, 49, 50, 61 and 114 Squadrons, a few days after the German invasion of Norway. Codenamed 'Gardening', the RAF's minelaying programme was directed at laying the weapons in areas which were taboo to Allied ships. Later, RAF minelaying operations extended from the Danish and Norwegian coasts to stretch along the whole German-occupied coast to Lorient. By the end of 1940 No. 5 Group's Hampdens had flown 1,209 minelaying oper-

Below: A pair of Hampdens of No. 44 Squadron, Waddington, in 1940. Nearest is AE257/KM-X, and behind is AE202/K-KM. (Rolls-Royce plc, Bristol)

ations, during which more than 700 mines were laid, but 21 aircraft failed to return from these missions. This was a casualty rate of less than 1.9 per cent, which, in cold figures, was statistically satisfying. Although considered less hazardous than operations over Germany, minelaying in enemy waters was nevertheless a difficult task.

Hampdens reverted to daylight operations during the Norwegian campaign, but again proved vulnerable to German fighters. On 12 April 1940, for example, a dozen Hampdens from Nos. 44 and 50 Squadrons tried to attack an enemy warship at Kristiansand South. Luftwaffe Bf 109s quickly appeared, and four Hampdens of No. 50 Squadron and two from No. 44 Squadron went down. Pilot Officer M. G. Homer, flying Hampden L4074, had a lucky escape when a Bf 109's cannon shell passed through the upper fuselage just behind his head and failed to explode. Such encounters again revealed that the Hampden's weakness lay in its puny defensive armament.

The AOC of No. 5 Group, Air Commodore A. T. Harris (later Air Chief Marshal Sir Arthur Harris, C-in-C Bomber Command), decided to cut through 'red tape' and improve the Hampden's rear armament. He requested Alfred Rose & Son of Gainsborough, Lincolnshire, to manufacture mountings for twin Vickers 'K' guns to be housed in the dorsal and ventral positions. This somewhat improved the Hampden's rear defence, but the two retained forward guns (one fixed and one moveable) were of little use in aerial combat. It is perhaps not so well known that some Hampdens of Nos. 44 and 49 Squadrons were employed temporarily as nightfighters when the Luftwaffe intensified its night 'blitz' against British cities late in 1940. Defensive night patrols were carried out by these Hampdens, which had a moveable machine-gun fired from a beam position in the fuselage by a gunner. No successes were recorded by these makeshift nightfighters, and they soon reverted to the bombing role.

Meanwhile, on the night of 19/20 March 1940, Hampdens of No. 5 Group joined No. 4 Group's Whitleys in making the first British air raid against a land target in the Second World War. The target was the minelaying-seaplane base at Hornum on the Isle of Sylt. Twenty Hampdens took part, fifteen bombing the target, three failing to find it and two being forced back early with faulty engines. Two months later, on 10 May, Germany launched its offensive against the Low Countries, and on the following night of 11/12 May eighteen Hampdens of No. 5 Group and an equal number of Whitleys of No. 4 Group made the first major concentrated attack by RAF bombers on the German mainland. This time, rail communications were the main targets, with Munchen Gladbach a primary objective in efforts to stem enemy advances toward Holland.

After the fall of France, Hitler's threat to invade England became real as Channel and North Sea ports

became crammed with German invasion barges for carrying troops, tanks and guns to Britain's coasts. These ports became Bomber Command's priority targets, and No. 5 Group's Hampdens played a major part in attacking them, one such target being Antwerp. It was over this city on the night of 15/16 September 1940 that eighteen-year-old Sergeant John Hannah, a wireless operator/air-gunner of No. 83 Squadron and crew member of Hampden P1355, won the Victoria Cross for outstanding gallantry. Hannah's aircraft was hit by enemy flak, which ruptured the fuel tanks, blew holes in the fuselage and caused fire to sweep into the Hampden's interior, engulfing the rear gunner's cockpit and navigator's position. The intense heat was causing the floor of the gunner's cockpit to melt, but Hannah forced his way aft to extinguish the flames, realising that the rear gunner had baled out. After managing to douse the fire amid exploding ammunition, blinding heat and fumes, using two fire extinguishers and finally his log book to beat out the flames, Hannah, although badly burned, returned to the front of the aircraft to find that the navigator had also baled out. Although he was in terrible pain, he passed the navigator's log and map to the pilot, whom he then assisted in nursing the crippled Hampden back to base.

Another Victoria Cross was won by Flight Lieutenant R. A. B. Learoyd of No. 49 Squadron in Hampden P4403. On the night of 12/13 August 1940 Learoyd was taking part in an attack by ten Hampdens from Nos. 49 and 83. Squadrons on an aqueduct carrying the important Dortmund-Ems canal. Five aircraft acted as decoys by bombing nearby lock gates and boats while the other five, including Learoyd's, attacked the aqueduct. This important target was heavily defended by two lines of anti-aircraft guns, and to reach and bomb the aqueduct the Hampdens were forced to fly the gauntlet of these guns. For this attack they carried delayed-action bombs, following each other in at two-minute intervals. In the murderous crossfire the first two aircraft were immediately shot down and two others received hits and serious damage, leaving Learoyd in P4403 to go in. He did so by diving through a hail of flak and attacking from 150ft (45.7m), his bombs badly damaging the aque-

duct and closing the canal for ten days. The damage suffered by Learoyd's aircraft included large holes in the starboard wing and a wrecked hydraulic system resulting in non-operational flaps and landing gear. Nevertheless, Learoyd returned safely to base at Scampton, where he made a successful belly landing and his crew walked away from the Hampden practically unscathed.

On the night of 1/2 July 1940 the first 2,000lb (907kg) bomb to be dropped on an enemy target by Bomber Command was released by Hampden L4070 during a raid on the German battlecruiser *Scharnhorst* as she lay in dry dock at Keil. Piloted by Flying Officer Guy Gibson (later Wing Commander Gibson, VC, of Dambuster fame), the Hampden made several dives at the target from 6,000ft (1,828m) in poor visibility, dropping its large semi-armour-piercing (SAP) bomb on the sixth attempt. But the bomb 'unshackled' too late, missed the warship and fell on Keil itself. The following month, on the night of 25/26 August 1940, Hampdens made their debut over Berlin during the RAF's first attack on Germany's capital. Hampden units taking part included Nos. 44, 49, 50, 61 and 83 Squadrons. Three months later, on 16/17 December, Bomber Command made its first 'area' attack on an industrial target by sending a force, including Hampdens, to bomb Mannheim.

During the spring of 1941 Bomber Command switched from attacking enemy industrial targets and concentrated much of its attention on the port of Brest, where the German warships *Scharnhorst*, *Gneisenau* and, later, *Prinz Eugen*, were docked. During one raid in May a Hampden of No. 44 Squadron scored a direct hit on the *Gneisenau* with a 2,000lb (907kg) SAP bomb. In July *Scharnhorst* moved to La Pallice, some 250 miles (2,509km) south, but all of these German capital ships were constantly attacked by Bomber Command. On 24 July a daylight attack was made on

Above: A TB.1 torpedo-bomber variant of the Hampden, AN127/XA-Y of No. 489 Squadron (Torpedo), RAF Coastal Command in 1942. (MAP)

Below: Hampden TB.1 torpedo-bomber AT137/UB-T of No. 455 (Australian) Squadron, RAF Coastal Command, circa 1941–42. (Aviation Photo News)

Brest by a force of Wellingtons, Hampdens and three RAF Boeing B-17C Flying Fortress Is. The raiders claimed six hits on *Gneisenau*, but two Hampdens failed to return. In a further effort to stop the three enemy warships reaching the open sea, on 13 December 1941 No. 44 Squadron sent three of its Hampdens out unescorted and in daylight to lay mines at the mouth of Brest Harbour (by then *Scharnhorst* had returned to Brest). The harbour defences were very fierce, and one Hampden, flown by Wing Commander S. T. Misselbrook, was shot down, and a second, piloted by Sergeant Hackney, was prevented from laying its mines in the correct position because of inadequate cloud cover. The remaining Hampden, AE202 piloted by Squadron Leader Burton-Giles, managed to lay its mines according to plan, but was hit several times by the German anti-aircraft defences. A wingtip was shot away and an aileron damaged, holes were blown through the wing, an engine fairing was ripped off, a propeller was damaged, one rudder was destroyed and a main wheel was punctured. But despite such punishment the Hampden limped home to base.

Hampdens continued to form part of Bomber Command's strategic night bombing offensive against Germany and targets in occupied Europe, and in the first week of March 1942 they participated in the well-known raid on the Renault works near Paris. This was the first time that Bomber Command employed the concept of concentrated attack in its proper sense, and led to the famous 1,000-bomber raids. The first of these was launched against Cologne on the night of 30/31 May 1942, and Hampdens were among the aircraft taking part. They also flew in the following two 1,000-bomber raids of mid-1942, but by then the Hampden was being phased out of Bomber Command as No. 5 Group received an increasing number of Lancasters. The last Hampden raid with Bomber Command took place on the night of 14/15 September 1942, when No. 408 'Goose' Squadron, RCAF, based at Balderton, raided Wilhelmshaven.

In addition to its strategic bombing activities, No. 5 Group also used its Hampdens on a number of night-intruder sorties. These were usually carried out against German shipping at sea, or searchlights and other suitable targets ashore. One very successful attack was made on the night of 3 November 1941 by Flight Lieutenant J. F. Craig, RNZAF, piloting Hampden AE309 of No. 144 Squadron. Patrolling near the Frisian Islands, Craig spotted a convoy of enemy ships through a break in the rain clouds and targeted the largest merchantman in a low-level attack. The vessel of some 10,000 tons (10,160 tonnes) was damaged and set ablaze, and it was later discovered that a high-ranking

German officer, Major-General Felix Varda, the head of Germany's western anti-aircraft system, was among those killed in the Hampden's attack. In April 1942 No. 144 Squadron was transferred to RAF Coastal Command, where Hampdens began another career in the torpedo-bombing role.

A torpedo-bomber derivative of the Hampden had been schemed in 1935 in response to Specification M.15/35; it was to be a shore-based twin-engine design with a gross weight of 13,600lb (6,169kg). Handley Page married the H.P.52 wings and tail unit to a fuselage of slightly greater width, sufficient to accommodate the largest air-launched torpedo and a power-operated dorsal turret. This tender was rejected by the Air Staff, who accepted Bristol's Type 152 Beaufort instead. However, the idea that torpedo-bombing could be the Hampden's forte was revived in 1941 by the RAE at Farnborough and put to Handley Page. It was found that an 18in (45.7cm) Mk. XII torpedo

Above: These Hampden TB.1s belong to No. 408 (Canadian) Squadron, RAF Coastal Command, formed at Lindholme in June 1941. The first aircraft is AT413. (MAP)

could be accommodated in the existing Hampden bomb bay. This necessitated using an adaptor for the 2,000lb (907kg) bomb shackles, and resulted in the torpedo protruding 3½in (8.9cm) beneath the bottom line of the bomb bay with the doors closed. Consequently the centre bomb doors were removed, the hinged side panels fixed open, internal alterations were made to the rear of the bay, and the ventral gun position fairing was modified. In addition to a torpedo, the converted Hampden could carry two 500lb (226kg) bombs on underwing racks and, weighing

Below: Handley Page H.P.53 Hereford prototype L7271 with Napier Dagger engines, early-type front canopy and sliding dorsal gun position. Note the overall shiny metal finish. (MAP)

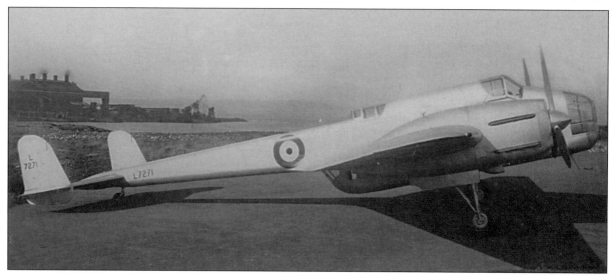

Above: The first production Hereford, L6002, used by maker Short & Harland of Belfast. It later became 3023M. (Author's collection)

23,500lb (10,659kg) gross, it had a range of 1,960 miles (3,154km).

During the spring of 1942 some half-dozen Hampdens underwent a series of torpedo aiming/dropping trials at the TDU, Gosport, among them L4037, L4182, L4211, P5388 and AT139. The type was accepted for Coastal Command service and designated Hampden TB Mk. I, a total of 144 being converted from Hampden bombers. One machine, N9106, had been the last Hereford rolled out at Short & Harland, subsequently being converted to a Hampden I and a TB.I in turn.

Below: The second production Hereford, L6003, was used at the A&AEE and by Napier, which produced its Dagger engines. (MAP)

Coastal Command Hampden TB.Is flew with the aforementioned No. 144 Squadron (ex-Bomber Command), No. 455 Squadron RAAF (ex-Bomber Command), No. 415 'Swordfish' Squadron RCAF (an ex-Beaufort unit) and No. 489 Squadron RNZAF (an ex-Blenheim IV unit).

In the first week of September 1942, 144 and 455 Squadrons sent sixteen Hampdens each to Russia as added protection for the North Russian convoys, especially PQ18. The Hampdens were destined for Vaenga airfield near Murmansk, where PQ18 was heading, but only 23 of the bombers arrived safely. Three of 144 Squadron's aircraft, P1344, P1273 and AT138, were shot down en route, one (AE310) forced-landed out of fuel, one (AE436) hit a Swedish mountain and another (AE356) was shot down accidentally by a Soviet Air Force Hurricane. Two Hampdens of No. 455 Squadron, AT109 and P5323, ran out of fuel and crash-landed, and a third, P5304,

Above: Hereford L6067 flew with No. 16 OTU at Upper Heyford in 1940. It crashed near Bicester on 1 August that year. (Author's collection)

Left: Herefords of No. 14 OTU (ex-No. 185 Squadron, a No. 5 Group Pool unit). The nearest aircraft is L6070/GL-A2. (MAP)

crashed in Sweden. After completing their Russian mission, Nos. 144 and 455 Squadrons' crews returned home, leaving their Hampdens to serve in the Soviet Air Force. All 23 Hampdens were transferred to the Russians and flew with the 3rd Squadron of the 24th Mine and Torpedo Aviation Regiment of the Northern Fleet. Four were lost in action in Russian service and nine were damaged, the remainder lasting only a short time, mainly through a lack of spares.

Coastal Command's Hampden TB.Is operated until 1943 and gave a good account of themselves, as can be judged from the tally of No. 489 Squadron, RNZAF, which alone sent 36,000 tons (36,576 tonnes) of enemy shipping to the bottom and damaged another 30,000 tons (30,480 tonnes). The operational careers

of the four Hampden TB.I squadrons ended on the following dates: No. 144, 18/19 January; No. 415, 23 September; No. 489, 26 October; and No. 455, 10 December. A detachment of the last unit, based at Sumburgh in the Shetlands, sank a German U-boat on 4 April 1943; by the end of the year it was being re-equipped with Beaufighters.

A number of Hampdens were updated to Met Mk. I meteorological reconnaissance standard and flew with Nos. 1403, 1404 and 1408 Flights (later Nos. 521, 517 and 519 Squadrons respectively), operating from Gibraltar and from Manston and Wick in the UK until the end of 1943. Two Hampdens are being restored in Canada and the UK at the time of writing. Hopefully they will find well earned places alongside the great aeroplanes of the Second World War.

Handley Page
Harrow

Although the aircraft featured here is the twin-engine Handley Page Harrow bomber of the late 1930s, as on several occasions in aviation history, nomenclature repeated itself. Handley Page had built a Harrow bomber in 1926, the H.P.31 Type E, albeit in prototype form only.

Intended to replace Blackburn's Dart, the Type E Harrow was an equal-span, single-engine biplane powered initially by a 470hp (350kW) Napier Lion V. It could carry either an 18in (45.7cm) torpedo or three 520lb (235.9kg) bombs. A 0.303in (7.7mm) Vickers machine-gun synchronised to fire through the propeller was provided for the pilot, and a 0.303in (7.7mm) Lewis gun was mounted on a Scarff ring in the rear cockpit. Two Harrow biplanes were produced, N205 and N206, both having interchangeable wheel and float undercarriages. Harrow N205 first flew on 24 April 1926, and N206 on 30 October. Built in response to Specification 21/23, the Harrow competed with the Avro Buffalo II and Blackburn Ripon, the winning contender being the Ripon. Aircraft N206 went into temporary storage before being used for wing-slot research, while N205 was updated to Mk. II standard with equal dihedral to upper and lower wings, an uprated Napier Lion XI (later XA), a slimmer nose and

retractable side radiators. For its seaplane trials at the Marine Aircraft Experimental Establishment (MAEE) at Felixstowe, N205 had twin floats fitted and was demonstrated to representatives from Argentina and Finland, but on 23 August 1928 it suffered tail damage and was struck off charge.

The origins of Handley Page's H.P.54 twin-engine Harrow bomber of 1936 can be traced back to Specification C.16/28, calling for a three-engine bomber-transport to replace the Handley Page Clive and Vickers Victoria. Handley Page responded with the H.P.43 prototype, J9833, on which work began in 1930. This was a large biplane with unstaggered, unequal-span wings braced by Warren-girder interplane struts. Three uncowled Bristol Pegasus IM3 radial engines were fitted, one in the upper centre section and two on the lower mainplanes. The aircraft had a monoplane tailplane with twin fins and rudders. Nose and tail gun positions were provided with

Below: This is the Handley Page Type E H.P.31 Harrow biplane bomber of 1926. Seen in Mk. II form, N205 was one of two built and has equal dihedral on upper/lower wings, an uprated Napier Lion engine, a revised nose and retractable side radiators. (MAP)

Above: The original Handley Page H.P.43 three-engine bomber-transport, J9833, with Bristol Pegasus engines. Note the Warren girder interplane struts and mudguards over the main wheels. (MAP)

Scarff gun rings, and an enclosed cockpit housed the pilot and navigator side-by-side and a wireless operator immediately behind them. The H.P.43 first flew on 21 June 1932, but subsequent test flights revealed a poor performance and control problems.

On 7 November 1933 plans were presented to the Air Ministry for a proposed monoplane conversion, the Handley Page H.P.51, in direct response to Specification C.26/31, issued after attempts to fulfil the requirements of C.16/28 had failed. The new specification called for a twin-engine bomber-transport monoplane particularly suited to tropical conditions. A gross weight limit of 18,000lb (8,164kg) was to include a military load of 3,050lb (1,383kg), capable of being carried over a range of 920 miles (1,480km), and the minimum cruising speed was set at 95mph (153km/h) at 10,000ft (3,048m).

Above: The original Handley Page H.P.43 three-engine bomber-transport, J9833, with Bristol Pegasus engines. Note the Warren girder interplane struts and mudguards over the main wheels. (MAP)

Two crew members in an enclosed cockpit were to act as pilot, navigator, wireless operator and bomb aimer, and gun positions were to be located in the nose and tail, each equipped with a 0.303in (7.7mm) Lewis machine-gun. There was to be provision to carry eight 250lb (114kg) bombs and eight 20lb (9kg) practice bombs. Other requirements included low-pressure, heavy-duty tyres, wheel brakes, a tailwheel, detachable wheel fairings or mudguards and buoyancy bags.

Handley Page designer Dr G. V. Lachmann based his cantilever monoplane wing on that of the earlier

HANDLEY PAGE HARROW MK. II DATA

Manufacturer
Handley Page Ltd, Radlett Aerodrome, Hertfordshire

Type
Five-seat heavy night bomber or 20-seat troop transport with a crew of three

Powerplant
Two 925hp (690kW) Bristol Pegasus XX air-cooled nine-cylinder radial engines

Performance
Maximum speed, 200mph (322km/h) at 10,000ft (3,050m). Cruising speed, 163mph (262km/h) at 15,000ft (4,570m). Initial climb, 710ft (216m)/min. Service ceiling, 22,800ft (6,950m). Range, 1,250 miles (2,012km)

Weights
Empty, 13,600lb (6,169kg). Loaded (maximum take-off), 23,000lb (10,433kg)

Dimensions
Span, 88ft 5in (26.97m). Length, 82ft 2in (25.04m). Height, 19ft 5in (5.92m). Wing area, 1,090sq ft (101.26sq m)

Armament
Four 0.303in (7.7mm) Lewis or Browning machine-guns, one each in nose and dorsal turrets and two in tail turret. Maximum bomb load, 3,000lb (1,361kg) carried internally

HANDLEY PAGE HARROW PRODUCTION

No prototype Harrow built, the first production machine, K6933, serving as

such (based on original H.P.51 troop transport)

Production order for 100 H.P.54 Harrows issued to Specification B.29/35. The first batch of 38 aircraft, K6933–K6970, built as Mk. Is at Radlett and delivered between June 1936 and July 1937. A second batch of 62 machines, K6971–K7032, built as Mk. IIs with Pegasus XX engines, followed. These were delivered between July and December 1937.

Tanker conversions for Flight Refuelling Ltd
K6933, became G-AFRG. To RCAF in 1939 and serialled 794
K7029, became G-AFRH. To RCAF in 1939 and cannibalised to keep 794 in service

H.P.47 general-purpose monoplane, K2773, built to Specification G.4/31. This aircraft had featured a fully slotted wing of 58ft (17.7m) span, with leading-and trailing-edge taper. Lachmann drew up a similar wing of 90ft (27.4m) span which he could marry to the H.P.43 fuselage and tail unit. An extra 31in (78cm) was added to the middle portion of the fuselage to allow for increased wing-root chord, and the twin fins and rudders were enlarged. Two Armstrong Siddeley Tiger II engines in long-chord Townend rings were to provide the power, and the H.P.43's serial, J9833, was retained for the H.P.51. By the end of 1934 J9833 was nearing completion in its monoplane form, with uprated Tiger IV engines, Lockheed hydraulic flap-operating equipment and a Tampier Bloctube engine control system.

In April 1935 the H.P.51 was ready at Radlett, Hertfordshire, the site acquired by Handley Page in 1929 for development of the company's new factory and airfield before moving from the old Cricklewood works. On 8 May the new bomber-transport took off on its initial flight in the hands of Handley Page's chief test pilot, Major J. L. Cordes. Performance and handling were greatly improved over the earlier biplane version, so much so that Handley Page decided to design a revised version, the H.P.54, intended as a production aircraft. It was thought that this layout would stand a good chance of winning the C.26/31 competition against Armstrong Whitworth's AW.23 and Bristol's Type 130. However, Major Cordes advised the adoption of a redesigned tail unit already drawn up by Lachmann but turned down by the Handley Page Board as an economy measure. This revised empennage was the result of wind-tunnel tests of a 1/32nd-scale model of the H.P.51 at Handley Page, followed by further tests at RAE Farnbor-

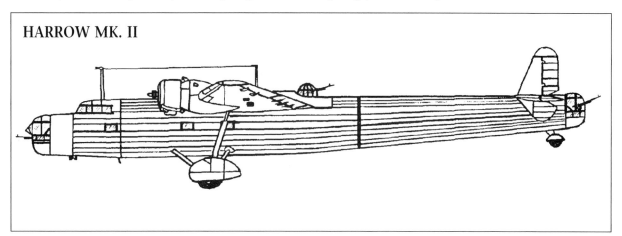

HARROW MK. II

K7027, became G-AFRL. Destroyed in German air attack on Ford, Sussex, 18 August 1940

RAF HARROW UNITS

No. 37 Squadron (Feltwell)
No. 75 Squadron (Driffield)
No. 93 Squadron (Middle Wallop)
No. 115 Squadron (Marham)
No. 214 Squadron (Feltwell)
No. 215 Squadron (Driffield)
No. 271 Squadron (Colerne, Doncaster and Down Ampney)

NB. No. 93 Squadron (Night Defence) was re-formed from No. 420 (LAM) Flight. Its Harrows were used for a time on minelaying duties. No. 271 Squadron was re-formed from No.

1680 Flight as a Harrow transport unit Examples of individual Harrows in RAF squadron service:
K7005, coded S-FJ, with No. 37 Squadron April 1937 to May 1939
K6947, coded 75-P (1937-style marking), with No. 75 Squadron September 1937 to July 1939
K7005, coded A-HN, with No. 93 Squadron December 1940 to June 1941 and used on LAM operations
K6962, coded M-BK, with No. 115 Squadron June 1937 to September 1939 (BK code introduced for 1938 Munich crisis)
K6988, coded J-UX, with No. 214 Squadron January 1937 to July 1939 (UX code introduced for 1938 Munich crisis)
K6937, coded C-BJ, with No. 271

Squadron May 1940 to 1945. This aircraft modified as a Sparrow with pointed nose, blanked-off tail turret; wore 1944 invasion stripes on wings and fuselage

For crew training, Harrows were employed as follows:
Nos. 2, 7, 8, 9 and 10 AOSs (Warmwell, Stormy Down, Evanton, Penrhos)
Nos. 7, 8, 9, 10 BGSs (same bases)
No. 8 Gunnery School (Evanton)
No 1 Air Armament School (Manby)
The Parachute Training School (Ringway)
No. 42 OTU (Andover)

NB. A number of Harrows were also attached to the RAE, Farnborough, and the A&AEE, Boscombe Down

ough, to determine the type's gliding properties when fitted with half-span slotted flaps. These, it was found, affected elevator response and made it possible for Lachmann to add the necessary refinements which would result in his new tail unit being adopted for the H.P.54.

To enable confirmation of the wind-tunnel tests by full-scale flight testing, the new tail was substituted for the original H.P.51 empennage, but additional external bracing was necessary and a new wooden elevator was built early in 1936. At the same time Bristol Pegasus III radials superseded the Tiger engines, and were fitted with four-bladed propellers. When first flown with the Pegasus IIIs early in September 1936, J9833 had its original tail, but the new tail unit was subsequently fitted. In the event, because it had been decided that the H.P.54 would replace ageing Vickers Virginias as an interim bomber crew trainer before becoming a transport, the H.P.51 was not entered in the C.26/31 competition, which was won by Bristol's Type 130 Bombay.

In its revised configuration the H.P.51 underwent numerous trials and equipment tests by the manufacturer before passing to the A&AEE at Martlesham Heath in January 1937 for performance trials. The following month it was transferred to the RAE, where further handling and acceptance trials were carried out. In May L9833 was used for radio equipment development trials, followed by five days in June over Salisbury Plain on troop-carrying exercises. It then flew with a fuel tanker installation at Ford, Sussex, with Flight Refuelling Ltd, but by October was back at the RAE for blind landing and artificial horizon trials. Further tests were undertaken with the Radio Flight on various equipment until November 1939, but although J9833 was still flying during January 1940, it was struck off charge soon afterwards.

Meanwhile, Dr Lachmann had been updating the original H.P.51 layout to produce the H.P.54. This design still employed H.P.51's tapered wing with slatted outer leading edges and trailing-edge flaps, but the fuselage was considerably altered. The length had been increased from 78ft 4in (23.9m) to 82ft 2in (25.04m), the cross-section improved by the use of stringers to produce a more oval shape, the nose and tail gun positions had been fitted with glazed turrets, and a new mid-upper turret was located above the wing. Then, owing to Government demands for over twenty extra bomber squadrons for its RAF expansion programme in May 1935, Handley Page received an 'off-the-drawing-board' order for 100 H.P.54s to be built as heavy night bombers to Specification B.29/35. This was, in fact, a stop-gap measure to provide a sufficient number of bombing aircraft in RAF service until squadrons could be equipped with modern types such as the Wellington and Whitley.

The name Harrow was adopted for the new bomber, and significantly it was the first production bomber for the RAF to wear the irregular dark earth and green camouflage pattern. There was no prototype Harrow as such, the first production machine, K6933, serving in this capacity. This aircraft made its initial flight from Radlett on 10 October 1936, piloted by Major Cordes. With its primary role now that of a heavy bomber, the Harrow required several structural modifications, an important one being to enable the aircraft to carry a 3,000lb (1,360kg) bomb load internally beneath the floor. This did not, however, have to detract from the Harrow's original ability to act as a

Above: The prototype/first production Handley Page H.P.54 Harrow heavy night bomber, K6933, at Radlett in October 1936. The front and rear gun turret positions were faired in at this stage. (Author's collection)

standby transport able to convey twenty fully-equipped troops.

The Harrow's high-set wing was built in three sections with sub-divisions. The D-section main spar carried the ribs and stringers, while duralumin flanges, tubular diagonals and vertical members formed an N truss which created a robust and torsionally rigid structure. The wing centre section, embodied in the top of the fuselage, carried the engine mountings at its outer extremities, to which the outer panels were attached. Handley Page slots were fitted along the outer leading edges of the wings, and slotted flaps located between the ailerons and fuselage on the trailing edges were activated by hydraulic jacks. Alclad skinning was employed forward of the main spar, fabric covering the after part of the mainplane surfaces.

The fuselage of the Harrow was constructed in three main portions. The nose was a duralumin monocoque structure with metal skinning, the centre portion was of steel-tube construction with bolted joints, and the rear section was a similar structure with welded joints. Internal struts and longerons were of steel, a light secondary structure of metal stringers forming the fuselage fairing. From the centre portion back the fuselage was fabric covered. Along the length of the fuselage an internal walkway linked crew positions. Below the floor of the centre portion was the bomb bay, in which could be carried the maximum 3,000lb (1,361kg) bomb load, the bombs being fused and dropped electrically by a Handley Page release gear. Four 0.303in (7.7mm) Vickers or Lewis machine-guns

comprised the initial defensive armament, these being mounted one each in nose, dorsal and tail cupolas.

The nose and tail positions initially had temporary fixed glazing, but after early production Harrows had appeared with their nose and tail gun positions covered in, power-operated turrets were installed in subsequent machines and retrospectively fitted to the earlier Harrows. The Hubbard nose and tail turrets had Frazer-Nash power controls, the turrets themselves being fixed while the guns traversed in a slit in the rotatable lower portion operated by a belt and end spools. Gun traverse and elevation was hydraulically operated, aiming was by means of a reflector sight, and the gun's weight was balanced by the seated gunner. For bomb-aiming a course-setting bomb sight was mounted above an optical flat panel protruding from the nose turret. These nose and tail turrets were produced as the Frazer-Nash FN14 and FN15 respectively. The manually-operated mid-upper cupola rotated with a mounting ring to which it was attached, and housed a single 0.303in (7.7mm) Lewis gun.

Of all-metal construction, the Harrow's empennage featured a metal-covered cantilever tailplane and fabric-covered elevators incorporating trim tabs. The twin fins, more triangular and rounded in profile than those of the H.P.51, were metal covered and had clip-on leading edges. The rudders were fabric covered and incorporated trim tabs. The main landing gear of the Harrow differed little from that of the H.P.51, but the Harrow's swivelling tailwheel was enclosed in a streamline fairing.

When the first Harrow, K6933, made its initial flights, both the nose and tail turrets were covered in and power was provided by two 850hp (634kW) Bristol Pegasus X radial engines, but when the second Harrow, K6934, first flew in January 1937, it had both FN turrets fitted and they housed Vickers 'K' guns.

Left: Handley Page Harrow prototype K6933 takes off from Radlett on its maiden flight, 10 October 1936. (Rolls-Royce plc, Bristol)

Above:: Harrow K6947 gets away from Radlett late in 1936. This machine was delivered to No. 37 Squadron at Feltwell. (MAP)

Two uprated 925hp (690kW) Pegasus XX radials had also been installed, which increased the top speed by 10mph (16km/h). Harrows K6933 and K6934 flew to Martlesham in November 1936 and January 1937 respectively, where various trials were undertaken. It was decided that some modifications were required, including a revised location for the navigator, a new blind-flying panel and better instrument lighting, a rest position for crew members, improved heating and air supply for the tail turret, an emergency exit for the pilot, increased oil tankage and the means to carry a 2,000lb (907kg) bomb.

In all, 38 Harrow Is powered by Pegasus X engines were delivered between June 1936 and July 1937, the remaining 62 (K6971–K7032) being produced by December that year as Mk. IIs. As well as having power-operated turrets, Harrow IIs had the Vickers and/or Lewis guns replaced by 0.303in (7.7mm) Brownings, and all were powered by Pegasus XX radials which gave a top speed of 200mph (321.8km/h) at 10,000ft (3,048m).

Left: The first Harrow with the initial fixed glazing fitted to nose and tail turrets. Harrows were the first RAF bombers to wear the then new irregular camouflage pattern. (MAP)

Eventually most Harrow Is had power-operated turrets fitted retrospectively, and in heavy-bomber mode carried a five-man crew consisting of the pilot, navigator/bomb-aimer, wireless operator/gunner, front gunner and tail gunner. The first six Harrow Is also had Pegasus XX engines installed later.

The first Harrow delivered to an RAF unit was K6935, which arrived at No. 214 Squadron's Scampton base on 13 January 1937, heralding replacement of the unit's Virginia biplanes. New Harrows were often collected from Handley Page's Radlett site by squadron pilots, familiarisation circuits of the aerodrome being a normal preliminary to the flight back to base. One such occasion proved the undoing of Harrow K6940. Flying very low on 25 March 1937, its wheels struck the roof of a carriage of a passing LMS express en route for Manchester. No one aboard the train was injured and, after a stop at the next station for inspection, it continued its journey. As for the Harrow, it made a forced landing in a nearby field, one crew member being slightly injured.

During April 1937 No. 214 Squadron transferred to Feltwell, Norfolk, and on the 29th of that month two of its Harrows, K6945 and K6950, collided in mid-air and crashed at Methwold. On 6 October the following year one of the Squadron's Harrow IIs, K6991, was struck by lightning while flying near Pontefract, Yorkshire, the entire crew tragically losing their lives in the ensuing crash. Other Bomber Command units to receive Harrows included No. 37 Squadron (Feltwell), Nos. 75 and 215 Squadrons (Driffield) and No. 115 Squadron (Marham). Like No. 214 Squadron, however, all of these units had exchanged their Harrows for more modern bombers by the outbreak of war in September 1939.

An unusual wartime task undertaken by a number of Harrows was the attempted disruption of enemy

Left: Harrow K6952 of No. 115 Squadron at Marham provides a good view of the rear FN15 turret, circa 1938. (MAP)

Bottom left: Harrow II K6987/R of No. 214 Squadron at its Feltwell base in 1937. (Aviation Photo News)

Below: Harrow II K7005 was destined to join No. 37 Squadron at Feltwell in 1937. It eventually finished up with No. 271 Squadron, lasting until 14 December 1943, when it crashed into Inishowen Head, Co. Donegal. (MAP)

charges slid down the wire and exploded on contact with the enemy aircraft. Harrows were initially chosen to carry the LAMs, of which 120 could be carried in the bomb bay on specially adapted racks. A special unit, No. 420 Flight (later No. 93 Squadron), was formed at Middle Wallop, and under the codename 'Mutton' Harrows began their operations in December 1940. Joined in this venture by Douglas Havocs (code-name 'Pandora'), the Harrows claimed three or four German bombers as 'kills' or probables. Harrows known to have participated in this scheme included K6993, K6994, K6963, K7005 and K7020. At least two machines wore a 'sharkmouth' insignia around the lower part of the nose.

Some Harrows went on to serve as trainers with several Air Observation and BGSs, but the majority were transferred for transport duties. A number were attached to various RAF units for the purpose of conveying spares and equipment between stations when bases were changed. After No. 271 Squadron had formed at Doncaster on 1 May 1940 as a transport unit, it operated Harrows alongside Bristol Bombays and some impressed civilian aircraft. In February 1944 the squadron moved to Down Ampney, Gloucestershire, the bulk of its aircraft being replaced by Douglas C-47 Dakotas. However, it retained a flight of Harrows (D Flight) which flew supply missions in support of Allied forces in North West Europe before becoming air ambulances.

On moving to the Continent D Flight was based at Airfield B56 near Brussels, where Bob Wilcock was an R/T operator for eighteen months. He says the Harrows operated what would now be called 'casevac' flights, moving out seriously wounded troops. Two of the Flight's Harrows were involved in the evacuation of wounded Allied troops from the Arnhem battle in September 1944. But during the Luftwaffe's 1945 New Year's Day attack on Continental bases of the Allied

bomber formations in night raids on Britain during the autumn of 1940. A weapon termed the Long Aerial Mine (LAM) had been produced, in which explosive charges were suspended beneath parachutes, below which was a 2,000ft (6,096m) length of piano wire. If an enemy bomber flew into the wires, the

2nd Tactical Air Force, Airfield B56 was targeted and seven Harrows were destroyed.

As a troop-carrier the Harrow could accommodate up to twenty fully equipped soldiers plus a crew of three, but the type flew mostly as a military freighter. Some dozen Harrows were modified by having their turrets replaced by streamlined fairings, these machines being dubbed 'Sparrows'. At least one Harrow (K6937) had windows inserted into the fuselage sides, Anson fashion, and at one period was used to carry VIPs and high-ranking enemy prisoners.

Another useful purpose was served by Harrows in the months leading up to the war. Three were loaned to Sir Alan Cobham's company, Flight Refuelling Ltd, for experimental in-flight refuelling of Imperial Airways C-class flying boats off Newfoundland and Foynes, Eire. The two Harrows operating on the Canadian side were shipped across, these being K6933, the first production Harrow registered as G-AFRG, and Mk. II K7029, registered G-AFRH. The Harrow used at Foynes was Mk. II K7027/G-AFRL. This aircraft was wrecked during an enemy air raid on Ford, Sussex, in

June 1940. G-AFRG was later impressed into the RCAF, numbered 794, and was seen languishing in a hangar at Dartmouth Air Station, Nova Scotia, in September 1941. Harrow G-AFRH was cannibalised for spares.

Royal Air Force transport Harrows/'Sparrows' retained the standard upper-surface camouflage scheme. Their wing roundels were red and blue, the fuselage roundels were red, white, blue and yellow, and the squadron codes were grey. The undersurfaces had a silver or 'sky' finish. One 'Sparrow' was coded 'N' aft of the fuselage roundel and had red, white and blue rudder stripes and the name *SPARROW* in black on each side of the nose. The last Harrow in RAF service, K7000, arrived at No. 19 MU, Kemble, in April 1945.

Left: Harrow II K6988/J of No. 214 Squadron, Feltwell, circa 1938. Note the squadron number painted on the fuselage sides. (Aviation Photo News)

Bottom left: Harrow II K7017/P of No. 37 Squadron visits RAF Harwell in April 1938. This aircraft crashed at Hendon on 23 July that year. (Mrs M. Hunt)

Below: Known as 'Sparrows', some Harrows had their turrets replaced by streamlined fairings and were used as transports. This is K6933/N, circa 1942. (MAP)

Bottom: Civil-registered as G-AFRG, this Harrow was one used by Flight Refuelling Ltd. Originally the first production Harrow, K6933, it later went to the RCAF as No. 794. (Aviation Photo News)

Short
Stirling

With the ominous expansion of Germany's Luftwaffe during the mid-1930s, Britain's Air Ministry, which until then had planned on the RAF's largest bombers being twin-engined, decided to opt for a four-engine heavy bomber. Specification B.12/36 was issued to British aircraft manufacturers, calling for a high-speed, long-range four-engine strategic bomber, the term 'high-speed' indicating a maximum speed of 230mph (370km/h), then considered likely to be the top speed achievable by this class of heavy bomber.

Assuming an overload take-off weight and the provision of some form of assisted take-off, a specified range of 3,000 miles (4,828km) carrying an 8,000lb (3,628kg) bomb load was envisaged (the development of catapult launching devices for heavy aircraft had been proceeding at Farnborough since the early 1930s). Under normal take-off conditions the B.12/36 design would be expected to carry 4,000lb (1,814kg) of bombs over a distance of 2,000 miles (3,218km). It was stipulated that maximum bomb load should be 14,000lb (6,350kg), and provision was to be made to include 2,000lb (907kg) armour-piercing bombs. Also, in keeping with an RAF tradition of using its bombers in the secondary role of troop-carriers, accommodation was to be provided for 24 fully equipped soldiers, with a level floor and a sufficient number of emergency-type push-out windows incorporated in the fuselage. A crew of six had to be carried, a reserve crew member was to be provided for and a rest area was required.

The response from the British aircraft industry was considerable, proposals being submitted by Armstrong Whitworth, Avro, Bristol, Handley Page, Hawker, Short Brothers, Supermarine and Vickers. The Air Staff selected the designs from Short Brothers and Supermarine for construction, the latter company's Types 317 and 318 prototypes being delayed by preoccupation with the Spitfire and finally destroyed in a Luftwaffe attack on Supermarine's works on 26 September 1940. This left Short Brothers with a clear field for its initial proposal, which used a wing similar to that of the company's Sunderland flying boat. Shorts chief designer, Arthur Gouge (later Sir Arthur), incorporated large flaps of his own design in the wing, which spanned 112ft (34.14m). Shorts calculated its new bomber would have an excellent high-altitude performance with a normal gross weight of 48,000lb (21,772kg) and, at a maximum overload weight of 65,000lb (29,484kg), would be able to operate from existing airfields without any assisted take-off device.

Air Ministry officials, however, appear to have adopted a rather short-sighted attitude regarding

Below: The half-scale Short S.31 M-4, a flying model of the Stirling built to provide information on the flying and handling qualities of the new full-scale four-engine bomber. (Aviation Photo News)

Right: The Stirling's wing planform was based on that of the Short Scion Senior, the S.31 half-scale Stirling having an essentially similar wing with modified components. Scion Senior VT-AGU, seen here, was a floatplane for Irrawaddy Flotilla and Airways Ltd of Burma. (Aviation Photo News)

Shorts' original design. They refused to accept a wingspan exceeding 100ft (30.48m), insisting that the aircraft had to conform with the dimensions of contemporary RAF hangars. Moreover, the Ministry restricted the size of individual components, as the airframe needed to be transportable in sections which existing RAF road vehicles and containers could accommodate. So it was literally back to the drawing board for Arthur Gouge and his team, the revised plans resulting in a reduced span of 99ft (30.17m), while the Gouge flaps were increased in size to 48 per cent of the chord to sustain performance at take-off. Thus the new bomber's wing became shorter and wider, which in turn meant revising estimates of the type's high-altitude performance.

With confirmation of further increases in Luftwaffe strength, the Air Ministry ordered two prototypes of Shorts' updated S.29 design in 1937 (contract No. 672299/37), followed by an initial production order for 100 machines 'off the drawing board', without waiting for prototype testing. At the same time the name Stirling was chosen for the new aircraft.

To test the characteristics of what was to be Shorts' largest landplane for a number of years, as well as its first featuring a retractable landing gear, the company built an all-wooden, half-scale flying replica of the Stirling with accommodation for a pilot and observer in tandem. The pilot was enclosed by a sideways-hinging cockpit canopy, but the hapless observer had to crouch in the fuselage immediately aft of the pilot's cockpit. Designated S.31, this mini-Stirling had wings based on those of the Short Scion Senior civil monoplane and was powered by four 90hp (67kW) Pobjoy Niagara III seven-cylinder radial engines driving two-bladed wooden propellers. A realistic slipstream was achieved, opening bomb doors were fitted to reveal

their effect on the behaviour of the full-size aircraft, and a fully retractable landing gear was installed. The S.31 emerged in an overall aluminium finish, carrying B condition marking 'M4' in black across the fin and rudder. Its first flight was made from Rochester on 19 September 1938 with Shorts' chief test pilot, John Lankester Parker, at the controls. After a dozen flights the S.31 was flown to the A&AEE at Martlesham Heath for a series of handling trials, and favourable reports were received. However, a 3° increase in wing incidence was recommended, the original 3½° having been set to obtain minimum cruise drag. This modification was considered essential to keep the aircraft's take-off and landing distances within certain limits, as it was envisaged that the full-size Stirling would grow heavier as military demands became greater. Shorts realised that such an alteration, with tooling then at an advanced stage, would mean a major redesign, inevitable long delays in production and no possible chance of meeting delivery dates.

To resolve the problem a compromise was reached by lengthening the main undercarriage legs to increase the ground angle by 3°. This modification was initially made to the S.31 mini-Stirling, which flew with the revised landing gear on 22 November 1938. The aircraft was then re-engined with four 115hp (85kW) Pobjoy Niagara IV engines, with which it flew on 10 January 1939, but a handling problem arose and, to improve longitudinal control, horn-balanced elevators were fitted before the next flight, on 14 January. A further modification in the form of a lengthened tailplane was introduced, and in this configuration the S.31 flew on 16 March 1938. After various tests the aircraft was accepted on 12 April and the investigation of Stirling handling characteristics continued.

Short Stirling

At the outbreak of war the S.31 was painted in the standard camouflage finish of brown and green upper surfaces with yellow (prototype- style) undersurfaces. In 1940 scaled-down Boulton Paul dorsal and ventral gun turrets were fitted to the mini-Stirling before it was sent to the RAE at Farnborough for wind tunnel tests. After removal of its experimental turrets, the S.31 was refurbished and continued flying in March 1942 but, with 110 flights logged, it was scrapped in 1943.

Meanwhile, in May 1939, the first prototype Stirling, L7600, had been completed at Rochester. High-speed taxying tests were carried out on 13 May, and the following day test pilot Lankester Parker took the big bomber for its maiden flight. During its first twenty minutes in the air the Stirling handled very satisfactorily, but after touching down on the airfield a brake seized, causing the landing gear to collapse. As a result L7600 was written off and the planned Stirling programme greatly retarded, for, with an obvious weakness revealed in the landing gear, modifications would be necessary. Consequently the second prototype, L7605, was not ready for testing until 21 Novem-

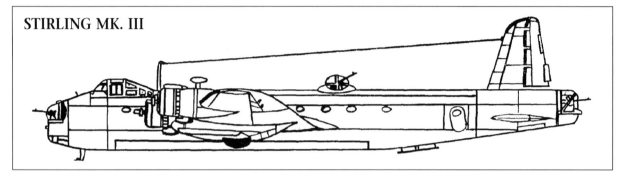

STIRLING MK. III

SHORT STIRLING MK. I DATA

Manufacturers
Short Bros Ltd, Rochester, Kent. Subcontracted to Short & Harland, Belfast; Austin Motors, Longbridge, Birmingham
Type
Seven-seat long-range heavy bomber
Powerplant
Four 1,500hp (1,119kW) Bristol Hercules XI air-cooled fourteen-cylinder radial engines
Performance
Maximum speed, 260mph (418km/h) at 10,500ft (3,200m). Cruising speed, 200mph (322km/h) at 10,000ft (3,050m) with maximum bomb load. Climb to 10,000ft (3,050m) with full load, 19.5min. Service ceiling, 18,000ft (5,486m). Range with 14,000lb (6,350kg) bomb load, 915 miles; with maximum fuel and 3,500lb (1,588kg) bomb load, 2,400 miles (3,862km)
Weights
Empty, 42,300lb (19,187kg). Loaded (normal), 53,000lb 24,040kg). Maximum overload, 68,000lb (30,845kg).
Dimensions
Span, 99ft 1in (30.20m). Length, 87ft 3in (26.59m). Height, 22ft 9in (6.93m). Wing area, 1,460sq ft (135.6sq m). Landing gear track, 23ft 6in (7.16m)

Armament (Mk. I Series 3)
Eight 0.303in (7.7mm) Browning machine-guns: two in FN5 nose turret, two in FN7 dorsal turret and four in FN20A tail turret (1,000rpg). Bomb load, 21 x 500lb (227kg) or seven 2,000lb (907kg) bombs and up to six 500lb (227kg) bombs in wing cells

SHORT STIRLING PRODUCTION

Two prototypes, L7600 and L7605. L7600 suffered undercarriage failure following its first flight, 14 May 1939. L7605 used as development aircraft
Stirling Is (Rochester-built):
   N3635–N3644; N3646; N3652–N3684; N3700–N3729; N3750–N3769; DJ972–DJ977; R9141–R9170; R9184–R9203; R9241–R9290; EF327–EF369 and EF384–EF400. Total = 260, of which N3645 and N3647–N3651 were destroyed in German bombing raid on works. Replaced as above by DJ972–'977
Stirling Is (Belfast-built): N6000–N6024; N6029–N6030; N6032–N6049; N6065–N6104; N6120–N6129; R9295–R9334; R9349–R9358; BF309–BF358; BF327–BF416 and BF434–BF454. Total = 261, of which N6025–N6028 and N6031 were

destroyed in German bombing raid on factory.
Note: N3657, N3711 and R9188 built as Mk. IIs before reconversion to Mk. I standard
Stirling Is (Austin-built): W7426–W7475; W7500–W7539; W7560–W7589; W7610–W7639; BK592–BK628 and BK644–BK647. Total = 191
Stirling IIIs (Rochester-built):
   EF401–EF413; EF425–EF470; EF488–EF518; LJ440–LJ483; LJ501–LJ529; LJ531–LJ544; LJ557–LJ596; LJ611–LJ653; LJ667–LJ670 and PW255–PW266. Total = 276, of which 21 machines converted to Mk. IV standard as follows: LJ615, '618, '620, '622, '624, '627, '629, '631, '633, '636, '638, '640, '643, '645, '647, '650, '652, '667, '668 and PW255, '257
Stirling IIIs (Belfast-built):
   BF455–BF483; BF500–BF534; BF561–BF580; MZ260–MZ264; EE871–EE918; EE937–EE975; EF114–EF613; EF177–EF217; EF231–EF277 and EF289–EF316. Total = 342, of which MZ260–MZ264 replaced N6025–N6028 and N6031, destroyed by enemy action as noted above
Stirling IIIs (Austin-built):

BK748–BK667; BK686–BK727;
BK759–BK784; BK798–BK818;
EH875–EH909; EH921–EH961;
EH977–EH996; EJ104–EJ127;
LK375–LK411; LK425–LK466;
LK479–LK521; LK535–LK576 and
LK589–LK624. Total = 429

Stirling IVs (Belfast-built):
EF317–EF323; LJ810–LJ851;
LJ864LJ899; LJ913–LJ956;
LJ969–LJ999; LK114–LK156;
LK169–LK211; LK226–LK257;
LK270–LK313; LK326–LK370;
PK225–PK237; PW384–PW425 and
PW438–PW465. Total = 450

Stirling Vs (Belfast-built): PJ878–PJ923;
PJ935–PJ959; PK115–PK158;
PK171–PK186. Total = 160

Total number of Short Stirlings produced, all marks including two prototypes = 2,371. The actual number built was 2,382, but eleven of these were destroyed on the factory sites by enemy action

NB. Stirlings built at the Swindon (South Marston) factory are included with the Rochester-built machines, while numbers of those listed as Belfast-built were produced at Queen's Island, Aldergrove, Long Kesh and Meghabery. It should also be remembered that some Stirling Is were later converted to Mk. III standard at RAF MUs, and similarly a number of Mk. IIIs were in turn converted to Mk. IVs

RAF STIRLING UNITS

Bomber Command (Mk. Is)

No. 7 Squadron (Leeming and Oakington)

No. 15 Squadron (Wyton and Bourn)

No. 75 Squadron (Newmarket)

No. 90 Squadron (Bottesford and Ridgewell)

No. 149 Squadron (Lakenheath)

No. 214 Squadron (Stradishall and Chedburgh)

No. 218 Squadron (Downham Market)

No. 620 Squadron (Chedburgh)

Bomber Command (Mk. IIIs)

No. 7 Squadron (Oakington)

No. 15 Squadron (Bourn and Mildenhall)

No. 75 Squadron (Newmarket and Mepal)

No. 90 Squadron (Ridgewell, West Wickham, Tuddenham)

No. 149 Squadron (Lakenheath and Methwold)

No. 171 Squadron (North Creake)

No. 196 Squadron (Witchford, Leicester East, Tarrant Rushton)

No. 199 Squadron (North Creake)

No. 214 Squadron (Chedburgh and Downham Market)

No. 218 Squadron (Downham Market)

No. 513 Squadron (Witchford)

No. 622 Squadron (Mildenhall)

No. 623 Squadron (Downham Market)

Transport Command (Mk. IVs)

No. 190 Squadron (Leicester East, Fairford, Great Dunmow)

No. 196 Squadron (Tarrant Rushton, Keevil, Wethersfield and Shepherds Grove)

No. 242 Squadron (Stoney Cross)

No. 295 Squadron (Harwell, Rivenhall)

No. 299 Squadron (Stoney Cross, Keevil, Wethersfield and Shepherds Grove)

No. 570 Squadron (Harwell, Rivenhall)

No. 620 Squadron (Fairford, Great Dunmow)

Transport Command (Mk. Vs)

No. 46 Squadron (Stoney Cross)

No. 51 Squadron (Leconfield, Stradishall)

No. 158 Squadron (Lisset, Stradishall)

No. 196 Squadron (Shepherds Grove)

No. 242 Squadron (Stoney Cross)

No. 299 Squadron (Shepherds Grove)

No. 1588 Flight (India/Middle East)

Examples of individual Stirlings in RAF squadron service

Mk. Is: N3641/D-MG of No. 7 Squadron; N3642/EM-G of No. 7 Squadron; N3667/T-LS of No. 15 Squadron; N3675/S-LS of No. 15 Squadron; N3680/Y-MG of No. 7 Squadron; N3683 of No. 75 Squadron (squadron code: AA, individual letter n/a); N3705/F-MG of No. 7 Squadron (captured by Germans after being forced down, flight-tested by Luftwaffe at Rechlin with damaged nose covered by tarpaulin, tailwheels in down position and undersurfaces yellow); N3706/S-MG of No. 7 Squadron; N6003/V-MG of No. 7 Squadron (later to No. 26 Conversion Flight and then to No. 1651 OCU); N6040/C-LS of No. 15 Squadron; R9197/U-YZ of No. 1651 Heavy Conversion Unit; R9198/M-BU of No. 214 Squadron; R9204/D-HA of No. 218 Squadron; R9241/L-HA of No. 218 Squadron; R9271/Q-WP of No. 90 Squadron; R9313/Q-HA of No. 218 Squadron; W7453/O-OJ of No. 149 Squadron; W7455/B-OJ of No. 149 Squadron; W7582/S-OJ of No. 149 Squadron; W7584/D-BU of No. 214 Squadron; BF382/Q-BU of No. 214 Squadron; EF369/Z-MG of No. 7 Squadron

Mk. IIIs: BF321/V-QS of No. 622 Squadron; BF475/T-LS of No. 15 Squadron; BF532/Y-MG of No. 7 Squadron; BF740/G-LS of No. 15 Squadron; BK621/Q-MG of No. 7 Squadron; BK665/D-WP of No. 90 Squadron; BK724/I-MG of No. 7 Squadron; BK770/? of No. 75 Squadron (squadron code was AA); BK777/? of No. 75 Squadron (squadron code was AA); BK784/M-WP of No. 90 Squadron; EF333/X-LS of No. 15 Squadron; EF445/K-BU of No. 214 Squadron; EH878/I-IC of No. 623 Squadron; EH887/Z-HA of No. 218 Squadron; EH895/M-BU of No. 214 Squadron; EH921/L-GI of No. 622 Squadron; EH943/B-OJ of No. 149 Squadron; EH934/K-EX of No. 199 Squadron; EJ112/Q-HA of No. 218 Squadron; EJ113/Q-GI of No. 622 Squadron; EJ115/C-EX of No. 199 Squadron; EJ121/Q-IC of No. 623 Squadron; EJ124/C-OJ of No. 149 Squadron; LJ444/A-GI of No. 622 Squadron; LJ454/E-IC of No. 623 Squadron; LJ525/R-EX of No. 199 Squadron; LJ582/L-EX of No. 199 Squadron

Mk. IVs: H-GI of No. 622 Squadron (serial n/a); E-QS of No. 620 Squadron (serial n/a)
Mk. IV PK237 was the 1,000th Stirling built at Belfast

Mk. Vs: PJ887/H-OZ of No. 196 Squadron; PK143 (KAW on nose) of No. 242 Squadron; E-KY of No. 242 Squadron (serial n/a)

ber 1939. Its initial flight was made on 3 December, when, to prevent a repetition of the first prototype's landing mishap, L7605 had its newly strengthened landing gear locked down. All went well, however, and during its second flight, on Christmas Eve, L7605 had its landing gear fully retracted and scheduled flight testing commenced. After eight manufacturer's test flights the second Stirling was sent for trials at the A&AEE, Boscombe Down, on 22 April 1940.

Despite the accident to L7600, plans for Stirling production went ahead, Scheme L under the RAF expansion programme of 1938 remaining as originally scheduled. This required the delivery of 3,500 heavy bombers to the RAF by April 1942, of which no fewer than 1,500 were to be Stirlings. To cope with this large order Short & Harland's Belfast factory was to be seconded to Rochester as a main production line, Austin Motors at Longbridge was to provide a third Stirling assembly line, and airframe components were to be subcontracted to more than twenty firms. These plans were thwarted, however, when an MAP directive gave special priority to the building of single- and twin-engine types. Moreover, six newly completed Stirlings were destroyed during a Luftwaffe attack on Shorts' Rochester works on 9 August 1940, and another five were lost six days later when the Belfast site was bombed. Consequently, although Rochester's first production Stirling, N3635, had flown on 7 May 1940, delivery of the new bomber was slower than anticipated, Belfast's first Stirling (N6000) not making its initial flight until 18 October. Thus only fifteen Stirlings had been delivered by the end of the year. Then a new shadow factory at South Marston, near Swindon, undertook Stirling production, although one final batch would be Rochester-built. Likewise, the

Above: The second prototype Stirling, L7605, with Hercules XI engines. The tail is raised off the ground by a special dolly ahead of the twin tailwheels, with a support jack at rear. (Author's collection)

Belfast Queen's Island site was complemented later by Stirling assembly at Aldergrove and Meghabery.

The Stirling was of all-metal construction, the wings being divided into sections to simplify production but designed to form complete port and starboard units which were attached directly to the fuselage sides, there being no centre section. For extra strength the two main-spar booms, constructed from tubular 'N' girders with extruded T-section flanges top and bottom, passed through the fuselage at the level of the main deck. Aft of the rear main spar the wing trailing edges were formed from a light tubular girder structure. The wing leading edges incorporated radiator and air conditioning intakes, early production machines exchanging leading-edge Dunlop de-icing units for armour to protect fuel tanks. Martin-Baker balloon cable cutters were installed, and the original fixed landing lights were replaced by retractable units.

Each wing root contained a 154 Imp gal (700lit) non-sealing fuel tank for maximum-range missions. Always emptied first after take-off, these tanks supplemented the four main self-sealing wing tanks between the spars and two between the rear spar and flap shroud. The total capacity of the fourteen wing tanks was 2,254 Imp gals (10,246lit). Also incorporated each side, inboard of the inner nacelles, were three bomb cells covered by electrically controlled doors. These could carry either six 500lb (227kg) bombs, or an extra 438 Imp gals (1,991lit) of fuel in six tanks. The aluminium alloy wing skinning was flush-riveted to the

Above: The Stirling cockpit, with the throttle bank prominent in the centre of picture and the brake lever to the left. (Ron Mackay)

spars and lattice-braced ribs, while the metal ailerons were fabric covered.

The Stirling was initially powered by four 1,375hp (1,025kW) Bristol Hercules II fourteen-cylinder sleeve-valve radial engines carried in four well spaced monocoque nacelles. The outboard engines were centrally mounted on the wing, but the inner two were set lower to allow room for the main landing gear legs to retract electrically into their nacelles. Cross-braced twin oleo legs and a system of double-jointed struts formed the landing gear, to which parts of the undercarriage doors were attached. The single, large-diameter wheels were partly exposed when retracted, but the twin castoring tailwheels retracted fully into the rear fuselage.

The fuselage, an all-metal structure of rectangular section with rounded corners, was formed from Z-section transverse frames, notched to accept longitudinal stringers, and was covered by a flush-riveted light aluminium alloy skin. It was built in four large sections, joined together during final assembly by tension bolts mounted in the webs of the end frames and external butt-straps which covered the skin joins. Although its bomb bay was 42ft (12.80m) long, the Stirling was restricted in its bomb carrying capacity because the main deck was carried on two deep longitudinal beams which divided the bay into three narrow compartments. Each bay could hold seven 500lb (227kg) bombs, which together with a maximum bomb load in the wing cells amounted to 13,500lb (6,129kg). Alternatively, if seven 2,000lb (907kg) bombs were carried, the load would comprise three in the centre bay and two in each outer bay, but no wing-cell bombs. This amounted to a total 14,000lb (6,356kg), which was in fact the Stirling's original specified maximum bomb load. Because each fuselage bomb bay was 19in (48.26cm) wide, bombs larger than 2,000lb (907kg) could not be carried owing to their greater diameter, that of a 2,000lb (907kg) armour piercing bomb being 13.5in (34.3cm), while a 4,000lb (1,814kg) bomb was 24.5in (62.2cm) in diameter. This restriction was an unfortunate legacy of the original 1936 specification.

Initially the Stirling's defensive armament consisted of a Frazer-Nash FN5 nose turret mounting twin 0.303in (7.7mm) Browning guns, an FN20A tail turret with four Brownings and a retractable FN25 ventral 'dustbin' turret housing two more Brownings. However, the ventral turret was soon removed because it was too cramped for prolonged occupation by any gunner, created additional drag when lowered in flight and slipped down on occasion when the aircraft was taxying owing to leaking hydraulic non-return valves, causing the guns to drag along the ground. At first it was replaced by a pair of 0.303in (7.7mm) Brownings pivot-mounted to fire one each side through beam hatches, these being fitted as standard for a time on the Stirling Mk. I Series 2. However, they proved inadequate in combat and were replaced in the Mk. I Series 3 by an FN7 dorsal turret with twin Browning guns, as used on the Blackburn Botha and Avro Manchester I. This turret, in turn, was later superseded on the Stirling III by an FN50 dorsal turret housing two 0.303in (7.7mm) Browning guns.

The Bristol Hercules II engines fitted to early production Stirlings were superseded by Hercules XIs as they became available. These engines, which had two-speed superchargers, were updated by Shorts to incorporate welded steel-tube mountings for the Stirling I Series 2, while Mk. I Series 3 aircraft were powered by wholly Bristol designed Hercules XIs. These uprated fourteen-cylinder double-row air-cooled radial engines, which were easier to remove and service, developed 1,590hp (1,186kW) at 2,900rpm for take-off and 1,020hp (760kW) at 2,500rpm for economical cruise. But use of hydraulic throttle controls caused a problem with these engines, a significant delay often occurring between moving the levers and any alteration in engine tone.

Accommodation was provided in the Stirling I for a crew of seven, comprising pilot, co-pilot, navigator/bomb-aimer, radio operator, flight engineer/gunner and two gunners. Entrance was via a door in the rear port side of the fuselage, and on the lengthy walk to the cockpit in original Mk. Is the retractable ventral turret had to be negotiated before passing the emergency devices for the landing gear and Gouge flaps, the primer and starter points for the engines, the fuel tank cocks and balance taps, the rest area with bunk and chair, the navigator's position, the radio operator's compartment and the flight engineer's panel.

The cockpit contained pilot and co-pilot's seats, each position having a control column and rudder bars. Between them was a bank of controls for the throttles, constant-speed propellers, mixture, landing gear selector, brakes and adjustment of the retractable landing lights. The cockpit roof control panel included main fuel cocks to the carburettors, slow-running shut-offs and tail and rudder trim handles. The flap operating switch and indicator were in the windscreen 'V', and in addition to normal instrumentation the panel had four boost gauges and four engine revolution counters.

Below: A Stirling awaits delivery to RAF Bomber Command as another passes overhead. (Ron Mackay)

Beneath the floor of the flight deck and nose gun turret was the bomb aimer's position, with the aiming window and bomb sight in the extreme lower nose, a bomb aiming control panel to the right, a prone-position couch and, immediately aft of that, an escape hatch. The tail gunner sat in an FN20A power-operated turret armed with four 0.303in (7.7mm) Browning machine-guns. Access to this turret was by means of a walkway and a four-rung ladder, and ammunition for the guns ran on tracks from magazines in the upper port side of the fuselage.

During 1941 arrangements were made to produce Stirlings in Canada. Designated Mk. II, these aircraft were to be powered by four 1,600hp (1,193kW) Wright R-2600-A5B Cyclone radials. Three UK-built Stirlings, (N3640, N3657 and N3711) had already been fitted with these engines for trials, as a safeguard against a shortage of Hercules. No such problem arose, however, and only the three British Stirling IIs were built, the first two eventually reverting to Mk. I configuration and the third being updated to Mk. III standard. A contract for 140 Stirling IIs to be built in Canada was rescinded.

By the end of 1942 Stirling IIIs had superseded Mk. Is on the production lines, Mk. Is R9188 and R9309

Below: This Belfast-built Stirling I, N6091, was delivered to No. 7 Squadron at Oakington. It failed to return from a raid against Berlin on 7/8 November 1941. (Author's collection)

having been converted to Mk. III standard and Austin-built Mk. IIIs BK648 and BK649 serving as prototypes. The Stirling III was powered by 1,635hp (1,219kW) Hercules XVI engines installed as 'power-eggs' complete with underslung 12in (30.5cm) oil coolers for ease of maintenance. This was the last bomber variant, and introduced the Frazer-Nash FN50 dorsal turret as used on the Avro Lancaster and fitted retrospectively to a number of Stirling I Series 3s. This mark also had increased-capacity fuel tanks, a modified interior and fewer oval windows in the rear fuselage.

During August 1940 No. 7 Squadron of Bomber Command's No. 3 Group began replacing its Vickers Wellingtons with Stirlings at Leeming, although only six production Stirling Is were available at the time. As well as being the first RAF unit to receive Stirlings, No. 7 Squadron had the distinction of becoming the RAF's first four-engine-bomber unit of the Second World War. The squadron began a working-up period on its Stirlings, which, despite some teething troubles, had good control and relatively light ailerons in view of the aircraft's size. Initial elevator movement was sluggish, but directionally and laterally the Stirling proved extremely stable and, except when the CG was in its most aft position with a loaded aircraft, was sufficiently longitudinally stable. With one engine shut down the Stirling could maintain altitude at any weight, but with two engines out of action it was difficult to maintain height at any weight exceeding

50,000lb (22,680kg). At a take-off weight of 70,000lb (31,752kg) a Stirling Mk. I cleared a 50ft (15.24m) obstacle within 1,400 yards (1,280m).

During October 1940 No. 7 Squadron moved to Oakington in Cambridgeshire, where in January 1941 HM King George VI and Queen Elizabeth (now the Queen Mother) inspected the unit's Stirlings and were given a flying demonstration by N3644. On the night of 10/11 February 1941 Stirlings made their operational debut when three from No. 7 Squadron (N3641, N3642 and N3644) took part in a raid on oil storage tanks at Rotterdam. This attack was led by Squadron Leader J. M.

Above: Stirling I BF382/BU-Q of No. 214 Squadron, Stradishall, in 1942. Note the Boulton Paul dorsal turret with twin Browning machine-guns. (Author's collection)

Below: An excellent underside-view of Stirling I OJ-N of No. 149 Squadron, Lakenheath, circa 1942. (MAP)

Right: The eighth production Stirling I, N3642, over well wooded English countryside in 1941. It first went to No. 7 Squadron, Oakington, moved to No. 15 Squadron, and then went to 1651 Conversion Flight (CF), finally becoming instructional airframe 3012M. (Author's collection)

Griffith-Jones, DFC, and 56 500lb (227kg) bombs were dropped. Attention was then turned to the French Atlantic port of Brest, where the German battlecruisers *Scharnhorst* and *Gneisenau* were harboured. The first attacks against Brest were nocturnal, but because the Stirling was exceptionally manoeuvrable for a large bomber, a number of daylight missions were undertaken, the first being against Emden on 27 April 1941.

Fighter escort was not provided on these early daytime raids, but Stirlings gave a good account of themselves and shot down a number of German fighters. Then, during an attack on Brest (the fifth operation by Stirlings), No. 7 Squadron sadly lost Squadron Leader Griffith-Jones and his crew in Stirling N3653, the first of the type to be shot down. A fortnight later one Stirling was sent to join a raid on Bremen, and on the night of 9/10 April 1941 three of No. 7 Squadron's Stirlings participated in an 80-aircraft raid on Berlin. This trio of machines was from 'B' Flight, but one aircraft (Flying Officer J. Sack) suffered a propeller problem and was forced to return to base, jettisoning its bombs in the sea en route. A second Stirling, N6005, managed to bomb Emden after being attacked by a Messerschmitt Bf 110 nightfighter, but the third, N6011, was shot down near Lingen. At about this time No. 7 Squadron was flying temporarily from Rowley Mile (Newmarket Racecourse) owing to Oakington's boggy grass surfaces, but operations had resumed from Oakington by the end of April.

April saw No. 15 Squadron exchanging its Wellington ICs for Stirlings at Wyton and, after a working-up period, joining No. 7 Squadron on the offensive, mainly against German warships until July. Much effort was spent attacking Brest in attempts to hit *Scharnhorst* and *Gneisenau*, and on 27 May twelve Stirlings made a number of sorties off Brest, unsuccessfully hunting for two other German warships, the *Bismarck* and *Prinz Eugen*. These anti-warship operations continued until the early evening of 23 July, when six unescorted Stirlings from Nos. 7 and 15 Squadrons attacked the *Scharnhorst* at La Pallice. Nine 2,000lb (907kg) armour-piercing bombs were dropped, the crew Stirling N6037 of No. 7 Squadron claiming a direct hit on the battleship's stern. This aircraft was then attacked by Messerschmitt Bf 109s, but the Stirling's rear gunner shot down two of the enemy aircraft and damaged a third. Stirling N6038 of No. 15 Squadron was not so lucky, ditching at sea after being hit by German fighters. During these operations some Stirlings from both Nos. 7 and 15 Squadrons carried specialised crew members from No. 109 Squadron (the redesignated A&AEE Wireless Intelligence Development Unit) using Trinity, an early apparatus for blind bombing, and a very basic form of Oboe (a navigational aid used by the RAF for precision marking and bombing). In December 1941 and early 1942 Trinity was employed during attacks against Brest.

Above: Austin-built Stirling I (W74??/MG-G) of No. 7 Squadron, Oakington, 'bombing-up' for a night raid on Germany in 1941. (Author's collection)

Production increased during 1941, and by the year's end twenty Stirlings a month were being rolled out. Subsequently No. 3 Group's squadrons became increasingly Stirling-equipped, No. 149 being operational before the end of 1941, while No. 218 was converting. During 1942 Nos. 75, 90 and 214 Squadrons received Stirlings, and in the following year the type entered service with Nos. 196, 199, 622 and 623 Squadrons. Other Bomber Command units which flew Stirling Is and IIIs included Nos. 171, 513 and 620 Squadrons. Thus the Stirlings of No. 3 Group's squadrons were much in evidence when Bomber Command launched its strategic bombing campaign against German industrial targets starting in March 1942. By then they had already bombed objectives further afield, such as the Skoda armament factory at Pilsen, Czechoslovakia, and had crossed the Alps to attack industrial sites at Turin and Milan in Northern Italy. During March/April 1942 Stirlings were equipped with Gee, a new radio/navigation/target identification system which had been tested the previous year by Wellingtons of No. 115 Squadron.

When Bomber Command dispatched its first 1,000-bomber raid against Cologne on the night of 30/31 May 1942, Gee-equipped Stirlings and Wellingtons led the attack. Navigating by Gee, they approached Cologne until visual identification of the target was made by moonlight. Incendiary bombs were dropped to start fires to guide in the following formations. The AOC of No. 3 Group, Air Vice-Marshal J. E. A. Baldwin, who had joined a Stirling crew in the leading formation, noted the high standard of accuracy in evidence, as fires were already burning only half a mile from the aiming point before the lead formation arrived. From

the RAF's point of view this first mass attack was successful, some 600 acres (242.82 hectares) of Cologne being destroyed. Two further 1,000-bomber raids were carried out by Bomber Command during 1942, on Essen and Bremen.

Stirlings formed part of the RAF's main bombing force until late 1943, and inevitably suffered casualties, but the amount of punishment these large bombers could absorb and still remain in the air was indeed a tribute to its robust construction. For example, on the night of 27/28 June 1942 Stirling N3751 of No. 214 Squadron was part of a force raiding Bremen. Having bombed the target the Stirling, piloted by Australian Sergeant F. M. Griggs, was on its way home when a pair of Messerschmitt Bf 110 nightfighters attacked it. The Stirling's nose and dorsal gunners retaliated, shooting down one enemy machine and causing the other to leave the scene, but by then the rear gunner was dead, the radio operator wounded, one engine had stopped and the electrical system, radio and intercom had been rendered useless. Griggs remained on course, but as they crossed the Dutch coast they were attacked by two Bf 109s. The nose gunner, attending to the wounded radio operator at the time, managed to reach his turret. Amazingly, both enemy fighters were shot down, but the Stirling was now unable to fly above 8,000ft (2,438m), which made it an easy target for any enemy flak ship. Another Bf 109 then attacked, and in taking evasive action Griggs lost control and the bomber went into a

ᅟ

ᅟ

Above: Stirling I W7455/OJ-B of No. 149 Squadron, Lakenheath, prepares for operations in 1942. (MAP)

dive. At practically wave-top height Griggs pulled out and regained enough control to limp home on three engines. Over the base an engine caught fire, but the flames were extinguished and Griggs crash-landed the Stirling on two engines. No other crew members were injured as the Stirling settled on terra firma.

Two Stirlings of No. 75 Squadron also reached home after taking heavy punishment. The first, flown by Flight Lieutenant G. Turner, collided over Hamburg with a Messerschmitt nightfighter and returned

Below: Stirling W7459/O shows off the type's profile to perfection. Note the early FN7 (Botha-type) dorsal turret. (MAP)

safely to base with four feet of its starboard wing missing. In the second instance, Pilot Officer Buck managed to fly his Stirling home with one engine out of action and the whole rudder shot away.

The Victoria Cross, Britain's highest military award for valour, was bestowed posthumously on two Stirling pilots. The first went to Australian Flight Sergeant R. H. Middleton of No. 149 Squadron, who, on the night of 28/29 November 1942, was flying Stirling I BF372 'H-Harry' against targets in the Italian city of Turin. The Stirling struggled to reach 12,000ft (3,657m) to cross the Alps, a climb that consumed excessive fuel and left a bare minimum for the return flight. Once over Turin Middleton flew across the city three times at a height of 2,000ft (609m) to make positive identification of the target, but the Stirling was

hit by flak. The port wing was badly damaged, making lateral control difficult, and a shell exploded in the cockpit and Middleton lost his right eye, the bone above his left eye was laid bare and he received body and leg wounds. He lost consciousness temporarily, but his co-pilot, Flight Sergeant L. A. Hyder, although bleeding badly himself from head and leg wounds, made efforts to regain control of the aircraft, succeeding when it was down to 800ft (243m). Hyder pulled the Stirling back to 1,500ft (457m) and managed to drop the bomb load. Middleton then regained

consciousness and ordered Hyder to go for first aid in the rest area while he himself, suffering great pain, managed to head the crippled bomber for home. After struggling with the controls for four hours, Middleton crossed the French coast at 6,000ft (1,828m) and the aircraft was again hit by flak. As the English coast appeared only five minutes' fuel remained, and Middleton ordered his crew to bale out as he flew along the coastline. The front gunner and the flight engineer, Flight Sergeants Mackie and Jeffery respectively, stayed with their skipper as long as possible,

Top left: 'Bombing-up' Stirling I N6101/E. This aircraft served with No. 149 Squadron, No. 26 CF and No. 1651 HCU. It crash-landed at Waterbeach on 9 December 1942. (Aviation Photo News)

Lower left: Stirling I R9304/U of No. 1651 CU, fitted with a Boulton Paul twin-gun dorsal turret. (Ron Mackay)

Above: Stirling IIIs of No. 199 Squadron, RAF Bomber Command, Lakenheath, with crews and ground crews, circa 1943–44. (Ron Mackay)

jumped too late and were drowned. Middleton remained with his Stirling and perished when it crashed into the sea at 0310 on 29 November. On 1 February 1943 the sea gave up Middleton's body at Dover and he was buried with full military honours. His posthumous Victoria Cross had already been gazetted on 15 January 1943.

The second posthumous VC awarded to a Stirling pilot went to Flight Sergeant A. L. Aaron, who was en route to Turin on the night of 12/13 August 1943 in Stirling III EF452 'O-Oboe' of No. 218 Squadron. Tragically, Aaron's wounds resulted from mistaken identity, the tail gunner in another Stirling opening fire on what he thought was an enemy nightfighter coming in from behind. At 0120 'O-Oboe' flew into a withering hail of bullets from the other Stirling's tail guns as they approached Turin. The result was horrendous. The windscreen fragmented, the nose and rear turrets were deactivated, the controls were badly damaged and three engines were hit. The navigator of 'O-Oboe'

was killed instantly, other crew members were wounded and terrible injuries were received by Flight Sergeant Aaron, who had part of his face torn off, his jaw smashed, a lung perforated and his right arm broken. Aaron collapsed over the control column and the Stirling dived several thousand feet, but the flight engineer managed to pull out at less than 4,000ft (1,219m) and the bomb-aimer took over the controls. Despite his terrible wounds, Aaron scribbled a note advising the bomb-aimer to make for England, but owing to the state of the aeroplane it was decided to head for Sicily. The bomb load was jettisoned after crossing the Italian coast, but an emergency call advised the Stirling to fly to Bone airfield on the North African coast. When Bone was sighted, Aaron, after some first-aid treatment, forced himself back into the pilot's seat and attempted to land the crippled bomber in spite of his failing strength. Bone's runway was blocked by a crashed Wellington, and Aaron twice tried to belly-land alongside it. By now the fuel tanks were practically empty and, when the gallant Aaron wanted to attempt a third landing, the bomb-aimer knew it was now or never and put the aircraft down himself. It was 0600 on Friday 13 August 1943, and nine hours later Flight Sergeant Aaron died from his wounds. He was buried in Bone cemetery with full military honours, and his VC was gazetted on 5 November 1943.

Meanwhile, during August 1942 No. 7 Squadron's Stirlings had joined three non-Stirling units to form the new Pathfinder Force (PFF) of No. 8 Group. These Stirlings helped guide the main bomber streams to

Left: Stirling N3657 in August 1941, as a prototype Mk. II powered by Wright Cyclone R-2600-A5B engines. (Shorts)

Centre left: Stirling III LK403/ZO-W of No. 196 Squadron, Witchford and Leicester East, in 1943–44. The Mk. III had 'power-egg' engine installations and an FN150 dorsal turret. (Ron Mackay)

Bottom left: Stirling III BF509 over Lough Neagh in 1943. (Aviation Photo News)

numerous targets, including the North Italian cities of Genoa, Milan and Turin. Sometimes weather was the worst enemy. On one mission, for example, eight Stirlings of No. 7 Squadron were sent to attack Turin, but only two reached the target. Over the Alps banks of cloud were over 20,000ft (6,096m) high, and the two Stirlings which reached Turin did so by dead-reckoning. One was promptly shot down, but the other, flown by Flight Lieutenant J. F. Barron, a New Zealander, successfully carried out its mission and returned safely to base. This same Stirling was part of a later raid on Munich, when it was attacked by two Junkers Ju 88 nightfighters. One was driven off by the tail gunner, but the other persisted in its attempt to down the British bomber, which by now had a badly damaged wing and tailplane, plus a ruptured fuel supply threatening both port engines with fuel starvation. But Barron evaded the nightfighter and, with the help of emergency repairs carried out by his flight engineer, coaxed the crippled Stirling back to base.

A new radar aid to navigation and target identification known as H₂S was introduced operationally on the night of 30/31 January 1943 by Stirlings of No. 7 Squadron and Halifaxes of No. 35 Squadron. Hamburg was targeted, and H₂S marked the area for Nos. 1 and 5 Groups' main bomber stream following behind. Some of this secret equipment fell into enemy hands the following month when a Stirling of No. 7 Squadron was shot down over Holland by a German nightfighter.

By now Lancasters were fast superseding Stirlings in Bomber Command's main force, Stirlings having suffered increasing losses, often due to their limited ceiling. They were consequently allotted 'easier' targets, such as V-1 flying-bomb launch sites in northern France. In addition, long-range support operations, dropping arms and supplies to the Maquis (French Resistance fighters) were carried out over occupied France by Stirlings of Nos. 149 and 199 Squadrons.

Another important task for Stirlings was minelaying in enemy waters, which, owing to the comparatively low altitude necessary for such operations, could prove very hazardous, with danger from flak ships, anti-aircraft guns and nightfighters. An improved method of sowing mines from a greater height resulted from a better parachute and better packaging to protect the mine's sensitive interior.

Mines could then be dropped from up to 15,000ft (4,572m), this technique being further enhanced by using H₂S, which provided the necessary aid to accuracy to allow concentrations of mines to be laid. On the night of 30/31 December 1943, three Stirling IIIs of No. 149 Squadron released their mines at 12,000ft (3,657m) near Bordeaux. Despite a heavy flak barrage by the German defences, all the mines were laid successfully.

The final raid by Stirlings as part of Bomber Command's Main Force occurred on 8 September 1944, when No. 149 Squadron joined an attack against Le Havre. By this time Stirlings had flown 18,440 missions and dropped 27,821 tons (28,268 tonnes) of bombs, but 606 Stirlings failed to return from operations and 163 were lost for other reasons.

In the meantime No. 199 Squadron at North Creake, Norfolk, had transferred to No. 100 Group in May 1944 as a Bomber Support Unit, continuing to fly its Stirlings until March 1945 in a radio countermeasures role. For this the Stirling IIIs were fitted with equipment known as Mandrel, used as a countermeasure against the German Freya early-warning system, and could be recognised by numerous aerials extending beneath their fuselages. Chutes were also incorporated from which Window was dropped to create

A Frazer-Nash FN150 dorsal turret with twin 0.303in (7.7mm) Browning guns, as fitted to the Stirling III. These turrets were produced by Parnall Aircraft Ltd at Yate, Gloucestershire. (TI Jackson Ltd, Yate)

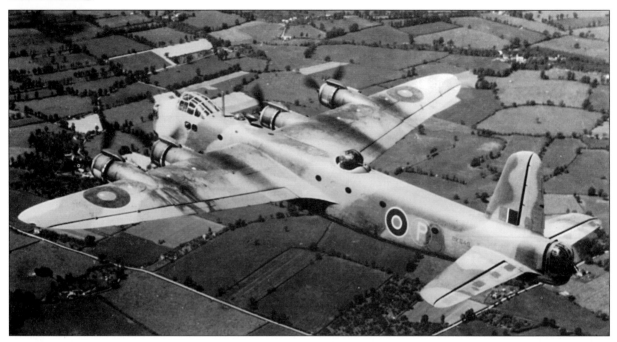

'spoof' raids, thus decoying enemy nightfighters from a major attack in another area.

The Stirling's design lent itself admirably to the concept of heavy transport and glider tug (as mentioned earlier, it was originally designed to serve in the secondary role of troop carrier), so there was no great problem in converting Mk. IIIs EF506 and LJ512 into Mk. IV prototypes, one for troop carrying and the other as a glider tug. The Mk. IV long-range troop transport version had its nose and dorsal gun turrets removed but kept the four-gun tail turret. A glazed fairing replaced the nose turret, a large opening was cut in the rear fuselage floor for paratroop dropping and the bomb cells were retained for carrying and dis-

tributing airborne supplies to ground forces. A crew of six was normal and, aft of the rear spar, accommodation was provided for 24 paratroops or 34 airborne soldiers with weapons and equipment. The glider tug variant, which also had a glazed nose and no dorsal turret, had ML glider towing gear attached to a yoke fitted round the rear fuselage. The tail gun turret was not always retained on Stirling glider tugs, which were delivered from October 1943 onwards. They could tow one large General Aircraft Hamilcar glider, two Airspeed Horsas or, on training exercises, up to five General Aircraft Hotspurs at the same time.

Stirling IVs went into action for the first time on D-Day, 6 June 1944, when aircraft of Nos. 190, 196, 299

and 620 Squadrons towed Horsas for release over dropping zones behind the beaches in Normandy. These Stirling IVs took part in the airborne assaults at Arnhem, Nijmegen and the Rhine crossing in March 1945. The type dropped arms and supplies to Allied troops in the front line and, as the 2nd Tactical Air Force moved on through Europe, the Stirlings kept them supplied with fuel, carrying loads of 120 x 5-gallon (22.73lit) drums to the airfields.

With its long range and supply dropping capability the Stirling proved ideal for the Special Operations Executive, responsible for clandestine missions behind enemy lines, which included dropping Allied agents. For this purpose two Stirling IV squadrons, Nos. 138 and 161, were classed as special-duty units and operated from Britain, while a third, No. 624 Squadron based in Algeria, undertook a similar role in North Africa. Stirling IVs were also issued for general supply duties in 1944 to some RAF Transport Command squadrons, including Nos. 190, 196, 295, 299, 570 and 620 Squadrons.

Bob Wilcock (RAF retired) told the author that his only association with Stirlings was at the B56 Brussels Airport. The aircraft were employed on Forces mail

delivery, dropping sacks of mail aimed at special markers set up on Allied continental airfields. Bob was an R/T operator on a VHF homing station, and sometimes the incoming aircraft was a Stirling, part of the Air Despatch Letter Service (ADLS). Always in the early morning a Stirling would arrive over the airfield, make an accurate drop and continue on to other bases. This operation had to be carried out at very low altitude, and Bob sadly recalled how one Stirling, having dropped its load of mail, stalled on the climb-out and crashed on the airfield boundary.

During August 1944 a final version of the Stirling appeared with the flight of Mk. V prototype LJ530. This was produced as an unarmed transport for RAF Transport Command, in anticipation of a support role in the planned Far East 'Tiger Force'. A lengthened nose with an upward hinging front section and a glazed cap provided access to a light cargo bay fitted with a beam block-and-tackle for loading purposes. The starboard side of the rear fuselage had a large door for freight and, although it was not structurally possible to remove the bomb bay, strengthening of the fuselage floor provided accommodation for forty troops, twenty fully equipped paratroopers, twelve stretcher cases or fourteen seated casualties. Alternatively, two jeeps with trailers, or one jeep plus a 6-pounder gun and trailer together with ammunition and crew, could be carried.

Stirling Vs, of which 160 production machines emerged from Short & Harland of Belfast, first entered service with No. 46 Squadron at Stoney Cross in January 1945 as part of Transport Command's No. 47 Group. The following month No. 242 Squadron began receiving Stirling Vs in place of its Wellington XVI transports. Other Stirling V equipped units included Nos. 51, 158, 196 and 299 Squadrons and No. 1588 Flight. The first operation by Stirling Vs was on 17 February 1945, when No. 46 Squadron inaugurated a

training route to Algiers (Maison Blanche). In the following month the unit extended flights to Tripoli
(Castel Benito) and in April to India. By May Nos. 46
and 242 Squadrons' Stirlings were making regular
flights to India via Tunisia, Libya, Palestine and Iraq,
carrying up to seventeen passengers, the entire journey taking twelve days. In June scheduled flights with
Stirling Vs were leaving RAF Lyneham, Wiltshire, for
India, and by August a regular Stirling V service was
being flown to the RAF base in the Azores.

Flying troops between the UK, the Middle East, Iraq
and India became a major role during 1945 for Stirling
V squadrons, each aircraft carrying 24 fully equipped

Above: The crew of Stirling IV LK128/8Z-B *Glorious Beer* of
No. 295 Squadron, Rivenhall, with their aircraft in 1945. Note
the rear entrance door ladder. (Ron Mackay)

Below: The prototype Stirling V, LJ530, with the redesigned
and longer nose. It first flew in August 1944. (Aviation Photo
News)

troops. After Japan surrendered, however, these flights
were greatly curtailed and Stirling Vs gave way to
Transport Command Avro Yorks on trunk routes. The
last first-line RAF Stirling V unit, No. 46 Squadron,
finally exchanged its four-engine machines for twin-

engine Douglas Dakotas in March 1946. Until July 1946 No. 1588 Heavy Freight Flight retained a few Stirling Vs at Bombay for its service between India and the Middle East. These Stirlings are believed to have been last of the type operated regularly by an RAF unit.

Shorts saw the Stirling as a potential airliner for early post-war service, and one Mk. V, PJ958, was converted at Belfast to Specification C.18/43, being fully insulated and furnished to seat 30 passengers. Known as the S.37 'Silver Stirling', it first flew in May 1945, but the main commercial interest was in the Handley Page Halifax C Mk. 8, a civil version of the bomber.

Above: The Stirling V unarmed military transport was similar to the Mk. IV but had a revised and lengthened nose section. This Mk. V is PJ897, circa 1945. Note the streamlined transparent nose and the faired-over tail turret position. (Author's collection)

Below: Stirling V PJ943 makes a fine picture, even if its extreme nose has been 'cut-off' by the photographer. (Ron Mackay)

Indeed, Shorts itself converted twelve Halifax C.8s into Haltons for BOAC, these carrying ten passengers and 8,000lb (3,629kg) of mail and/or cargo in an underfuselage pannier. As for the S.37 'Silver Stirling',

it received little attention from the civil market and became instructional airframe 5797M.

Another Mk. V Stirling, PK148, flew in civil markings as G-AKPC during January 1948, and was ferried from RAF Polebrook to Airtech Ltd at Thame. There it was scheduled for overhaul and updating in readiness for sale to the Belgian operator Trans-Air, but this fell through and PK148 was scrapped in 1948. However, Trans-Air purchased twelve Stirling V conversions by Airtech, the first of ten from RAF Polebrook (PK172) flying out on 12 April 1947 to become the Belgian registered OO-XAC. These Stirlings were refurbished as passenger transports with 36 seats or as freighters. One route they operated was from Blackbushe to Shanghai, but in October 1947 the converted Stirling Vs passed to Air Transport SA, one machine, OO-XAD, being sold to Egypt a year later.

So ends the Stirling saga, a story which, if the makers had been given a free hand by the Air Ministry at the start, might have been very different. Nevertheless, the Stirling was Britain's first four-engine heavy bomber of the Second World War designed as such, and without doubt earned itself a significant place in the annals of RAF history.

Above: A Stirling V of No. 196 Squadron, Shepherds Grove, on finals early in 1946, shows its overall silver finish. (MAP)

Below: This Stirling V is seen at Blackbushe in 1949, having been converted to civil transport configuration and sold to Belgian operator Trans-Air as OO-XAS. (MAP)

Vickers
Wellesley

The first standard RAF bomber to employ the geodetic form of construction devised by the late Sir Barnes Wallis, the Vickers Armstrong Wellesley monoplane made headlines in November 1938 by capturing the long-distance-flight world record for Great Britain. Two years later Wellesleys were operating against Italian forces during the East African campaign.

The Wellesley's origins can be traced back to the Vickers Type 207, built to Specification M.1/30 as a naval torpedo-bomber. Designed by Rex Pierson, this aircraft, S1641, incorporated ideas on light alloys put forward by Barnes Wallis, who was Vickers (Aviation) Ltd's chief designer on structures from 1 January 1930. Unfortunately S1641 was wrecked after a high-speed dive on 23 November 1933.

Barnes Wallis next applied his knowledge of light alloy construction to the Vickers Type 253, designed to Specification G.4/31 calling for a general-purpose aeroplane capable of day and night bombing, dive-bombing, land reconnaissance, photography and ambulance duties. An added clause of October 1931 required the roles of torpedo-bomber and coastal reconnaissance aircraft to be included in the list of capabilities.

In conjunction with Rex Pierson, Barnes Wallis decided to incorporate his geodetic method of construction in the fuselage of the Type 253 biplane, although the wings would be of conventional design. However, so convinced was Barnes Wallis of the potential of his geodetic structure that he persuaded the Vickers Board of Directors to go ahead with a private-venture machine, the Type 246 monoplane, which would also meet with the requirements of G.4/31, and which was to be constructed entirely on the geodetic principle. The fuselage was very similar in structure and outline to that of the Type 253 biplane, but the wide-span monoplane wing was also geodetic and had a high aspect ratio of 8.85 to 1.

With his geodetic method of construction applied wholly to the Type 246, Barnes Wallis proved that a fabric-covered airframe could be quite light and yet retain considerable torsional stiffness. He worked on the principle that a bent member under compression formed a bow, and that this bowing would be restrained by cross-bracing it with another member at its mid-point.

Below: The Wellesley's progenitor was the G.4/31 biplane K2771, which had a similar geodetic fuselage structure. (Vickers Photographic and Audio Dept.)

WELLESLEY

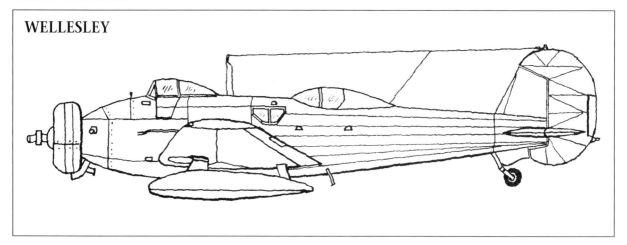

VICKERS TYPE 287 WELLESLEY DATA

Manufacturer
Vickers (Aviation) Ltd, Weybridge, Surrey

Type
Two/three-seat, high-performance, long-range day or night bomber and general-purpose monoplane

Powerplant
One 925hp (690kW) Bristol Pegasus XX air-cooled nine-cylinder radial engine with combined Townend cowling and exhaust ring

Performance
Maximum speed, 191mph (307km/h) at sea level; 228mph (367km/h) at 19,680ft (5,998m). Cruising speed, 180mph (289km/h) at 15,000ft (4,572m). Initial climb, 1,090ft (332m)/min; climb to 19,680ft (5,998m) in 17.5min. Service ceiling, 33,000ft (10,058m). Range, 2,590 miles (4,168km) at 188mph (302km/h) at 15,000ft (4,572m)

Weights
Empty, 6,369lb (2,889kg). Loaded (normal), 11,100lb (5,035kg); maximum overload, 12,500lb (5,670kg)

Dimensions
Span, 74ft 7in (22.76m). Length, 39ft 3in (11.97m). Height, 12ft 4in (3.77m). Wing area, 630sq ft (58.5sq m). Landing gear track, 17ft (5.18m)

Armament
One fixed forward-firing 0.303in (7.7mm) Browning machine-gun in starboard wing; one 0.303in (7.7mm) Vickers 'K' gun on moveable mounting in rear cockpit. Bomb load, up to 2,000lb (907kg) in underwing panniers; provision to carry one 18in (45.72cm) aerial torpedo beneath fuselage

Vickers Wellesley Production

One prototype Type 246 built as private venture to Air Ministry Specification G.4/31. Temporary SBAC B-conditions marking 0-9. Sold to Air Ministry (contract 436980/35) September 1935 as K7556 under revised Specification 22/35

Production order for 96 Wellesley bombers in two batches of 79 and 17 aircraft to Specification 22/35 (contract 435442/35). First batch, K7713–K7791, delivered between March and October 1937. Second batch, K8520–K8536, delivered during October and November 1937. First production machine, K7713, to A&AEE for evaluation on 4 March 1937
Second production order received for 80 Wellesley bombers to same specification (contract 537135/36). These machines, L2637–L2716 inclusive, delivered between February and May 1938

RAF WELLESLEY SQUADRONS AND UNITS

UK
No. 7 Squadron (Finningley)
No. 35 Squadron (Worthy Down and Cottesmore)
No. 76 (Finningley)
No. 77 Squadron (Honington and Driffield)
No. 148 Squadron (Scampton and Stradishall)
No. 207 Squadron (Worthy Down)

Abroad
No. 14 Squadron (Transjordan and Sudan)
No. 45 Squadron (Egypt and Aden)
No. 47 Squadron/47 Squadron Operational Echelon (East Africa)
No. 223 Squadron (Nairobi and Asmara)

Other Units
LRDU; ATDU; A&AEE; RAE; CFS; No. 70 OTU; No. 71 OTU
Communication Flights, Iraq, Khartoum and Khormaksar
Wellesleys K7728, K7735 and K8531 sold to Royal Egyptian Air Force in February 1940
Wellesleys K7727, K7746, K8534 and K8536 became instructional airframes 1029M, 1041M, 1092M and 1066M respectively
Wellesleys used experimentally: K7717 (LRDU); K7736 (intensive flying trials); K7740 (fuel jettisoning tests and extended glazed cockpit canopy); K7772 (Bristol Hercules engine testbed); K7791 (gun mounting and reflector sights); L2641, L2642, L2679, L2682 and L2716 (various experimental tests at RAE)

In his design for the wing structure of the Type 246, Barnes Wallis located the main spar one-third of the chord back from the leading edge. Two diagonal systems of members, curved to the required contour, crossed each other at right angles, so that one set of bracings was in compression and the other set in tension.

Four longerons were used in the construction of the fuselage, and the 'geodesics' (bracing members) were spirally arranged in both directions, following the fuselage shape. The geodetic method was also applied to the tailplane and fin. In this form of structure the need for internal load-carrying struts and formers was dispensed with, allowing extra unobstructed space within the aircraft. Additionally, a near-perfect streamlined shape could be obtained, and as stressed skinning was not an important factor in a geodetic airframe, fabric could be employed as the main covering material, which again saved weight.

As in the Type 253 biplane (K2771), power for the Type 246 monoplane was provided by a 690hp (514kW) Bristol Pegasus IIIM.3 nine-cylinder air-cooled radial engine. An improvement in the new monoplane was the fitting of a fully retractable, manually-operated landing gear in which the main units

Above: The Vickers G.4/31 monoplane, O-9, with its original landing gear, a Pegasus IIIM3 engine and an open front cockpit. After crashing on 19 July 1935 it was rebuilt as Wellesley prototype K7556. (Cambridge University Library)

folded inwards, the wheels resting in wells in the wing roots. The tailwheel was fixed and enclosed by a two-piece streamlined fairing.

When it emerged, the Vickers Type 246 had a lower tare weight and a superior performance with a higher payload than the Type 253 biplane. Bearing the Vickers B-conditions number 0-9, it made its first flight from Brooklands on 19 June 1935, piloted by Captain J. 'Mutt' Summers, Vickers' chief test pilot, who was also responsible for test flying the Type 253, which had initially flown ten months previously. The biplane had already undergone its trials at the A&AEE at Martlesham Heath and, in June 1935, stood beside the new Type 246 monoplane in the New Types Park at the annual RAF Display at Hendon.

Below: Wellesley prototype K7556, in its definitive form, takes off from Brooklands in 1936. Note revised landing gear and front cockpit; an uprated Pegasus X engine was installed. (MAP)

Above: The prototype Wellesley in overall silver finish on test in 1936. Note the underwing bomb panniers, enclosed cockpit and faired tailwheel. The engine is a Bristol Pegasus X. (Vickers (Aviation) Ltd)

Considerable enthusiasm for the Type 246 was aroused, but unfortunately it came to grief on 23 July in a crash-landing caused by undercarriage problems. By then the Air Ministry, although aware of the new monoplane's potential, had chosen the Type 253 biplane as a successful contender among the nine prototypes from various manufacturers entered in the G.4/31 competition. A contract for 150 of the new biplanes was drawn up with Vickers, but thanks to the perseverance of the company's Chairman, Sir Robert McLean, the Air Ministry was persuaded to cancel the biplane order in favour of the Type 246 monoplane. A new contract was signed for the production of 96 Vickers Wellesley day or night bombers, the name Wellesley being adopted after the famous British soldier Arthur Wellesley (later the Duke of Wellington).

Specification 22/35 defined the production standard required for the new bomber, the Air Ministry by then having had second thoughts about the general-purpose concept contained in Specification G.4/31. The original private-venture Type 246 prototype was also ordered as a pre-production machine and converted to the Type 281, bringing it more into line with production standards.

In place of the original open cockpits it now had sliding canopies, a broader-chord rudder and a less complex tailwheel fairing. The retractable landing gear was now hydraulically-operated, and an uprated Pegasus X engine driving a Fairey-Reed fixed-pitch, three-bladed metal propeller was installed. Because of the geodetic structure it was considered unwise at the

time to have a cut-out in the lower fuselage of the Wellesley to provide a bomb bay. Instead, bomb-carrying panniers were adopted, built by the Heston Aircraft Company, one being attached beneath each wing and carrying up to 1,000lb (453kg) of bombs each internally. Defensive armament comprised a 0.303in (7.7mm) Browning machine-gun in the starboard wing with 97 rounds, and an 0.303in (7.7mm) Vickers 'K' gun on a moveable mounting in the rear cockpit with 600 rounds.

Thus, early in 1936, the original Type 246 emerged as the Type 281 Wellesley prototype, K7556, and in March it was sent to the A&AEE for trials. In consequence a number of modifications were introduced as a result of the flight test programme.

The first Type 287 production Wellesley, K7713, did not fly until 30 January 1937, delays having occurred through constructional problems with the new geodetic system. In addition, a number of exhaustive static tests were needed to convince the RAF of the integrity of this form of structure. The standard powerplant for production Wellesleys was the 925hp (690kW) Bristol Pegasus XX radial, driving a de Havilland Standard three-bladed propeller.

After the first eight production aircraft had been built, wing strengthening was introduced on all fol-

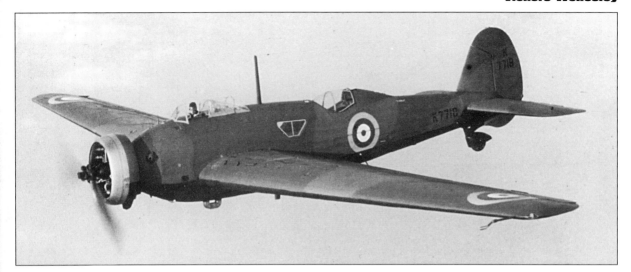

lowing production Wellesleys, which became the Type 294. A second contract was then placed with Vickers for a further 80 Wellesley bombers, making a total of 176 production machines ordered. Both contracts had been completed by March 1938.

The 60th production Wellesley, K7772, went to the Bristol Aeroplane Co Ltd at Filton on 24 August 1937. Designated Vickers Type 289, it was employed as a flying test-bed for the Bristol Hercules two-row sleeve-valve radial engine. Another machine, the 28th production Wellesley, K7740, led to what has been unofficially dubbed the Wellesley Mk. II. This aircraft was in fact the experimental Type 402, in which fuel jettisoning tests were carried out, and which changed the normal Wellesley profile by having a long glazed canopy running between the front and rear cockpits. This was fitted in connection with RAF interest in having a third crew member, avoiding the necessity of the navigator doubling as rear gunner.

As it was, Wellesleys usually flew with a crew of two, pilot and bomb-aimer/gunner, though provision

Above: The sixth production Wellesley, K7718, which went initially to No. 7 Squadron at Finningley. Note the Bristol/Townend cowling integral exhaust collector ring, the faired tailwheel and 1937-style RAF camouflage and markings. (Vickers (Aviation) Ltd)

was made between the two for a navigator if required, but without the extended canopy as fitted to K7740. This aircraft was also used on torpedo trials during December 1940, carrying an 18in (45.72cm) aerial torpedo with a dummy warhead at the Air Torpedo Development Unit.

Other Wellesleys were used on various trials: K7717, the fifth production machine (initially with Nos. 76 and 148 Squadrons), was used as development

Below: Unofficially dubbed Wellesley Mk. II, K7740 was temporarily fitted with a glazed canopy, as seen here, and underwent fuel jettisoning trials at the RAE. After a spell with the TD Flight it went to No. 223 Squadron, but crashed en route to the Middle East on 6 April 1940. (Vickers (Aviation) Ltd)

Left: A line-up of three Wellesleys of No. 148 Squadron, K7733 (nearest), K7732 and K7735, at Scampton in 1938. (Cambridge University Library)

Right: Wellesley K7717 (in No. 148 Squadron markings) with Vickers as trials aircraft for the LRDU. Note the long-chord engine cowling. (MAP)

aircraft with the Long Range Development Unit (LRDU) at Upper Heyford, and also test-flew the Bristol Pegasus XVIII engine for tropical use as well as testing the Type 294 strengthened wing. Wellesley K7791 was tested with special gun mountings and reflector sights, L2641, '42, '79 and '82 were flown at the RAE on de-icing experiments, and L2716 had armoured wing leading edges for trials involving barrage balloon cable-cutting.

The first Wellesleys to enter RAF service were delivered to No. 76 Squadron at Finningley in April 1937, this unit having been formed from 'B' Flight of No. 7 Squadron the same month. Next to receive Wellesleys was No. 148 Squadron at Scampton during the summer, while at the same time No. 35 Squadron began replacing its Fairey Gordon biplanes with Wellesleys at Worthy Down. This was also the base of No. 207 Squadron, whose Wellesleys started to arrive that September. Two months later No. 77 Squadron at Honington replaced its Hawker Audax biplanes with the new Wellesley monoplane bombers.

Wellesleys were also sent to RAF Middle East units, No. 45 Squadron at Helwan, Egypt, exchanging its Gordons for the type during November 1937. March 1938 saw Amman-based No. 14 Squadron giving up its

Gordons for Wellesleys, and during June No. 223 Squadron in East Africa began receiving Wellesleys in exchange for its Vickers Vincent biplanes. A year later at Khartoum No. 47 Squadron began taking Wellesleys on charge, but a few of its Vincents were retained for use in the rough conditions of the Sudan.

In the meantime, January 1938 had seen the setting-up at Upper Heyford of the RAF's LRDU in connection with a proposed attempt on the world non-stop long-distance flight record by Wellesley bombers. With its comparatively light weight and generous internal space, the Wellesley was an obvious choice for the attempt.

Five standard Wellesleys, L2637, L2638, L2639, L2680 and L2681, were chosen for conversion by the RAE to LRDU requirements, these aircraft being delivered to the LRDU in the spring of 1938. Alterations included the fitting of a drag-reducing NACA-type long-chord cowling faired to the front fuselage, with controllable cooling gills to improve cooling and reduce drag, the installation of a 1,010hp (753kW) Bristol Pegasus XXII engine running on 100 octane lead-free aviation fuel and driving a Rotol constant-speed propeller, a revised landing gear with stronger members, heavy-duty tyres and an improved retrac-

tion system, extra fuel capacity amounting to 1,290 Imp gal (5,864lit), oil tankage increased to 60 Imp gal (272lit), the deletion of all military equipment, the fitting of an RAE Mk. IV automatic pilot, the provision of accommodation for a third crew member (navigator) and a slight increase in forward fuselage width to allow the installation of a sleeping bunk.

The first LRDU Wellesley conversion, L2637, was held as reserve aircraft and did not take part in the long-distance flights, the first of which was a preliminary experience-gaining flight which started from RAF Cranwell on 7 July 1938. Four Wellesleys, led by the unit's chief pilot, Squadron Leader R. Kellett, flew to the Persian Gulf and back to Ismailia, where they landed after a flight of 4,300 miles (6,919km) in an elapsed time of 32 hours.

All four aircraft then returned to Upper Heyford, when it was decided that the record attempt would

start from Ismailia, taking a route to Darwin, Australia, via Saudi Arabia, India and the Dutch East Indies. The Wellesleys would weigh 18,400lb (8,346kg) for take-off (almost double their normal weight), which meant that a special take-off strip some 1,200 yards (1,096m) long had to be prepared at Ismailia.

On 5 November 1938 the three LRDU Wellesleys (L2638, L2639 and L2680) took off from Ismailia and, after a 45-minute climb to their 10,000ft (3,048m) operating height, set course eastwards. Bad weather was encountered over the Bay of Bengal, and worse followed as they crossed the Dutch East Indies, where they flew through heavy rain and

Below: Wellesley L2639 of the LRDU, with revised engine cowling and other refinements. It was piloted by Flight Lieutenant H. A. V. Hogan on the world long-distance record flight in November 1938. (MAP)

thunderstorms and were faced with massive banks of cumulus cloud. Flight Lieutenant H. A. V. Hogan in L2639 was forced to make a refuelling stop at Kupang, Timor, before continuing to Australia, but the other two Wellesleys, flown by Squadron Leader Kellett and Flight Lieutenant A. N. Combe, landed at Darwin after a flight lasting just over 48 hours and covering a distance of 7,157 miles (11,517km) non-stop. This record stood for eight years. The three Wellesleys stood up to the ordeal well, ripped fabric being the only damage inflicted by the extreme weather conditions encountered en route. The Bris-

Above: The three Wellesleys (L2638, L2639 and L2680) which set a new world non-stop distance record on 5/7 November 1938. (Vickers (Aviation) Ltd)

tol Pegasus engines performed faultlessly over the whole distance.

By the outbreak of the Second World War most home-based Wellesleys (except No. 76 Squadron, operating as an OTU) had been replaced in RAF Bomber Command units. The majority had been transferred to Africa and the Middle East as front-line equipment, with a Vokes air-cleaner and sand filter mounted beneath their engine cowlings.

When Italy joined forces with Germany on 10 June 1940, Nos. 14, 47 and 223 Squadrons' Wellesleys were based respectively at Port Sudan, Erkowit and Summit

Below: Wellesley K7729 spent its time with Vickers, the A&AEE at Martlesham Heath and RAE Farnborough until it crashed at Bunces Farm, Farnham, on 5 October 1938. (MAP)

Above: These two Wellesleys, L2697/U and L2706/W, seen over typical Middle East terrain, are from No. 14 Squadron, based at Amman, Transjordan. (MAP)

in the Sudan. At dusk the next day No. 14 Squadron sent a force of nine aircraft, commanded by Squadron Leader A. D. Selway, the CO, to attack Italian-held Massawa. Two leading sections of six aircraft dropped their assortment of 40lb (18kg) and 20lb (9kg) high-explosive and incendiary bombs from 600ft (182m), direct hits being scored on bulk fuel tanks in the harbour and on hangars and buildings at Otumlo airfield. The three Wellesleys following in the third section, carrying 250lb (113kg) bombs, attacked from 3,500ft (1,066m) to score direct hits on a hangar and nearby railway installations. It was confirmed afterwards that

780 tons (792 tonnes) of fuel had been destroyed in the attack on fuel tanks in the harbour. All nine Wellesleys engaged in the action, including K7223, K7725, K7741, L2645, L2647, L2649, L2652 and L2710, returned safely to base.

Further attacks were carried out by No. 14 Squadron, not only on Massawa, but against other targets in Eritrea including the Italian airfields at Gura and Asmara. To protect the Wellesley's vulnerable belly, No. 14 Squadron designed a ventral gun mounting for a second 'K' gun. In consequence, on 26 June 1940, when the unit joined No. 47 Squadron's Welles-

Below: An unidentified Wellesley of No. 47 Squadron, which operated in East Africa against the Italians. Note the Vokes air filter under the cowling for tropical operations. (MAP)

leys for a raid on Gura, No. 14's aircraft flew at a lower altitude to provide extra protection against attacks from below. The Wellesleys were engaged by a formation of Fiat C.R.42 Falcos of the Regia Aeronautica, and although no British bombers were lost, three were damaged. In return, two Fiats were claimed as probables, one leaving the scene pouring smoke and a second descending rapidly, apparently out of control.

The following month No. 14 Squadron's 'B' Flight operated with twin guns mounted in the dorsal position. These were fitted to mountings, again of the squadron's own design, which allowed the gunner a wider field of fire. As the squadron's Wellesleys were returning from a raid, thus armed, they sighted an Italian Savoia-Marchetti S.M.81 Pipistrello three-engined bomber which had been trying to shadow an Allied convoy. Wellesley K7723, flown by Flying Officer G. S. R. Robinson, attacked the enemy bomber, which plunged into the sea and broke up.

By the end of August 1940, after nearly three months of operating against the Italians in East Africa, No. 14 Squadron had flown its Wellesleys on 22 bombing missions, each of which necessitated over six hours in the air. They had dropped some 43 tons (43.7 tonnes) of bombs for the loss of two Wellesleys over Italian territory. The following month the squadron began to receive Bristol Blenheim IV replacements, its Wellesleys being transferred to Nos. 47 and 223 Squadrons.

Meanwhile, in May 1940, No. 47 Squadron, which had flown its Wellesleys on patrol sorties before Italy entered the war, moved from its base at Khartoum to Erkowit, near the Red Sea. On 11 June the unit's first bombing raid was made against the airfield at Asmara, and in July the squadron moved to Carthago. Attacks continued against Italian airfields, especially those at Azoza and Gondar. Then, on 16 October, a formation of eight Italian aircraft raided Gedaref airfield, where

Above: This unusual shot, albeit distant, shows No. 148 Squadron's Wellesleys taking off from Scampton en masse in 1938. (Cambridge University Library)

Right: Wellesleys of No. 45 Squadron (Egypt and Aden) on patrol over Middle East terrain circa 1938–39. The nearest aircraft is K7783, with K7773 next to it. (MAP)

No. 47 Squadron had a detachment of Wellesleys. Eight were reduced to burnt-out hulks during the attack. The squadron also had a detachment at Khartoum, and made this its headquarters at the end of October. Two other detachments operated from Kassala and Argordat, from where attacks were made on enemy guns and troop positions, as well as photographic reconnaissance sorties being carried out. After the Italian capitulation in Abyssinia during May 1941, No. 47 Squadron established itself on Asmara aerodrome.

Third Wellesley unit in the Middle East when war broke out was No. 223 Squadron in the Sudan, but they were transferred during June 1940 to Aden. On 18 August five of the squadron's Wellesleys left an advanced base at Perim Island to attack enemy airfields near Addis Ababa. Flying over very hostile terrain and through severe icing conditions and thick cloud, four of the Wellesleys reached their targets. They met with fierce anti-aircraft fire and the attentions of a Fiat C.R.32 fighter, but all returned safely to base, including the fifth, which had become lost en route and landed in French Somaliland before rapidly taking off again! The results of this raid were four Savoia-Marchetti S.M.79 Sparviero bombers destroyed, plus three hangars.

From the start of the East African campaign No. 223 Squadron had deployed its Wellesleys against Italian targets along the Red Sea coast, fuel dumps at Gura and the port of Massawa. Enemy aircraft and hangars were destroyed at Tessenei airfield, and raids were made on communications and airfields in Somaliland. Afterwards the squadron supported British troops driving into Eritrea, where enemy airfields and ground forces were attacked. The Eritrean battle had been won by April 1941, and No. 223 Squadron was moved to Shandur, Egypt, as an OTU, where its Wellesleys were replaced by twin-engine Martin Maryland bombers supplied to the RAF.

The Wellesley units contributed much to the East African and early Middle East conflicts. During the

battle of Keren, support was provided by Nos. 47 and 223 Squadrons, each making a number of bombing raids against the Italian stronghold. Keren itself was finally overwhelmed on 27 March 1941. In another action by No. 223 Squadron, an Italian destroyer flotilla sailing from Massawa on 3 April for Port Sudan was attacked by the unit's Wellesleys and Blenheim IVs of No. 14 Squadron, all the enemy vessels being sunk, beached or scuttled. Shortly afterwards most of East Africa was in British hands, and the RAF moved the majority of its units north to Egypt, where they bolstered Allied forces fighting in the Western Desert.

Ironically, when No. 47 Squadron came to re-equip with new Bristol Beauforts in Egypt, its intended new mounts had all been allocated to another squadron. A number of Wellesleys were subsequently overhauled and on 16 April 1942 an operational echelon of Wellesleys was formed as No. 47 Squadron Operational (Wellesley) Air Echelon at Landing Ground 89 (LG89).

After establishing itself at Asmara earlier, No. 47 Squadron had launched bombing raids on Amba Alagi and, after this had fallen to the Allies, its Wellesleys flew supply dropping missions to Allied troops at Dabarach until the final battle of the East African Campaign was fought at Gondar on 28 November 1941. During that period No. 47 Squadron had been the only RAF unit operating in the area, apart from South African Air Force (SAAF) units. Now, as No. 47 Squadron Air Echelon, the unit operated anti-subma-

rine patrols, reconnaissance and sea navigation flights and convoy escort duties over the Eastern Mediterranean area, first from Burgh-el-Arab, then out of Shandur, St Jean, LG227, LG08 and finally LG07. Sorties continued to be flown from LG07 until 3 March 1943, when No. 47 Squadron Operational (Wellesley) Echelon was disbanded. As for No. 47 Squadron, it had been re-established as a fully equipped Bristol Beaufort squadron during September 1942, after the merging of elements from Nos. 39 and 42 Squadrons.

The Wellesley's part in the early war years was a gallant effort by crews flying an aeroplane already considered obsolete. Quite a number were shot down by enemy ground fire or fell victim to the Regia Aeronautica's Fiat C.R.42 Falco biplane fighters operating in the East African war zone. Nevertheless, the Wellesley justified Barnes Wallis's faith in his geodetic concept, and the type did much to pave the way for its illustrious successor, the Vickers Wellington twin-engine bomber.

Below: A rare shot of Wellesley K7774 in the Nubian Desert, en route for delivery to No. 223 Squadron. It was later transferred to No. 47 Squadron, crash-landing at Summit in the Sudan on 21 October 1940. (MAP)

Bottom: Receiving much attention at Aboukir in 1938 is Wellesley L2649 of No. 14 Squadron. Note the lowered side flap on the front cockpit and unit badge on the fin. (MAP)

Glossary

AASF	Advanced Air Striking Force		MAEE	Marine Aircraft Experimental Establishment
A&AEE	Aeroplane & Armament Experimental Establishment		METS	Middle East Training School
ACC	Army Co-operation Command		MU	Maintenance Unit
AFDU	Air Fighting Development Unit		NACA	National Advisory Committee for Aeronautics
AGS	Air Gunnery School			
AOC	Air Officer Commanding		OCU	Operational Conversion Unit
AS	Anti-submarine		OTU	Operational Training Unit
AOS	Air Observers School		PFF	Pathfinder Force
BEF	British Expeditionary Force		PV	private venture
BGS	Bombing and Gunnery School		RAAF	Royal Australian Air Force
BOAC	British Overseas Airways Corporation		RAE	Royal Aircraft Establishment
CAA	Canadian Associated Aircraft Ltd		RAF	Royal Air Force
CATP	Commonwealth Air Training Plan		RCAF	Royal Canadian Air Force
CFS	Central Flying School		RNAS	Royal Naval Air Station
CG	Centre of gravity		RNZAF	Royal New Zealand Air Force
CO	Commanding Officer		rpg	rounds per gun
COW	Coventry Ordnance Works		rpm	revolutions per minute
CSBS	Course Setting Bomb Sight		R/T	radio transmitter
DAP	Department of Aircraft Production (Australia)		SAAF	South African Air Force
			SAP	semi armour-piercing
D/F	direction finding		SBAC	Society of British Aircraft Constructors
DFC	Distinguished Flying Cross		SD	Special Duties
DFM	Distinguished Flying Medal		SoTT	School of Technical Training
FIU	Fighter Interception Unit		SRAF	Southern Rhodesian Air Force
GO	Gas operated		TDU	Torpedo Development Unit
GP	general purpose		VC	Victoria Cross
HCU	Heavy Conversion Unit		w/o	write-off
LRDU	Long Range Development Unit			

Bibliography

AIR 27, Piece No 98 (1923–1941), PRO, Kew.

AIR 27, Piece No 435 (1916–1941), PRO, Kew.

AIR 27, Piece No 1233 (1916–1942), PRO, Kew.

Air Enthusiast: Nos 9; 10; 14; 16; 18

Air International: April 1974; March 1975; November 1978; July 1980; March 1981; December 1981; November 1984

Aircraft of the Fighting Powers: Vol I (1941); Vol II (1942); Vol IV (1944); Vol VI (1945), Harborough Publishing Co.

Armstrong Whitworth Aircraft Since 1913: O. Tapper, Putnam 1973

Avro Aircraft Since 1908: A. J. Jackson, Putnam 1965

Blackburn Aircraft Since 1909: A. J. Jackson, Putnam 1989

Bomber Command: HMSO 1941

Bomber Offensive: Sir Arthur Harris, Collins 1947

Bristol Aircraft Since 1910: C. H. Barnes, Putnam 1970

Bristol Blenheim: Chaz Bowyer, Ian Allan 1984

Bristol Blenheim in Action: R. Mackay, Squadron Signal Publications 1988

Coastal Command: HMSO 1942

British Aircraft of World War II: D. Mondey, Temple Press 1982

Fairey Aircraft Since 1915: H. A. Taylor, Putnam 1974

Famous Bombers of the Second World War: W. Green, Vol 1 1959 and Vol 2 1960, Macdonald & Co

FlyPast: July and August 1983

Handley Page Aircraft Since 1907: C. H. Barnes, Putnam 1976

Jane's All the World's Aircraft, 1938: David & Charles 1972 (reprint)

Planes: Nos. 11, 12 and 13

Planemakers: 4 Shorts: M. J. H. Taylor, Jane's Publishing 1984

Profile Publications: Nos. 34, 58, 65, 93, 142, 153, 256, 260

RAF Squadrons: Wing Commander C. G. Jefford, Airlife 1988

RAF Yearbooks; 1978, 1981, 1982

Royal Air Force Bombers of World War Two, Vol 2: P. J. R. Moyes, Hylton Lacy 1968

Vickers Aircraft Since 1908: C. F. Andrews and E. B. Morgan, Putnam 1988 (2nd edition)

Wings of War; An Air Force Anthology: Batsford 1943

Index

General Index

Index